"LOCATION OF INDIAN TRIBES IN THE SOUTHEAST ABOUT THE YEAR 1650." From John R. Swanton, *The Indians of the Southeastern United States*, BAE Bull. 137, Map. 1. *Courtesy of the Smithsonian Institution, Bureau of American Ethnology.*

SOUTHEASTERN INDIANS

LIFE PORTRAITS

To

my father

ALBERT DONLIN FUNDABURK

Other Book by the Editor

SUN CIRCLES AND HUMAN HANDS

The Southeastern Indians

Art and Industries

1957

SOUTHEASTERN INDIANS

LIFE PORTRAITS
A Catalogue of Pictures
1564 - 1860

Edited by
EMMA LILA FUNDABURK
1958

SCARECROW REPRINT CORPORATION
METUCHEN, NEW JERSEY. 1969

Illustrations

APPRECIATION

The owners of the pictures shown herein are indicated by the courtesy lines. I wish to thank the museums, libraries, and individuals who granted permission for the use of reproductions of their paintings, drawings, and engravings. This book would not have been possible without their cooperation. The individuals in the various institutions who patiently supplied the photographs and descriptive information performed an invaluable service in the total combined effort necessary to produce this book.

The Smithsonian Institution, Bureau of American Ethnology—Dr. Frank H. H. Roberts, Director; Dr. William C. Sturtevant, Ethnologist; Mrs. Margaret Blaker, Archivist; and the photographic department— was especially helpful in making available photographs and information and in suggesting other sources of pictures. The Alabama Department of Archives and History—Peter A. Brannon, Director; Mrs. Leonard Cobb, Librarian; and Alex L. Bush, Photographer—aided in providing research materials. The Montgomery Public Library—Mrs. Dixie L. Fisher, Director —secured several dozen rare books by interlibrary loan from many libraries, including the New Orleans Public Library; Jacksonville (Florida) Public Library; Providence (R. I.) Public Library; Birmingham Public Library; Tennessee State Library and Archives; Florida State Library; the University Libraries of Alabama, Florida, Georgia, North Carolina, South Carolina, Kentucky, Virginia, and Oklahoma; Alabama Polytechnic Institute Library; the Library of Congress and others. I am also grateful to the New York Public Library which made available prints of many pictures, and supplied useful information about various publications. Bibliographical lists from Washington University, St. Louis, the New York State Library, and others were helpful. I appreciate the correspondence regarding rare books and microfilms which I received from various libraries including the Harvard University Library, University of Pennsylvania Library, the Pennsylvania Historical Society Library, the Virginia Historical Society and others. I am also grateful to many individuals—among them Dr. Ben C. McCary, William and Mary College and Dr. Charles H. Fairbanks, University of Florida—who suggested sources of pictures and information.

I want to thank my sister, Mary Douglass Fundaburk Foreman, for suggesting the basic design of this book; my aunt, Helen Douglass Bradley for proof reading and making the index; Beverley Colomb Bricken for secretarial work and prepublication advertising copy; the Alabama Engraving Company for artwork and engraving; the Birmingham Printing Company for composition and printing; and the many individuals to whom I have corresponded seeking information. I am also grateful to the prepublication subscribers. I hope they and others will find this a useful research document.

This book has not been the work of one person. It represents the combined effort of many individuals and institutions. To each who has helped in any way with this—I deeply thank you!

De Bry after Le Moyne

TIMUCUA INDIANS. 1564-1565. FLORIDA. Engravings from Theodore de Bry, *Brevis Narratio Eorvm Qvae in Florida Americae Provicia. . . .* (Voyages, America, Part II), Frankfurt-am-Main, 1591. Engraved on copper by De Bry after the paintings of Jacques le Moyne de Morgues (d. 1588), cartographer and artist for the French Huguenot colony, Fort Caroline, St. Johns River, Florida. They were the first paintings representing native life in the area now the United States. *Courtesy of The New York Public Library.*

1. "THE PROMONTORY OF FLOR-IDA, AT WHICH THE FRENCH TOUCHED; NAMED BY THEM THE FRENCH PROMONTORY." Engraving number 1 from De Bry, 1591. 6¼ x 8¼ inches. After LeMoyne. Florida. 1564. *NYPL.*

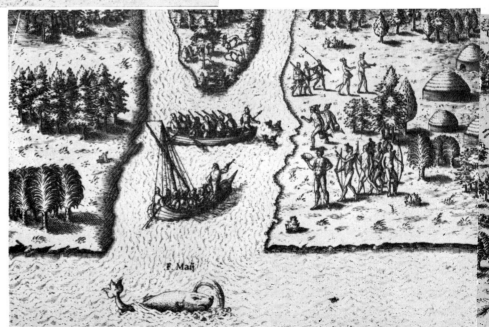

2. "THE FRENCH SAIL TO THE RIVER OF MAY." Engraving number 2 from De Bry, 1591. 6¼ x 8¼ inches. After Le Moyne. Florida. 1564. *NYPL.*

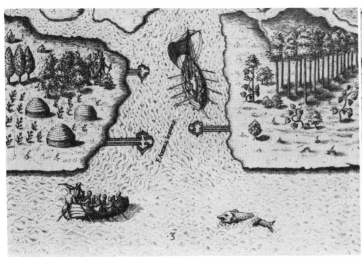

3. "LEAVING THE RIVER OF MAY, THE FRENCH DISCOVER TWO OTHER RIVERS." Engraving number 3 from De Bry, 1591. 6¼ x 8¼ inches. After Le Moyne. Florida. 1564. *NYPL*.

4. "SIX OTHER RIVERS DISCOVERED BY THE FRENCH." Engraving number 4 from De Bry, 1591. 6¼ x 8¼ inches. After Le Moyne. Florida. 1564. *NYPL*.

5. "THE FRENCH REACH PORT ROYAL." Engraving number 5 from De Bry, 1591. 6¼ x 8¼ inches. After Le Moyne. Florida. 1564. *NYPL*.

6. "THE FRENCH COMMANDER ERECTS A COLUMN WITH THE ARMS OF THE KING OF FRANCE." Engraving number 6 from De Bry, 1591. 6¼ x 8¼ inches. After Le Moyne. Florida. 1564. *NYPL*.

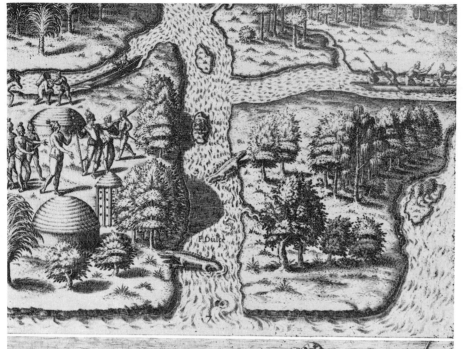

7. "THE FRENCH LEFT IN FORT CHARLES SUFFER FROM SCARCITY OF PROVISIONS." Engraving number 7 from De Bry, 1591. 6¼ x 8¼ inches. After Le Moyne. Florida. 1564. *NYPL.*

8. "THE NATIVES OF FLORIDA WORSHIP THE COLUMN ERECTED BY THE COMMANDER ON HIS FIRST VOYAGE." Engraving number 8 from De Bry, 1591. 6¼ x 8¼ inches. After Le Moyne. Florida. 1564. *NYPL.*

9. "THE FRENCH SELECT A PLACE FOR BUILDING A FORT." Engraving number 9 from De Bry, 1591. 6¼ x 8¼ inches. After Le Moyne. Florida. 1564. *NYPL.*

10. "PICTURE OF FORT CARO-LINA." Engraving number 10 from De Bry, 1591. 6¼ x 8¼ inches. After Le Moyne. Florida. 1564. *NYPL*.

11. "CEREMONIES PERFORMED BY SATURIOUA BEFORE GOING ON AN EXPEDITION AGAINST THE ENEMY." Engraving number 11 from De Bry, 1591. 6¼ x 8¼ inches. After Le Moyne. Florida. 1564. *NYPL*.

12. "O U T I N A , GOING AT THE HEAD OF HIS ARMY AGAINST THE ENEMY, CONSULTS A SORCERER ON THE EVENT." Engraving number 12 from De Bry, 1591. 6¼ x 8¼ inches. After Le Moyne. Florida. 1564. *NYPL*.

13. "OUTINA, WITH THE HELP OF THE FRENCH, GAINS A VICTORY OVER HIS ENEMY POTANOU." Engraving number 13 from De Bry, 1591. 6¼ x 8¼ inches. After Le Moyne. Florida. 1564. *NYPL.*

14. "ORDER OF MARCH OBSERVED BY OUTINA ON A MILITARY EXPEDITION." Engraving number 14 from De Bry, 1591. 6¼ x 8¼ inches. After Le Moyne. Florida. 1564. *NYPL.*

15. "HOW OUTINA'S MEN TREATED THE SLAIN OF THE ENEMY." Engraving number 15 from De Bry, 1591, 6¼ x 8¼ inches. After Le Moyne. Florida. 1564. *NYPL.*

16. "TROPHIES AND CERE-
MONIES AFTER A VICTORY."
Engraving number 16 from De Bry,
1591. 6¼ x 8¼ inches. After Le
Moyne. Florida. 1564. *NYPL*.

17. "EMPLOYMENTS OF THE HER-
MAPHRODITES." Engraving number 17 from De Bry, 1591. 16¼ x 8¼
inches. After Le Moyne. Florida. 1564.
NYPL.

18. "THE CHIEF APPLIED TO
BY WOMEN WHOSE HUS-
BANDS HAVE DIED IN WAR
OR BY DISEASE." Engraving
number 18 from De Bry, 1591,
6¼ x 8¼ inches. After Le
Moyne. Florida. 1564. *NYPL*.

19. "CEREMONIES OF WOMEN MOURNING FOR THEIR DECEASED HUSBANDS." Engraving number 19 from De Bry, 1591. 6¼ x 8¼ inches. After Le Moyne. Florida. 1564. *NYPL.*

20. "MODE OF TREATING THE SICK." Engraving number 20 from De Bry, 1591. 6¼ x 8¼ inches. After Le Moyne. Florida. 1564. *NYPL.*

21. "MODE OF TILLING AND PLANTING." Engraving number 21 from De Bry, 1591. 6¼ x 8¼ inches. After Le Moyne. Florida. 1564. *NYPL.*

22. "INDUSTRY OF THE FLORIDIANS IN DEPOSITING THEIR CROPS IN THE PUBLIC GRANARY." Engraving number 22 from De Bry, 1591. 6¼ x 8¼ inches. After Le Moyne. Florida. 1564. *NYPL.*

23. "BRINGING IN WILD ANIMALS, FISH, AND OTHER STORES." Engraving number 23 from De Bry, 1591. 6¼ x 8¼ inches. After Le Moyne. Florida. 1564. *NYPL.*

24. "MODE OF DRYING FISH, WILD ANIMALS, AND OTHER PROVISIONS." Engraving number 24 from De Bry, 1591. 6¼ x 8¼ inches. After Le Moyne. Florida. 1564. *NYPL.*

25. "HUNTING DEER." Engraving number 25 from De Bry, 1591. 6¼ x 8¼ inches. After Le Moyne. Florida. 1564. *NYPL*.

26. "KILLING CROCODILES." Engraving number 26 from De Bry, 1591. 6¼ x 8¼ inches. After Le Moyne. Florida. 1564. *NYPL*.

27. "FLORIDIANS CROSSING OVER TO AN ISLAND TO TAKE THEIR PLEASURE." Engraving number 27 from De Bry, 1591. 6¼ x 8¼ inches. After Le Moyne. Florida. 1564. *NYPL*.

28. "PREPARATIONS FOR A FEAST." Engraving number 28 from De Bry, 1591. 6¼ x 8¼ inches. After Le Moyne. Florida. 1564. *NYPL*.

29. "PROCEEDINGS OF THE FLORIDIANS IN DELIBERATING ON IMPORTANT AFFAIRS." Engraving number 29 from De Bry, 1591. 6¼ x 8¼ inches. After Le Moyne. Florida. 1564. *NYPL*.

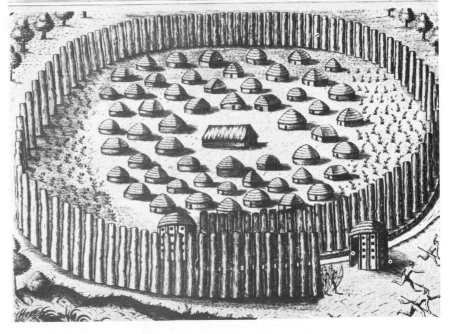

30. "CONSTRUCTION OF FORTIFIED TOWNS AMONG THE FLORIDIANS." Engraving number 30 from De Bry, 1591. 6¼ x 8¼ inches. After Le Moyne. Florida. 1564. *NYPL*.

31. "HOW THEY SET ON FIRE AN ENEMY'S TOWN." Engraving number 31 from De Bry, 1591. 6¼ x 8¼ inches. After Le Moyne. Florida. 1564. *NYPL.*

32. "HOW SENTINELS ARE PUNISHED FOR SLEEPING ON THEIR POSTS." Engraving number 32 from De Bry, 1591. 6¼ x 8¼ inches. After Le Moyne. Florida. 1564. *NYPL.*

33. "HOW THEY DECLARE WAR." Engraving number 33 from De Bry, 1591. 6¼ x 8¼ inches. After Le Moyne. Florida. 1564. *NYPL.*

34. "FIRST-BORN CHILDREN SACRIFICED TO THE CHIEF WITH SOLEMN CEREMONIES." Engraving number 34 from De Bry, 1591. 6¼ x 8¼ inches. After Le Moyne. Florida. 1564. *NYPL.*

35. "SOLEMNITIES AT CONSECRATING THE SKIN OF A STAG TO THE SUN." Engraving number 35 from De Bry, 1591. 6¼ x 8¼ inches. After Le Moyne. Florida. 1564. *NYPL.*

36. "THE YOUTH AT THEIR EXERCISES." Engraving number 36 from De Bry, 1591. 6¼ x 8¼ inches. After Ie Moyne. Florida. 1564. *NYPL.*

37. "THE DISPLAY WITH WHICH A QUEEN ELECT IS BROUGHT TO THE KING." Engraving number 37 from De Bry, 1591. 6¼ x 8¼ inches. After Le Moyne. Florida. 1564. *NYPL.*

38. "SOLEMNITIES AT THE RECEPTION OF THE QUEEN BY THE KING." Engraving number 38 from De Bry, 1591. 6¼ x 8¼ inches. After Le Moyne. Florida. 1564. *NYPL.*

39. "THE KING AND QUEEN TAKING A WALK FOR THEIR AMUSEMENT." Engraving number 39 from De Bry, 1591. 6¼ x 8¼ inches. After Le Moyne. Florida. 1564. *NYPL.*

40. "CEREMONIES AT THE DEATH OF A CHIEF OR OF PRIESTS." Engraving number 40 from De Bry, 1591. 6¼ x 8¼ inches. After Le Moyne. Florida. 1564. *NYPL*.

41. "MODE OF COLLECTING GOLD IN STREAMS RUNNING FROM THE APALATCY MOUNTAINS." Engraving number 41 from De Bry, 1591. 6¼ x 8¼ inches. After Le Moyne. Florida. 1564. *NYPL*.

42. "MURDER OF PIERRE GAMBRÉ, A FRENCHMAN." Engraving number 42 from De Bry, 1591. 6¼ x 8¼ inches. After Le Moyne. Florida. 1564. *NYPL*.

De Bry after White

SOUTHERN ALGONQUIAN INDIANS. 1585. NORTH CAROLINA. Engravings from Theodore de Bry, *Admiranda Narratio Fida Tamen, de Commodis et incolarvm Ritibvs Virginiae, . . . Viv ae Imagines . . . et ad viuum expreffa* of Joanne With. . . . (Voyages, America, Part I), Frankfurt-am-Main, 1590. Engraved on copper by De Bry after the water colors of John White, artist with Sir Walter Raleigh's first colony to Roanoke Island in 1585, and Governor of the second Virginia colony in 1587. *Courtesy of The New York Public Library.*

43. "THE ARRIUAL OF THE ENGLIFHEMEN IN VIRGIN-IA." Engraving number 2 from De Bry, 1590. 8¾ x 6 inches. After White. North Carolina. 1585. *NYPL.*

44. "A WEROAN OR GREAT LORDE OF VIRGINIA." Engraving number 3 from De Bry, 1590. 8¾ x 5⅞ inches. After White. North Carolina. 1585. *NYPL.*

45. "ONE OF THE CHEIFF LADYES OF SECOTA." Engraving number 4 from De Bry, 1590. 8¾ x 5⅞ inches. After White. North Carolina. 1585. *NYPL.*

46. "ONE OF THE RELIGEOUS MEN IN THE TOWNE OF SECOTA." Engraving number 5 from De Bry, 1590. Engraved by G. Veen. 8¾ x 6¼ inches. After White. North Carolina. 1585. *NYPL.*

47. "A YOUNGE GENTILL WOEMAN DOUGHTER OF SECOTA." Engraving number 6 from De Bry, 1590. Engraved by G. Veen. 8¼ x 5⅞ inches. After White. North Carolina. 1585. *NYPL.*

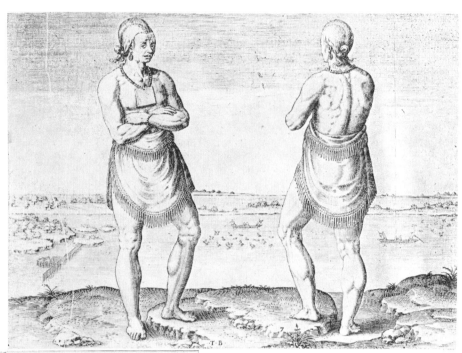

48. "A CHEIFF LORDE OF RO-ANOAC." Engraving number 7 from De Bry, 1590. 8¾ x 6⅜ inches. After White. North Carolina. 1585. *NYPL.*

49. "A CHEIFF LADYE OF POME-IOOC." Engraving number 8 from De Bry, 1590. 8½ x 5¾ inches. After White. North Carolina. 1585. *NYPL.*

50. "AN AGED MANNE IN HIS WINTER GARMENT." Engraving number 9 from De Bry, 1590. 8⅝ x 6 inches. After White. North Carolina. 1585. *NYPL.*

51. "THEIR MANNER OF CA-
REYNGE THER CHILDREN
AND ATYERE OF THE CHEIFFE
LADYES OF THE TOWNE OF
DASAMONQUEPEUC." Engraving
number 10 from De Bry, 1590.
8⅜ x 5⅝ inches. After White.
North Carolina. 1585. *NYPL.*

52. "THE CONIUERER." Engraving
number 11 from De Bry, 1590. Engraved
by G. Veen. 8½ x 6 inches. After White.
North Carolina. 1585. *NYPL.*

53. "THE MANNER OF MAK-
INGE THEIR BOATES." Engraving number 12 from De Bry, 1590.
8½ x 5⅞ inches. After White.
North Carolina. 1585. *NYPL.*

54. "THEIR MANNER OF FISHYNGE IN VIRGINIA." Engraving number 13 from De Bry, 1590. 12½ x 10⅜ inches. After White. North Carolina. 1585. *NYPL*.

55. "THE BROVVYLLINGE OF THEIR FIFHE OUER THE FLAME." Engraving number 14 from De Bry, 1590. 8⅜ x 5¼ inches. After White. North Carolina. 1585. *NYPL*.

56. "THEIR FEETHEYNGE OF THEIR MEATE IN EARTHERN POTTES." Engraving number 15 from De Bry, 1590. Engraved by G. Veen. 8¼ x 5⅝ inches. After White. North Carolina. 1585. *NYPL*.

57. "THEIR FITTING AT MEATE." Engraving number 16 from De Bry, 1590. 8½ x 6 inches. After White. North Carolina. 1585. *NYPL*.

58. "THEIR MANNER OF PRAINGE VVITH RATTELS ABOWT THE
FYER." Engraving number 17 from De Bry, 1590. 10⅛ x 7¼ inches. After
White. North Carolina. 1585. *NYPL*.

59. "THEIR DANFES VVHICH THEY VFE ATT THEIR HYGHE FEAFTES." Engraving number 18 from De Bry, 1590. 12⅝ x 10½ inches. After White. North Carolina. 1585. *NYPL.*

60. "THE TOVVNE OF POMEIOOC." Engraving number 19 from De Bry, 1590. 8¾ x 11½ inches. After White. North Carolina. 1585. *NYPL.*

61. "THE TOVVNE OF SECOTA." Engraving number 20 from De Bry, 1590. 9 x 12¼ inches. After White. North Carolina. 1585. *NYPL.*

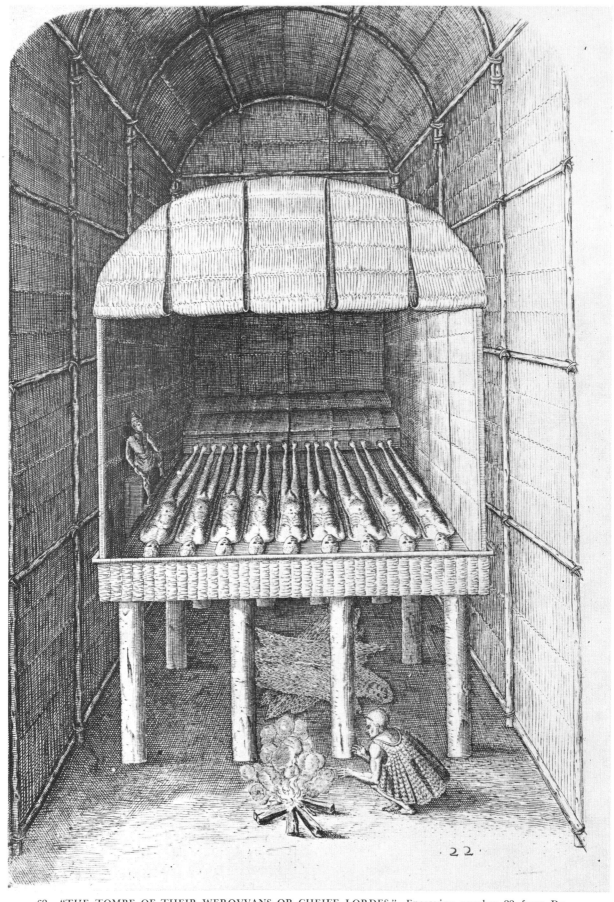

62. "THE TOMBE OF THEIR WEROVVANS OR CHEIFF LORDES." Engraving number 22 from De Bry, 1590. 9 x 12¾ inches. After White. North Carolina. 1585. *NYPL.*

63. "THER IDOL KIVVAFA." Engraving number 21 from De Bry, 1590. 8½ x 6⅛ inches. After White. North Carolina. 1585. *NYPL*.

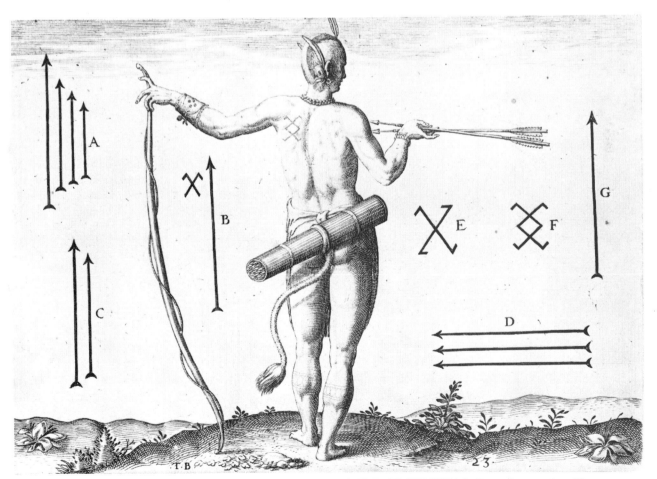

64. "THE MARCKES OF FUNDRYE OF THE CHEIF MENE OF VIRGINIA." Engraving number 23 from De Bry, 1590. 8¾ x 6⅜ inches. After White. North Carolina. 1585. *NYPL*.

White

SOUTHERN ALGONQUIAN INDIANS. 1585. NORTH CAROLINA. The following 18 pictures were reproduced from photographs of water colors painted by John White. The originals are owned and copyrighted by the British Museum. John White was the artist and cartographer for the first Virginia colony in 1585, and governor of the second in 1587. In that year, he stayed in the colony only a few months. When he returned to Roanoke Island in 1590 the colony had disappeared. *Courtesy of the British Museum, London.*

65. John White. "THE MAN-
NER OF THEIR ATTIRE . . ."
10½ x 6 inches. *BM.*

66. John White. "THE WYFE
OF AN HEROWAN OF SECO-
TAN." 10½ x 5½ inches. *BM.*

67. John White. "ONE OF
THEIR RELIGIOUS MEN." 10⅜
x 6 inches. *BM.*

68. John White. "ONE OF THE WYUES OF WYNGYNO." 9¼ x 5⅜ inches. *BM.*

69. John White. "A CHEIFE HEROWAN." 10⅜ x 5¾ inches. *BM.*

70. John White. "A CHEIFE HEROWANS WYFE . . ." 10 x 5⅝ inches. *BM.*

71. John White. "THE AGED MAN IN HIS WYNTER GARMENT." 10⅜ x 5⅞ inches. *BM.*

72. John White. "THE WYFE OF AN HEROWAN OF POMEIOOC." 10⅜ x 5⅞ inches. *BM.*

73. John White. "THE FLYER." 9⅝ x 6 inches. *BM.*

74. John White. "THE MANNER OF THEIR FISHING." 14 x 9¼ inches. *BM*.

75. John White. "THEIRE SITTING AT MEATE." 8⅜ x 8½ inches. *BM*.

76. John White. CEREMONY OF SITTING ROUND A FIRE. 8½ x 8 inches. *BM*

77. John White. RELIGIOUS DANCE. 10¼ x 14 inches. *BM*.

78. John White. "SECOTON. . . ." 12½ x 7⅞ inches. *BM.*

79. John White. "THE TOMBE OF THEIR CHER-OUNES OR CHEIFE PERSONAGES, ..." 11⅝ x 8 inches. *BM.*

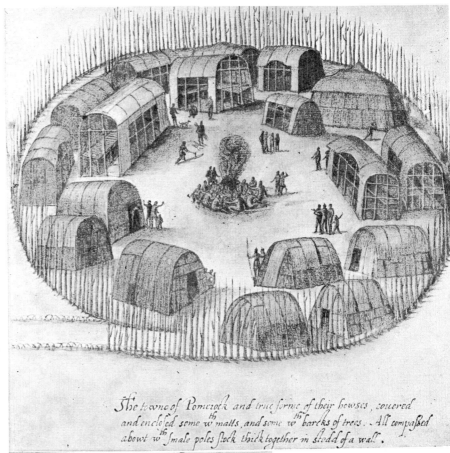

80. John White. "THE TOWNE OF POMEIOCK AND THE TRUE FORME OF THEIR HOWSES, ..." 8¾ x 8½ inches. *BM*.

The towne of Pomeiock and true forme of their howses, couered and enclosed some wth matts, and some wth barcks of trees. All compassed abowt wth smale poles stock thick together in stedd of a wall.

81. John White. "OF FLOR-IDA." 10¼ x 5⅜ inches. *BM*.

82. John White. "OF FLOR-IDA." 10⅝ x 5⅜ inches. *BM*.

Smith and Others

POWHATAN (SOUTHERN ALGONQUIAN). 1607-1645. VIRGINIA. English and Spanish traders were active on the Atlantic coast and penetrating westward. Late in the century, Frenchmen pushed into the middle and lower Mississippi Valley. This set the stage for the bitter clashes among these nations and their Indian allies during the next century. Explorers and traders from Virginia led the way. For a bibliography see, Ben C. McCary, *Indians in Seventeenth Century Virginia*. Published by the Virginia 350th Anniversary Celebration Corporation, Williamsburg, 1957.

83. "CAPTAIN JOHN SMITH'S MAP OF VIRGINIA. 1607." From Capt. John Smith, *Works, 1608-1631*, Edition edited by Edward Arber, English Scholar's Library. No. 16. Birmingham, 1884. *Photograph Courtesy of the Smithsonian Institution, Bureau of American Ethnology. Neg. S. I. 34543.*

Ætatis suæ 21. Aᵒ. 1616.

Matoaks als Rebecka daughter to the mighty Prince Powhatan Emperour of Attanoughkomouck als Virginia converted and baptized in the Christian faith, an Wife to the Worᵗ Mᵗ Tho: Rolff.

84. Artist unknown. British School. POCA-HONTAS. Oil on Canvas. 30 x 25 inches. England. 1616. _Courtesy of the National Gallery of Art, Washington, D. C., Mellon Collection, NPG 21._

· MATOAKA ALS REBECCA FILIA POTENTISS · PRINC · POWHATANI IMP · VIRGINIÆ ·

Matoaks als Rebecka daughter to the mighty Prince Powhatan Emperour of Attanougskomouck als virginia converted and baptized in the Christian fauts, and wife to the worᵗ Mr Joh Rolff.

S. Pass: sculp: Compton Holland exc.

85. Simon van de Pass. MATOAKA (POCAHONTAS). Line engraving. 6¾ x 4½ inches. London. 1616. _Courtesy of the British Museum._

86. Wencelaus Hollar. INDIAN OF VIRGINIA. MALE. Etching. 4 x 3 inches. England. 1645. _Courtesy of the New York Public Library._ (Plates 85 and 87 have been omitted).

Michel and Others

POWHATAN (SOUTHERN ALGONQUIAN) AND TUS-
CARORA (IROQUOIAN). 1701-1711. VIRGINIA AND
NORTH CAROLINA. "Michel made two journeys to Amer-
ica, between the years 1702-1704. His lettters and reports
show that he aimed at settling a Swiss colony in America.
In this he was not directly successful, but his letters led to
the organization of a joint-stock company, known as George
Ritter and Co., under whose auspices Christopher von Graffenried founded the German colony of New Berne, N. C., in
the year 1710, at the mouth of the Trent and Neuse rivers."
W. J. Hinke, ed., "Report of the Journey of Francis Louis
Michel . . ." Quoted *Courtesy of the Virginia Historical Society.* See Note 89.

88. Christopher von Graffenried. "CHRISTOPHER V. GRAFFENRIED (1661-1743) AND THE ENGLISH SURVEYOR
LAWSON AND THEIR NEGRO-SERVANT AT THE RED INDIAN TRIBUNAL IN CATECHNA (N. C.), 1711." Tuscarora. Original pen drawing with black washing, in: *Relations du Voyage d'Amèrique que le Baron de Graffenried a
fait en y amenant une colonie Palatine et Suisse, et son retour en Europe.* Size 34,5 x 20,5 cm. The drawing is not
dated, but the event represented took place in 1711. Call number: Burgerbibliothek Bern, Mül. 466 (1). *Courtesy of
the Burgerbibliothek Bern, Switzerland. Photograph by Stadt- und Universitätsbibliothek, Kesslergasse 41, Bern.*

89. Francis Louis Michel. "DREY AMER-ICANER." Three Americans. Powhatan? Southern Algonquian. Original pen drawing, washed with watercolor, in; *Franz Ludwig Michels (1675-1720) kurze amerikanische Reissbeschreibung, 1702.* The original manuscript is lost. This document is a contemporary copy made by his brother John Louis Michel. Size: 16 x 13,5 cm. Call number: Burgerbibliothek Bern, Mss. hist. helv. X.152, fol. 64a. *Courtesy of the Burgerbibliothek Bern, Switzerland. Photograph by Foto Zumstein, Kasinoplatz 8, Bern. Description of 88 and 89, by Dr. H. Haeberli, Director, Burgerbibliothek Bern.*

90. Lassus. CANOE WITH INDIANS. A detail view from "Veüe et perspective de la Nouvelle Orléans. Dessin à la plume rehaussé d'aquarelle. 1 mètre 52 x 0, 49. 1726." *Courtesy of the Ministère de la France d'Outre-Mer, Paris. Dépôt des Fortifications des Colonies, Louisiane, No 71. Photograph by J. Colomb-Gérard, 25, Bonne-Nouvelle, Paris.*

Du Pratz

NATCHEZ (MUSKHOGEAN) AND CHITIMACHA (TUNI-CAN) INDIANS. 1718-1734. LOUISIANA AND MISSIS-SIPPI. Woodcuts from Antoine Simon Le Page Du Pratz (c. 1690-1775), *Histoire de la Louisiane*, 3 volumes, Paris, 1758. Eleven of the 39 woodcuts therein depict Indians. Others picture the area's flora and fauna; one is a map of New Orleans. Du Pratz reached Dauphin Island in August, 1718. He later settled at Bayou St. John near New Orleans for two years. He next lived among the Natchez for eight years. *Courtesy of the Smithsonian Institution, Bureau of American Ethology.*

98. "MORTUARY RITES OVER THE TATTOOED-SERPENT (MORT ET CONVOI DU SERPENT PIQUE)" Woodcut from Du Pratz, 1758, Vol. 3, opp. p. 55. Natchez Temple. *SI-BAE* Neg. 1168-b

99. THE CEREMONY OF THE CALU-MET . . . BETWEEN THE CHITIMACHA INDIANS AND THE FRENCH, 1718 (MARCHE DU CALUMET DE PAIX)." Woodcut from Du Pratz, 1758, Vol. 1, opp. p. 105. *SI-BAE* Neg. 1168-b-9.

100. "NATIVE IN SUMMER (NATURELS EN ETÉ)" Woodcut from Du Pratz, 1758, Vol. 2, opp. p. 308. *SI-BAE* Neg. 2860-ff-2.

101. "WINTER CLOTHING OF A NATCHEZ MAN (NATURELS EN HYVER)." Woodcut from Du Pratz, 1758, Vol. 2, p. 309. *SI-BAE* Neg. 1168-8-5 (1).

102. "GENERAL DANCE OF THE NATCHEZ INDIANS (DANCE GENERALE)." Woodcut from Du Pratz, 1758, Vol. 2, opp. p. 376. Natchez tribe. *SI-BAE* Neg. 1168-b-3.

103. "A WOMAN AND HER DAUGHTER (FEMME ET FILLE)." Woodcut from Du Pratz, 1758, Vol. 2, opp. p. 310. *SI-BAE* Neg. 2860-ff-4.

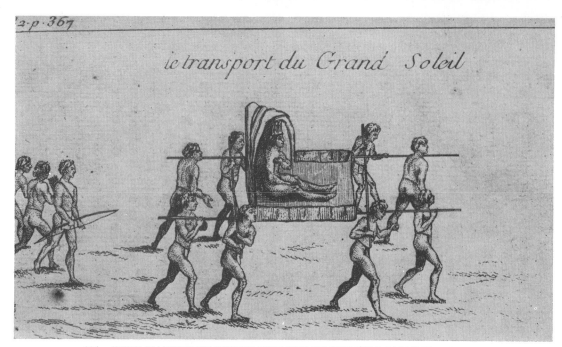

104. "THE MANNER IN WHICH THE GREAT SUN WAS CARRIED TO THE HARVEST FESTIVAL OF THE NATCHEZ (LE TRANSPORT DU GRAND SOLEIL)." Woodcut from Du Pratz, 1758, Vol. 2, opp. p. 367. Natchez tribe. *SI-BAE* Neg. 1168-b-2.

105. "PLAN OF A FORT AND PRISONER IN THE FRAME FOR EXECUTION (PLAN DU FORT. PRISONIER AU CADRE)." Woodcut from Du Pratz, 1758, Vol. 2, opp. p. 429. *SI-BAE* Neg. 2860-ff-7.

Naturels du Nord qui vont en chasse d'hyver avec leur Famille

106. "INDIANS OF THE NORTHWEST OF LOUISIANA LEAVING IN WINTER . . . FOR A HUNT." Woodcut from Du Pratz, 1758, Vol. 3, opp. p. 164. Kansa tribe. *SI-BAE* Neg. 45,068-A.

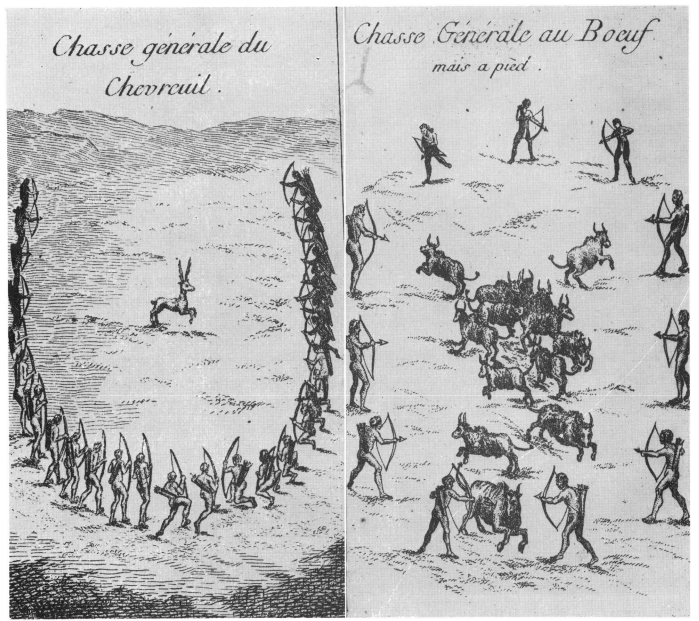

Chasse générale du Chevreuil.

Chasse Générale au Boeuf mais a pied.

107. "DEER HUNT (CHASSE GENERALE DU CHEVREUIL)." Woodcut from Du Pratz, 1758, Vol. 2, opp. p. 71. Natchez tribe. *SI-BAE* Neg. 45,068.

108. "BISON HUNT (CHASSE GENERALE AU BOEUF MAIS A PIED)." Woodcut from Du Pratz, 1758, Vol. 3, opp. p. 210. Natchez tribe. *SI-BAE* Neg. 45,068-B.

Faber and Others

CHEROKEE (IROQUOIAN), YAMACRAW OR YAMAS-SEE? (MUSKHOGEAN) AND OTHERS. 1730. TENNESSEE AND THE CAROLINAS. During the seventeenth, eighteenth, and nineteenth centuries European powers, vying for control of the new world, transported many Indian groups and individuals to Europe. Some were forced to go, while others volunteered. In Europe the Indians were objects of great curiosity; often royally entertained, as in England; and sometimes fell prey to commercial purposes. Several accounts of such trips are found in Carolyn Thomas Foreman, *Indians Abroad*. 1493-1938, University of Oklahoma Press, 1943.

109. "CHIEFS . . . FROM CAROLINA." Cherokee. Engraving, 18½ x 22 inches, by Isaac Basire, London, 1730. After a painting by Markham. 1 to r. O Onaconoa, K Skalilosken Ketagustah (Prince) (Catergusta), K Kollannah (Caulunna), OK Oukah Ulah (King) (Oukah Olah), T Tathtowe, C Clogoittah (Clogoitta), U Ukwaneequa (Attakullakulla or Little Carpenter, then a youth). These Cherokee Indians accompanied Sir Alexander Cuming to England, 1730. See Forman, pp. 44-55. *Courtesy of the Smithsonian Institution, Bureau of American Ethnology,* Neg. 1063-h-2. *Engraving, British Museum.*

110. **"TOMO-CHI-CHI AND OTHER YAMACRAWS PRESENTED TO THE TRUSTEES OF THE COLONY OF GEOR-GIA."** After an oil painting by Verelst, said to be in the possession of the descendants of the Earl of Shaftesbury, a Trustee of the Georgia colony? From a copy owned by the State of Georgia? *Courtesy of the Georgia Department of Archives and History.* Print, Smithsonian Institution, Bureau of American Ethnology, Neg. 1129-C. Swanton, BAE Bull. 137, Pl. 30.

111. **"THE REVEREND CHARLES WESLEY, PREACHING TO THE AMERICAN INDIANS IN 1736."** Engraving by F. Bromley. 16¾ x 22 inches. On India paper. Printed by R. R. McIan. Published by Joseph Laing, London. Edinburgh, Glasgow and 107 Fulotn Street, New York. 1870? *Courtesy of the University of Georgia Libraries, Athens. De Renne Collection.*

112. **"TOMO CHACHI AND HIS NEPHEW.** Engraving (mezzotint) by John Faber, after a painting by William Verelst, Flemish painter, 1734. 13⅞ x 9⅞ inches. c. 1735. *Courtesy of the Bureau of American Ethnology* Neg. 1129-a.

De Batz

CHOCTAW, ACOLAPISSA, NATCHEZ (MUSKHOGEAN), TUNICA, ATAKAPA (TUNICAN) AND OTHERS. 1732-1735. LOUISIANA AND MISSISSIPPI. Drawings by A. de Batz. The captions and notes accompanying these are quoted from David I. Bushnell, Jr., "Drawings by A. DeBatz in Louisiana, 1732-1735," (with six plates) *Smithsonian Miscellaneous Collections*, Vol. 80, No. 5, Publication 2925, Washington, 1927. Though little is known about DeBatz, his signature is also found on a church plan, New Orleans, and two maps. Drawings herein are from the Bushnell Collection. *Courtesy of the Peabody Museum, Harvard University.*

113. A. de Batz. "CHOCTAW SAVAGES PAINTED AS WARRIORS, CARRYING SCALPS (SAUVAGES TCHAKTAS NATACHEZ EN GUERRIERS QUI PORRENR DES CHEVETURES). Drawing in color. 8¼ x 14⅞ inches. *PM-HU* Neg. 16630. Spec. 41-72.

114. A. de Batz. "DRAWING OF SAVAGES OF SEVERAL NATIONS, NEW ORLEANS. 1735. (ILLINOIS, FOX, AND ATAKAPA). Drawing in color. 11¾ x 17⅞ inches. *PM-HU* Neg. 16629. Spec. 41-72.

SAUVAGE matachez en Guerrier, ayant fait trois Chevelure
c'est a dire ayant tuez trois Hommes Natchez.
Brida les Boeufs Chef des Thonicas, il remply la place de
son predecesseur que les natchez Tuerrent au mois de juin
dernier. Femme chef Veufue du ... defunt F. Jacob. fils
du defunt H cheuelures matachée et ... le baton ... pareillemen
tesinez ... d'apres nature sur ... les ... lieux,
Redigez ... a la n^lle orleans le 22. ... Juin 1732. De ...

Sauvage en habit d'hiver.

115. A. de Batz.
"S A V A G E
ADORNED AS
W A R R I O R ,
HAVING TAK-
EN THREE
SCALPS. (BUF-
FALO TAMER,
CHIEF OF
THE TUNICA.
1732.)" Drawing
in color. 12⅞ x
9⅛ inches. PM-
HU Neg. 16627.
Spec. 41-72.

116. A. de Batz.
"A SAVAGE
I N WINTER
DRESS." Draw-
ing in color. 9½
x 4½ inches.
P M - H U Neg.
16631. Spec. 41-
72.

TEMPLE des Sauvages, constuit de Poteaux en
terre, revêtù de ... natte de Canne, et
Couvert de même, ... terminé par trois pi...
de Bois, de 3. pieds ... de long 18. pouces ...
et 4 p.^ d'aipaisseur, ... matachez et Scul...
grossierement les ... 3. pyramides So...
natte garnie de ... canes pointu...
garentir, que ... son ne puiss...
monter aux ... figures qui rep-
-resente des ... d'Indes par is...
corps et ... la queüe, la
teste rep... esente celle
de l'Aigle ... ce qui nous'a
parù de ... plus a prochan...

CABANE du Chef de poteaux en garnie de Bauge ou mortie...
de terre, Couverte aussy ... de natte.
Le temple a 22. pieds de ... longueur et 14 pieds de large
il sert de Sepulture aux ... Chefs de la Nations
Toutes les Caban... des Sauvages sont de
pareille Construct... ion, etante toutes.
Ronde, celle cy ... 18. pieds de
diametre.

Relevés et dessinez au Village des Cotas-Pissas le quinze avril de la pr...
unne. Redigez a la nouvelle Orleans le Vingt et deux Juin 1732.

Echelle de Six ... Piedts

ARBRE inconû: Cet Arbre est actuellement Sur pied. aux natch...
Les Sauvages le Conservoient et le tenoient en grande Veneration, en preu...
quelque Branches ou Rameaux, pour mettre dans le feu Sacré, qu'ils en...
-tenoient perpetuelement dans leur Temple. qui étoit Construit proche ...
Arbre, les Francois Bruleren... detruirent ce Temple en fevrier 1730. Su...
Raport des plus encient de, Cette Colonie, Cet Arbre est le...
Seul et unique de cette Province! A Branche garnie de...
Feüilles de grandeur et Couleur natu... ref... B Fleure...
Couleur Blanche et pâle. C. La...
noissance il reste une...
elle tombe qui for...
Bouton et son peu...
Combien il a prodit feüil...

L'Arbre ... dessine d'apres nature a...
13. may ... Redigez a la n...
... orleans le 22 Juin 1732.

117. A. de Batz. "TEMPLE, AND CABIN
OF THE CHIEF. ACOLAPISSA. 1732." Pen
and ink drawing. 12⅝ x 9 inches. PM-HU
Neg. 19413. Spec. 41-72-16.

118. A. de Batz. "TREE NEAR SITE OF
NATCHEZ TEMPLE. 1732." Drawing in col-
or. 12⅝ x 9⅛ inches. PM-HU Neg. 16628.
Spec. 41-72.

Parsons and Others

CHEROKEE (IROQUOIAN). 1762. TENNESSEE AND THE CAROLINAS. Little Carpenter (Attakullakulla), the peace chief, of the Upper Cherokee in November, 1761, requested that the commander of Fort Patrick Henry send an officer to his people to convince them of the friendship of the English. Destruction had resulted to both sides in the Cherokee-English war of 1759-1761, and bitterness remained. Lt. Henry Timberlake volunteered for the mission. He later took three Cherokees to London. *Memoirs of Lieutenant Henry Timberlake*, London, 1765, is a valuable record of his observations.

The Three Cherokees came over from the head of the River Savanna to London 1762
& their Interpreter that was Poisoned.

119. "THE THREE CHEROKEES. CAME OVER FROM THE HEAD OF THE RIVER SAVANNA TO LONDON, 1762." l to r. The interpreter. Outacite or Man-Killer. Austenaco (Judd's Friend). Uschesees ye Great Hunter (Cunne Shote?). Copperplate engraving, colored by hand. 9 5/16 x 11 13/16 inches. Sold in May's Buildings, Covent Garden, according to Act, by G: Bickham. London, 1762. *Courtesy of the Smithsonian Institution, Bureau of American Ethnology* Neg. 1063-h-1.

120. Francis Parsons. CUNNE SHOTE. Chero-
kee. Oil on canvas. 28 x 35 inches. London. 1762.
*Courtesy of the Thomas Gilcrease Institute of
American History and Art, Tulsa.*

OUTACITE,
Chief of the CHEROKEES

121. "OUTACITE, Chief of the
Cherokees." From Drake, 1837.
Book IV, opp. p. 32. *Courtesy of
the Smithsonian Institution.* BAE
Neg. 1063-h-3.

Engraved for the Royal Magazine.

AUSTENACO, Great Warriour.
Commander in Chief of the Cherokee Nation.

122. "AUSTENACO, GREAT
WARRIOR." Engraving from the
Royal Magazine. 1762? *Courtesy of
the Smithsonian Institution,* BAE
Neg. 1063-g.

CUNNE SHOTE.
*Chef des Chiroquois
d'apres Parson*

123. "CUNNE SHOTE, CHEF DES
CHIROQUOIS." d'aprés Parson.
Engraving, colored. *Courtesy of the
University of Georgia Libraries,
Athens. De Renne Collection.*

Bartram and Romans

CHOCTAW, CREEK, CHICKASAW, SEMINOLE (MUSK-HOGEAN), AND CHEROKEE (IROQUOIAN). 1755-1790. SOUTHEASTERN UNITED STATES. William Bartram (1739-1823), a naturalist and artist of the flora and fauna of the Eastern United States, produced valuable records of Indian life in the Southeast. See Notes 124 and 125. Bernard Romans (c. 1721-1784), Dutch botanist, surveyor, and engraver, came to America from England in 1755. He worked in Florida for several years. There he recorded his careful observations of the customs and activities of native life.

124. "MICO CHLUCCO THE LONG WARIOR OR KING OF THE SIMINOLES." F r o m William Bartram, *Travels. . .*, 1791. J. Trenchard, Sculp. *Courtesy of the Yale University Library, New Haven.*

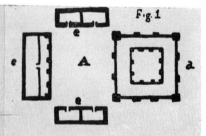

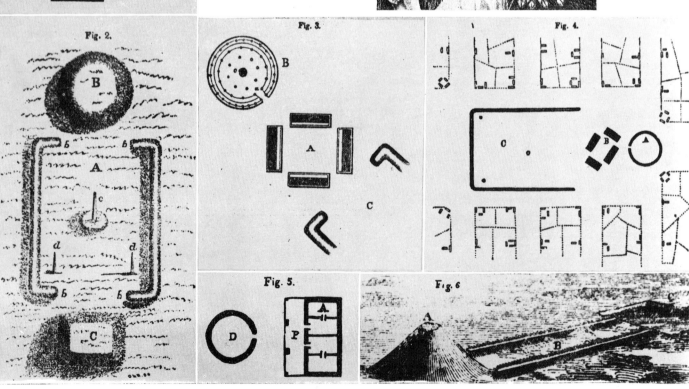

125. "ANCIENT INDIAN MONUMENTS. . ." From William Bartram, (Manuscript 1789. Published 1853). Figure 1. "Villa of the Chief of the Town of the Apalachians." Figure 2. "Plan of the Ancient Chunky-Yard." Figure 3. "The Public Square." Figures 4 and 5. "Creek Towns." Figure 6. "Ancient Remains." *Courtesy of the University of Pennsylvania Library.*

126. "CHOCTAW BURIALS." From Bernard Romans, *A Concise Natural History of East and West Florida*, Vol. 1, 1775, opp. p. 89. *Courtesy of the Smithsonian Institution, Bureau of American Ethnology* Neg. 1102-d.

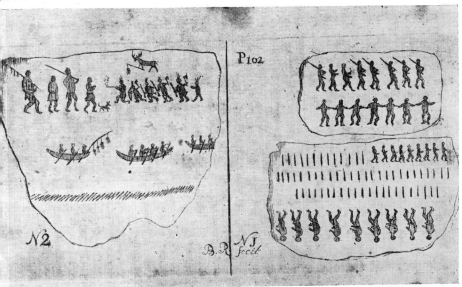

127. "PICTOGRAPHS." Left. ". . . made by Creek war party." Right. ". . . made by Choctaw." From Romans, Vol. 1, 1775, p. 102. *SI-BAE* Neg. Pictograph 8.

128. "CHARACTERISTIC BUSTS OF CHOCTAW INDIANS." From Romans, Vol. 1, 1775, p. 82. *SI-BAE* Neg. 1102-e.

129. "CHARACTERISTIC CHICASAW HEAD." From Romans, Vol. 1, 1775, p. 59. *SI-BAE* Neg. 1071-b.

130. "CHARACTERISTIC HEAD OF A CREEK WAR CHIEF." From Romans, Vol. 1, 1775, p. 93. *SI-BAE* Neg. 1166-b.

Tidball
and
Trumbull

CREEK (MUSKHOGEAN). 1790-1791. ALABAMA AND GEORGIA. For the sketch shown below, John Caldwell Tidball (1825-1906) probably referred to written sources and to his observations of Creek Indians on Western reservations. He was with Lt. Whipple's expedition to the Pacific, 1853-1854, and journeyed through many Indian reservations including that of the Creeks. John Trumbull (1756-1843) was an artist and soldier. He produced sketches of five Creek Indians in New York, July 1790, while they were attending a conference there.

131. "A LOG HABITATION, 1791." Creek. Engraving from H. R. Schoolcraft, *Historical . . . Information . . . Respecting . . . the Indian Tribes of the United States,* 6 vols. Philadelphia, 1851-1857. After a drawing by J. C. Tidball, U. S. A. *Courtesy of the Smithsonian Institution, Bureau of American Ethnology Neg. 1169-a.*

132. John Trumbull. "HOPOTHLE MICO, . . ." Creek. Pencil drawing. 4⅞ x 4 inches. "New York, July 1790." *Courtesy of the Fordham University Library, New York. Photograph by the Frick Art Reference Library, New York, Neg. FARL 21170.*

133. John Trumbull. "TUSKATCHE MICO, . . ." Creek. Pencil drawing. 3 11/16 x 4 11/16 inches. New York. 1790. *Courtesy of the Yale University Library, New Haven, Cat. No. 1947.497.*

134. "STIMAFUTCHKI, . . ." Creek. Engraving from Trumbull, Autobiography, Pl. 20. After a pencil drawing, New York, 1790. *Courtesy of the Smithsonian Institution, BAE Neg. 1169-L-3.*

135. John Trumbull. "JOHN—A CREEK." Pencil drawing. 4 x 2¾ inches. New York. 1790. *Courtesy of the Yale University Library, New Haven, Cat. No. 1947.496.*

136. "HYSAC, . . ." Creek. Engraving from Trumbull, *Autobiography*, Pl. 19. After a pencil drawing, New York, 1790. *Courtesy of the Smithsonian Institution, BAE Neg. 1169-L-2.*

King and Others

CREEK, CHOCTAW, SEMINOLE (MUSKHOGEAN), YU-CHI, AND CHEROKEE (IROQUOIAN) INDIANS. 1820-1830. ALABAMA, TENNESSEE, FLORIDA, MISSISSIPPI AND GEORGIA. Charles Bird King (1785-1862) painted oil portraits of many Indian leaders who visited Washington. Some of his portraits became the models for copies by Henry Inman (Peabody Museum, Harvard University Collections) and for the lithographs published by Thomas L. McKenney and James Hall (See Pls. 144-180.) Most of King's portraits formerly in the Indian Gallery were destroyed in the Smithsonian Institution fire in 1865.

137. Charles B. King. DAVID VANN. Cherokee. oil on wood. 13¾ x 17¼ inches. Washington. 1825. *Courtesy of the Thomas Gilcrease Institute of American History and Art. Tulsa.*

138. Charles B. King. TULCEE-MATHLA. Seminole. Oil on canvas. 17½ x 13½ inches. Washington. 1826. *Courtesy of the University Museum, Philadelphia,* Neg. 46927.

139. Charles B. King. PUSH-MATAHA. Choctaw. Oil on wood. 17½ x 13½ inches. Washington. 1824. *Courtesy of the Redwood Library and Athenaeum, Newport, 201.*

140. Charles B. King. MISTIP-PEE. Creek. Oil on wood. 17½ x 13½ inches. Washington. 1826. *Courtesy of the Redwood Library and Athenaeum, Newport, 176.*

141. Charles B. King. TIMPO-OCHEE BARNARD. Yuchi. Oil. 17½ x 13½ inches. Washington. 1825. *Courtesy of the Redwood Library and Athenaeum, Newport, 196.*

142. Baroness Hyde de Neuville. CHEROKEE. Watercolor on paper. 11⅛ x 7¼ inches. Tennessee? 1820? *Courtesy of the New-York Historical Society, New York City, Neg. 37253.*

143. Washington Allston. WILLIAM McINTOSH. Creek. Oil on Canvas. 92 x 52 inches. Washington? 1820's. *Courtesy of the Alabama Department of Archives and History, Montgomery. Photograph by John E. Scott, Jr.*

McKenney and Hall

CREEK, CHOCTAW, SEMINOLE (MUSKHOGEAN), YU-CHI, AND CHEROKEE (IROQUOIAN) INDIANS. 1820-1830. ALABAMA, TENNESSEE, FLORIDA, MISSISSIPPI, AND GEORGIA. Thomas L. McKenney and James Hall were neither artists nor engravers. They were the authors—publishers of *The Indian Tribes of North America*, 3 vols., 1838-1842. The books contained 120 colored lithographs (size 19¼ x 13½ inches) after oil paintings by C. B. King, owned by the United States Government. Most of those oil portraits were destroyed by fire in 1865. See Notes 138 and 144. *Photographs courtesy of the Smithsonian Institution, Bureau of American Ethnology.*

144. McINTOSH. Creek. From Mc-Kenney and Hall, undated. SI-BAE Neg. 45,111-B.

145. MISTIPPEE. Creek. From Mc-Kenney and Hall, undated. SI-BAE Neg. 45,111-C.

146. ME-NA-WA. Creek. From Mc-Kenney and Hall, 1838. SI-BAE Neg. 1119-b.

147. LEDAGIE. Creek. From Mc-Kenney and Hall, undated. SI-BAE Neg. 45-111-A.

148. TUSTENNUGGEE EMATH-LA. Creek. From McKenney and Hall, undated. SI-BAE Neg. 45,-111-J.

149. SE-LOC-TA. Creek. From Mc-Kenney and Hall, undated. SI-BAE Neg. 45,111-H.

150. YOHOLO-MICCO. C r e e k .
From McKenney and Hall, 1842.
SI-BAE Neg. 43,796.

151. OPOTHLE YOHOLO. Creek.
From McKenney and Hall, 1842.
SI-BAE Neg. 45,111-F.

152. APAULY-TUSTENNUGGEE.
Creek. From McKenney and Hall,
undated. SI-BAE Neg. 45,111.

153. OCHE-FINCECO. Creek. From
McKenney and Hall, undated. SI-
BAE Neg. 45,111-E.

154. NAH-ET-LUC-HOPIE. Creek.
From McKenney and Hall, undated. SI-BAE Neg. 45,111-D.

155. PADDY CARR. Creek. From
McKenney and Hall, undated. SI-
BAE Neg. 45,111-G.

156. TIMPOOCHEE BARNARD.
Yuchi. From McKenney and Hall,
undated. SI-BAE Neg. 45,113.

157. PUSH-MA-TA-HA. Choctaw.
From McKenney and Hall, undated. SI-BAE Neg. 1092-A.

158. PO-CA-HON-TAS. Powhatan.
From McKenney and Hall, undated. SI-BAE Neg. 876.

159. SPRING FROG. Cherokee. From McKenney and Hall, undated. SI-BAE Neg. 45,113-C.

160. DAVID VANN. Cherokee. From McKenney and Hall, undated. SI-BAE Neg. 45,113-D.

161. TAH-CHEE. Cherokee. From McKenney and Hall, 1838. SI-BAE Neg. 1045.

162. SE-QUO-YAH. Cherokee. From McKenney and Hall, 1838. SI-BAE Neg. 991-a.

163. JOHN RIDGE. Cherokee. From McKenney and Hall, undated. SI-BAE Neg. 45,113-A.

164. JOHN ROSS. Cherokee. From McKenney and Hall, undated. SI-BAE Neg. 988-B.

165. MAJOR RIDGE. Cherokee. From McKenney and Hall, undated. SI-BAE Neg. 45,113-B.

166. TENS - KWAU-TA-
WAW. Shawnee. From
Mc-Kenney and Hall,
1838. SI-BAE Neg. 769-b.

167. KISH - KAL - WA.
Shawnee. From McKen-
ney and Hall, undated.
SI-BAE Neg. 45,113-F.

168. QUA - TA- WA-PEA.
Shawnee. From McKen-
ney and Hall, undated.
SI-BAE Neg. 45,113-H.

169. PAYTA - KOOTHA.
Shawnee. From McKen-
ney and Hall, undated.
SI-BAE Neg. 45,113-G.

170. CA - TA-HE-CAS-SA.
Shawnee. From McKen-
ney and Hall, undated.
SI-BAE Neg. 45,113-E.

171. YAHA-HAJO. Seminole. From McKenney and Hall, undated. SI-BAE Neg. 45,112-H.

172. MICANOPY. Seminole. From McKenney and Hall, undated. SI-BAE Neg. 45,112-C.

173. OSCEOLA. Seminole. From McKenney and Hall, undated. SI-BAE Neg. 45,112-E.

174. TUKO-SEE-MATHLA. Seminole. From McKenney and Hall, undated. SI-BAE Neg. 45,112-F.

175. CHITTEE YOHO-
LO. Seminole. From Mc-
Kenney and Hall, un-
dated. SI-BAE Neg. 45,-
112.

176. TULCEE-MATHLA
Seminole. From McKen
ney and Hall, undated.
SI-BAE Neg. 45,112-G.

177. FOKE - LUSTE-HA-
JO. Seminole. From Mc-
Kenney and Hall, un-
dated. SI-BAE Neg. 45,-
112-A.

178. NEA - MATH - LA.
Seminole. From McKen-
ney and Hall, undated.
SI-BAE Neg. 45,112-D.

179. ITCHO - TUSTIN-
NUGGEE. Seminole.
From McKenney and
Hall, undated. SI-BAE
Neg. 45,112-B.

180. BILLY - BOWLEGS
Seminole. From McKen-
ney and Hall, edition?
SI-BAE Neg. 1174-a.

Lesueur

CHOCTAW (MUSKHOGEAN). 1825-1837. TENNESSEE, MISSISSIPPI AND LOUISIANA. Charles Alexandre Lesueur (1778-1846), a French artist, lived in the United States between 1816 and 1837. In 1825 he moved from Pennsylvania to Indiana. There he produced biological engravings and taught art. Several times he traveled the Mississippi to New Orleans. On these trips he made sketches of Indians. *Courtesy of the Muséum d'Histoire Naturelle, Le Havre, France. Photographs by V. Genetier, Paris.*

181. Charles A. Lesueur. "INDIAN CA-BANNE." Memphis? open, lean-to, brush shelters held up by forked poles. *MNH, Havre 576.*

182. Charles A. Lesueur. "JAMES. JAMY. CHAWTAS. A PETIT GOLPHE MISSISSIPPI. April 16, 1830." *MNH, Havre 732.*

183. Charles A. Lesueur. "CHACTAS". Four seated figures and a profile head. *MNH, Havre 636.*

184. Charles A. Lesueur. "JEU DE PEAUNE INDIEN Á LA NELLE OR-LEANS." Indian Ball Play. Players hold two ball sticks. *MNH, Havre* 637.

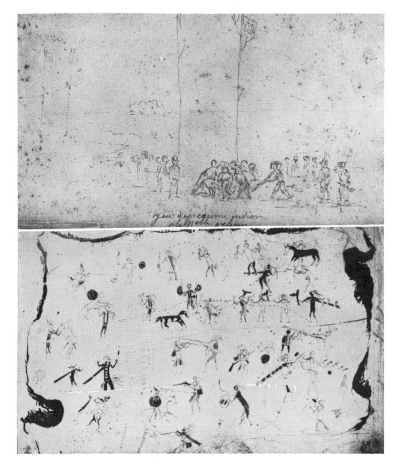

185. Charles A. Lesueur. "PEAU DE BISON DECOREE DE PEINTURES PAR UN INDIEN." Water color of a military record on a buffalo skin. This and pipes in his 728 may apply to Plains Indians. *MNH, Havre* 727.

186. **Charles A. Lesueur. "CHAWCTAS. INNABE. AN-NABE. Memphis. 6 April 1830."** *MNH, Havre* 731.

187. Charles A. Lesueur. "CHAWCTAS. BASTA-LABE. BASTA LLA BA. A Memphis le 16 April 1830." MNH, *Havre* 726.

Catlin

CHEROKEE (IROQUOIAN), CHOCTAW, CREEK, SEMI-
NOLE (MUSKHOGEAN), YUCHI (U C H E A N), and
SHAWNEE (ALGONQUIAN). 1830's. OKLAHOMA. FORT
MOULTRIE, SOUTH CAROLINA, AND FLORIDA. More
pictures of the Indians west of the Mississippi were produced
by George Catlin (1796-1872) than by any other painter. For
three decades following 1830, he produced several hundred
portraits and scenes of native life, copied them many times,
and exhibited his work on three continents. See Plates and
Notes 188-283, *Courtesy of the Smithsonian Institution,
United States National Museum.*

188. "George Catlin. "STEEH-
TCHA-KO-ME-CO, the Great
King, called 'Ben Perryman.'"
Creek. *SI-USNM* Neg. 42,095-E.

189. George Catlin. "HOL-TE-
MAL-TE-TEZ-TE-MEEK-EE, 'Sam
Perryman.'" Creek. *SI-USNM* Neg.
42,095-G.

190. George Catlin. "HOSE-PUT-
O-KAW-GEE." Creek. *SI-USNM*
Neg. 31,643-B.

191. George Catlin. "TEL-MAZ-
HA-ZA." Creek. *SI-USNM* Neg.
31,554-M.

192. George Catlin. "TCHOW-
EE-PUT-O-KAW." Creek. *SI-
USNM* Neg. 31,639-D.

193. George Catlin. "WAT-AL-
LE-GO." Creek. *SI-USNM* Neg.
31,560-C.

194. George Catlin. "COL-LEE." Cherokee. *SI-USMN* Neg. 42,095-F.

195. George Catlin. "TEH-KE-NEH-KEE, the Black Coat." Cherokee. *SI-USNM* Neg. 31,551-E.

196. George Catlin. "ETCH-EE-FIX-E-CO, the Deer without a Heart, called 'Euchee Jack.'" Yuchi. *SI-USNM* Neg. 31,642-D.

197. George Catlin. "CHEE-A-EX-E-CO." Yuchi. *SI-USNM* Neg. 31,939.

198. George Catlin. "TEN-SQUAT-A-WAY, the Open Door; called the Shawnee Prophet." *SI-USNM* Neg. 42,094-E.

199. George Catlin. "LAY-LOO-AH-PEE-AI-SHEE-KAW, G r a s s, Bush, and Blossom." Shawnee. *SI-USNM* Neg. 31,940-A.

200. George Catlin. "PAW-TE-COO-CAW, the Straight Man." Shawnee. *SI-USNM* Neg. 38,752-C.

201. George Catlin. "LAY-LAW-SHE-KAW, He who goes up the River." Shawnee. *SI-USNM* Neg. 42,094.B.

202. George Catlin. "OSCEOLA, the Black Drink."
Seminole. *SI-USNM* Neg. 42,096-H.

203. George Catlin. "MICK-E-NO-PAH." Seminole.
SI-USNM Neg. 42,800.

204. George Catlin. "CO-EE-HE-JO." Seminole. *SI-
USNM* Neg. 31,939-B.

205. George Catlin. "YE-HOW-LO-GEE, the Cloud."
Seminole. *SI-USNM* Neg. 31,939-A.

206. George Catlin. "BEAUTIFUL SAVANNAH IN THE PINE-WOODS OF FLORIDA." *SI-USNM* Neg. 31,568-G.

207. George Catlin. "WHITE SAN BLUFFS, ON SANTA ROSA ISLAND; AND SEMINOLES DRYING FISH, NEAR PENSACOLA, ON THE GULF OF FLORIDA." *SI-UNM* Neg. 31,539-H.

208. George Catlin. "A SEMINOLE WOMAN." *SI-USNM* Neg. 31, 602-A.

209. George Catlin. "EE-MAT-LA, King Phillip." Seminole. *SI-USNM* Neg. 31,-939-L.

210. George Catlin. "OSCEOLA NICKA-NOCHEE." Seminole. *SI-USNM* Neg. 37,100.

211. George Catlin. "LAH-SHEE, the Licker, called 'Creek Billy.'" Seminole, *SI-US NM* Neg. 31,939-D.

212. George Catlin. "KUT-TEE-O-TUB-BEE, How Did He Kill?" Choctaw. *SI-USNM* Neg. 31,949-K.

213. George Catlin. "MO-SHO-LA-TUB-BEE, He Who Puts Out and Kills." Choctaw. *SI-USNM* Neg. 3348-B.

214. George Catlin. "WOMAN." Choctaw. *SI-USNM* Neg. 31,643-H.

215. George Catlin. "HA-TCHOO-TUC-KNEE, the Snapping Turtle, 'Peter Pinchlin.'" Choctaw. *SI-USNM* Neg. 31,939-C.

216. George Catlin. "TUL-LOCK-CHISH-KO, He Who Drinks the Juice of the Stone." Choctaw. *SI-USNM* Neg. 31,943-K.

217. George Catlin. "TUL-LOCK-CHISH-KO." See 216. Choctaw. *SI-USNM* Neg. 42,093-A.

218. George Catlin. "EAGLE DANCE." Choctaw. *SI-USNM* Neg. 43,459.

219. George Catlin. "BALL PLAY OF THE CHOCTAWS—BALL UP." *SI-USNM* Neg. 43,882-A.

220. George Catlin. "BALL PLAY OF THE CHOCTAWS—BALL UP." Variant of Catlin 428. See 219, above. *SI-USNM* Neg. 37,193.

221. George Catlin. "BALL PLAY. BALL IS DOWN." Choctaw. *SI-USNM* Neg. 30,946-H.

222. George Catlin. "BALL PLAY DANCE." Choctaw. *SI-USNM* Neg. 30,946.

223—227. *Courtesy of the New York State Library. Albany. From George Catlin, Souvenir of the North American Indians.* MS. London. 1852. A bound volume containing 99 water colors, page size 10½ x 14 inches, with descriptive copy on the page opposite each painting. Most portraits are bust-head instead of full-length. Those shown here measure from 5 to 8 inches high.

223. George Catlin. "HOL-TE-MAL-TE-TEZ-TE-NEEK-E." Creek *NYSL* 90.

224. George Catlin. "TUCH-EE." Cherokee. *NYSL* 85.

225. George Catlin. "OS-CE-O-LA." Seminole. *NYSL* 78.

226. George Catlin. "YE-HOW-LO-GEE." Seminole. *NYSL* 77.

227. George Catlin. "LA-SHEE." Seminole. *NYSL* 76.

228. George Catlin. "CHOCTAW EAGLE DANCE." Oil on cardboard. *Courtesy of the American Museum of Natural History.* New York. Cat. No. A 245. 324241.

229. George Catlin. "BALL PLAY DANCE. CHOCTAW." Oil on cardboard. *Courtesy of the American Museum of Natural History.* New York. Cat. No. A 250. 324679. (variation, 324681).

230. George Catlin. "TULLOCK CHISH KO." Choctaw. *NL* 215.

231. George Catlin. "HAH - CHOO - TUCK - NEE." Choctaw. *NL* 203.

232. George Catlin "MO - SHO - LA - TUB - BEE." Choctaw. *NL* 202.

230—248. *Courtesy of the Newberry Library. Chicago. Ayer Collection.* From George Catlin, *Portraits of North American Indians.* MS. 2 vols. London. 1852. Pages on which the sketches appear are a uniform size— 10¼ x 13½ inches. Each picture is numbered, and a description of it is found on the opposite page. Ewers (1956, p. 526) describes this manuscript:

"Bound volumes comprising 217 pencil portraits, one to a page. Title page signed 'Geo. Catlin, 1852.' Includes portraits of Indians west of Rockies not seen by Catlin until 1850's."

233. George Catlin. "TEN - SQUA-TA-WAY." Shawnee. *NL* 93.

234. George Catlin "LAY - LAW-SHE-KAW." Shawnee. *NL* 90.

235. George Catlin "PAH - TEE-COO-SAW." Shawnee. *NL* 92.

236. George Catlin. "KAY-TEE-QUA." Shawnee. *NL* 91.

237. George Catlin. "LA - SHEE." Seminole. *NL* 135.

238. George Catlin "MIC-E-NO-PAH." Seminole. *NL* 130.

239. George Catlin "EE-MAT-LA." Seminole. *NL* 132.

240. George Catlin. "OS-CE-O-LA." Seminole. *NL* 129.

241. George Catlin "SEMINOLEE WOM-AN." Seminole. *NL* 134.

242. George Catlin "SEMINOLEE WOM-AN." Seminole. *NL* 136.6.

243. George Catlin "OS-CE-O-LA." Seminole. *NL*. 136.

244. George Catlin. "YE - HOW - LO - GEE." Seminole. *NL* 133.

245. George Catlin "STEE - CHA - CO - ME-CO." Creek. *NL* 204.

246. George Catlin "HOL-TE-MAL-TE-TEZ-TE-NEEK-E." Creek. *NL* 205.

247. George Catlin "JOL - LEE." Cherokee. *NL* 211.

248. George Catlin. "TUCH-EE." Cherokee. *NL* 212.

249. George Catlin. "MIC - E - NO - PA." Seminole. *Y U L*, 129.

250. George Catlin. "LA-SHEE." Seminole. *YUL*, 133.

251. George Catlin. "OS - CE - O - LA." Seminole. *Y U L*, 128.

252. George Catlin. "EE - MAT - LA." Seminole. *Y U L*, 134.

253. George Catlin. "YE - HOW - LO - GEE." Seminole. *YUL*, 131.

254. George Catlin. "HOW-E-DA-HE." Seminole. *Y U L*, 130.

255. George Catlin. "S E M I N O L E E WOMAN." Seminole. *YUL*, 132.

256. George Catlin. "OS - CE - O - LA." Seminole. *Y U L*, 135.

257. George Catlin. "SHAWNO WOM-AN." Shawnee. *YUL*, 83.

258. George Catlin. "PAH - TEE-COO-S A W." Shawnee. *YUL*, 84.

249—260. *Courtesy of the Yale University Library. New Haven. Western Americana Collection. Pencil sketches by George Catlin, from Souvenir of the North American Indian. This manuscript is on pages, size 8¼ x 11 inches. A description of each picture appears on the page opposite the picture. Ewers (1956, p. 526) describes this manuscript:*

"Two bound volumes comprising 216 pencil portraits, one to a page. Similar to (the collection of portraits in the Newberry Library). Also 3 oil portraits on cardboard."

259. George Catlin. "TEN - SQUA-TA-W A Y ." Shawnee. *YUL*, 85.

260. George Catlin. "LAY - LAW-SHE-K A W ." Shawnee. *YUL*, 82.

261. George Catlin. "CHEROKEE WARRIORS." l to r. "Tuch-ee, called 'Dutch'" (with rifle) and "Jol-lee" (with pipe). 11 x 12 inches. *HLAG* 113.

262. George Catlin. "CHOCTAW CHIEF AND YOUNG HALF-CASTE." l to r. "Ha-choo-tuck-ne" (hands on legs) and "Mo-sho-la-tub-be, chief. . . ." (hands crossed in lap). 10 x 15 inches. *HLAG* 107.

263. George Catlin. "CREEK CHIEF 'BEN PERRYMAN' AND HIS BROTHER." l to r. "Hol-te-mal-te-tez-te-neek-e, 'Sam Perryman' " and "Stee-cha-co-me-co (the great king) called 'Ben Perryman' " (gun in hand) and unidentified woman and child. 11 x 15 inches. *HLAG* 104.

261—265. *Courtesy of the Henry E. Huntington Library and Art Gallery. San Marino, California. From George Catlin, The North American Indians in the Middle Nineteenth Century. MS.* 1871. Ewers (1956, p. 526) describes this manuscript:

"155 pencil drawings, many identical to those in New York Public Library, and 50 oil-on-paper cartoons, many identical to those in the American Museum of Natural History."

264. George Catlin. "SEMINOLE CHIEF AND WOMEN." l to r. "Two wives of Os-ce-o-la. Os-ce-o-la (with gun). Mick-e-no-pa, head chief of tribe. How-e-da-hee, Seminolee woman, wife of chief Mick-e-no-pa." 10½ x 18 inches. *HLAG* 106.

265. George Catlin. "SEMINOLE WARRIORS." l to r. standing. "Os-ce-o-la, a Boy. Ee-mat-la. (and) Ye-how-lo-gee." sitting. "Wont-now . . . wife of one of the warriors. La-shee. Co-ee-ha-jo." 10½ x 16 inches. *HLAG* 105.

266. George Catlin. "CREEK." l to r. "Wife and child of the chief. Ste-cha-co-me-co, chief. Hol-te-mal-te-tez-te-neek-e." N-YHS Pl. 64. Neg. 33064 A.

266—274. *Courtesy of the New-York Historical Society, New York City.* From a collection of separate pencil drawings by George Catlin. These are not in a folio, are undated, and on paper 18⅛ x 24 inches, within double border-lines, size 13⅛ x 8⅞ inches. See H. Maxson Holloway, "Drawings by George Catlin." *New-York Historical Quarterly,* Vol. 26, No. 1, 1942. Ewers (1956, p. 526) describes this manuscript:

"221 pencil and pen-and-ink drawings, many of them very similar if not identical to (those in the collection of the New York Public Library)."

267. George Catlin. "SEMINOLEE." l to r. standing. "Ye-how-lo-gee. Ee-mat-la. Os-ce-o-la, sitting. Co-ee-ha-jo. La-shee. Wont-now, wife of one of the warriors." N-YHS Pl. 68. Neg. 33068 A.

268. George Catlin. "SHAWANO." l to r. "Kay-te-qua, the Female Eagle; daughter of the Chief. Pah-te-coo-saw, hunter. Lay-law-she-kaw, chief. Unidentified children. Ten-squa-ta-way. N-YHS Pl. 75. Neg. 33075 A.

269. George Catlin. "CHEROKEE." l to r. Jol-lee.
Tuch-ee. *N-YHS* Pl. 72. Neg. 33072 A.

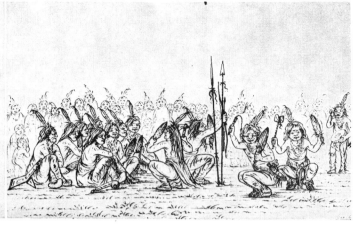

270. George Catlin. "EAGLE DANCE (CHOCTAW)."
N-YHS Pl. 153. Neg. 33153 A.

271. George Catlin. "CHOCTAW." l to r. "Mo-sho-la-
tub-be. Ha-choo-tuck-nee." *N-YHS* Pl. 65. Neg. 33065 A.

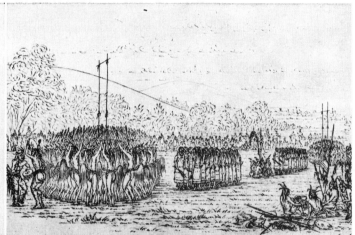

272. George Catlin. "BALL-PLAY DANCE (CHOC-
TAW)." *N-YHS* Pl. 164. Neg. 33164 A.

273. George Catlin. "BALL PLAYERS." l to r. "Tul-
lock-chish-ko. We-chush-ta-doo-ta. Ah-no-Je-nahge." *N-
YHS* Pl. 83. Neg. 33083 A.

274. George Catlin. "BALL-PLAY (CHOCTAW). *N-YHS*
Pl. 165. Neg. 33165 A.

275. George Catlin. "SEMINOLEE." l to r. "Wife and child of the Chief. Mik-e-no-pa, head chief. Os-ce-o-la, celebrated warrior. Two wives and child of Os-ce-o-la." *NYPL* Vol. I, 48 (150-153).

276. George Catlin. "CHOCTAW." l to r. "Mo-sho-la-tub-bee. Hah-tchoo-tuck-nee." *NYPL*. Vol. II, 74.

277. George Catlin. "SEMINOLEE." l to r. standing. "Ye-how-lo-gee. Ee-mat-la (with pipe). Os-ce-o-la. sitting. Co-ee-ha-jo. La-shee. "Woman and child." *NYPL* Vol. I, 49 (154-159).

278. George Catlin. "CREEK." l to r. "Steeh-cha-co-me-co. Hol-te-mal-te-tez-te-neek-ee." *NYPL* Vol. II, 75 (231-232).

279. George Catlin. "SHAWANO." l to r. "Kay-te-qua, daughter of the Chief. Pah-te-coo-saw, warrior. Lay-law-she-kaw, chief . Ten-squa-tah-way." *NYPL* Vol. I, 31 (96-99).

280. George Catlin. "CHEROKEE." l to r. "Jol-lee. Tuch-ee." *NYPL* Vol. II, 78 (238-239).

281. George Catlin. "SIOUX AND CHOCTAW BALL PLAYERS, in Ball Play Costume. Tullock-chish-ko. We-chush-ta-doo-ta. Ah-no-je-nahge." *NYPL* Vol. II, 79 (240-242).

275—283. *Courtesy of the New York Public Library, New York City. From George Catlin, Souvenir of the North American Indians.* MS. 3 vols. 1871. The drawings are on sheets 17¼ x 22⅞ inches, enclosed within a border 13¼ x 19 inches. Ewers (1956, p. 526) describes this manuscript:

"Bound volumes containing 167 plates of pencil drawings with page of explanation opposite each plate. Drawings executed in Europe ante 1852. Includes many replicas of original Indian Gallery subjects. Portraits commonly full-length and three or more to a plate. In addition there are portraits of Indians of North America west of Rockies seen by Catlin in 1850's and facsimiles of painted buffalo robes presumably owned by the artist."

282. George Catlin. "CHOCTAW BALL PLAY." *NYPL* Vol. III, 135.

283. George Catlin. "CHOCTAW BALL-PLAY DANCE." *NYPL* Vol. III, 134.

Vinton and Others

SEMINOLE (MUSKHOGEAN). 1830-1860. FLORIDA AND FORT MOULTRIE, SOUTH CAROLINA. Osceola was the most frequently pictured warrior of the Seminole war. Captain John Vinton, United States Army, drew and painted Osceola at Lake Monroe, Florida. After he was taken prisoner and sent to Fort Moultrie, South Carolina, Catlin, Curtis, Laning, and others painted and sketched his picture. Since there were no photographers in 1837, newspaper, magazine, and book publishers depended on the work of artists, whose original work was usually engraved by other copyartists.

284. "OSEOLA." Seminole. Lithograph from a sketch by John Rogers Vinton. 10⅛ x 8¼ inches. Lake Monroe, Florida. *Courtesy of the P. K. Yonge Library of Florida History, The University of Florida Libraries, Gainesville.*

285. John Rogers Vinton. "OSEOLA AT LAKE MONROE DURING THE ARMISTICE, May 1837." Seminole. Pencil drawing signed "JRV.—1845." 8¾ x 5⅜ inches. *Reproduced by permission of Mark F. Boyd, Photograph by L'Avant Studios, Tallahassee.*

286. George Catlin. OSCEOLA. Seminole. Oil on canvas. 23¼ x 28½ inches. 1838. *Courtesy of the American Museum of Natural History, New York, 33771.* Catlin's Catalog, 1848, lists as no. 308, a full-length portrait of Osceola.

287. W. M. Laning. "OSCEOLA, CHIEF OF THE SEMINOLES." Oil on canvas. 36⅛ x 28 inches. *Courtesy of the National Gallery of Art, Washington. Collection of Edgar William and Bernice Chrysler Garbisch, 463.*

288. John Rogers Vinton. "OCEOLA." Seminole. Pencil drawing. 2¾ x 3 inches. Undated. Unsigned. *Courtesy of the Museum of the American Indian, Heye Foundation, New York, Neg. 26048. Print. 18412.*

289. John Rogers Vinton. "OSEOLA." Oil on board. 10 x 13 inches. Undated. *Courtesy of Major General W. F. Tompkins, USA, Retired, Richmond.*

290. "O-CE-O-LA OBT. JANY. 30, 1838" Seminole. Engraving. 11½ x 14¾ inches. After J. R. Curtis. Sullivan's Island, S. C. *Courtesy of the South Caroliniana Library, University of South Carolina, Columbia. Photograph by Kent of Columbia, Inc.*

291. Robert John Curtis. OSCEOLA. Seminole. Oil on canvas. 24 x 30 inches. Ft. Moultrie, South Carolina. January, 1838. *Painting in the collection of the Charleston Museum, Charleston. Print supplied by Mr. E. Milby Burton, the Director of the Museum.*

292. George Catlin. OSCEOLA. Seminole. Lithograph from studio portrait. 19½ x 26½ inches. *Courtesy of the Thomas Gilcrease Institute of American History and Art, Tulsa.*

293. Winslow Homer. "INDIAN HUNTER IN THE EVERGLADES." Watercolor. 14 x 9¼ inches. *Courtesy of the Museum of Fine Arts, Boston.*

OSEOLA.

wm Butler 1858

294. "OSEOLA." Seminole. Engraving. from John L. Williams, *Territory of Florida* . . . 1837.

295. OSCEOLA. Seminole. Lithograph in color, from Charles De Wolf Brownell, *Indian Races* . . . 1857.

296. "OSEOLA OR POWELL THE SEMINOLE CHIEF." From M. M. Cohen, *Notices of Florida* . . . 1836.

297. "BILLY BOW-LEGS, Chief of the Seminoles." Line reproduction. *Harper's Weekly*, June 12, 1858.

298. "BEN BRUNO, Negro Slave and Favorite." Line reproduction. *Harper's Weekly*, June 12, 1858.

299. "LONG JACK, Billy Bowleg's Lieutenant." Line reproduction. *Harper's Weekly*, June 12, 1858.

300. "NO-KUSH-AD-JO, INSPECTOR-GENERAL." Line reproduction. *Harper's Weekly*, June 12, 1858.

301. "YOUNG WIFE OF BILLY BOW-LEGS." Line reproduction. *Harper's Weekly*, June 12, 1858.

302. "NEGRO ABRAHAM." Giddings, 1858, opp. p. 33.

303. "GOPHER JOHN, INTERPRETER." Giddings, 1858, opp. p. 64.

304. "THLOCK-LO TUSTENUGGEE, Tiger Tail." Giddings. 1858.

305. "COACOOCHEE, Wild Cat." Giddings, 1858, opp. p. 176.

306. "'BILLY BOWLEGS,' AND HIS SUITE OF INDIAN CHIEFS." Line reproduction from *Illustrated London News*, Vol. 22, No. 623, May 21, 1853, p. 396. *Print from a photostat negative loaned by W. C. Sturtevant.*

307. "VILLAGE INDIEN SUR L'APPA-LACHICOLA." Seminole. From Comte Francis de Castelnau, *Vues et souvenirs de l'Amerique du Nord.* Paris: Arthus Bertrand, 1842, Pl. 9, fig. 1. *Print from a photostat negative loaned by W. C. Sturtevant.*

308. "MASSACRE OF THE WHITES BY THE INDIANS AND BLACKS IN FLOR-IDA." Woodcut from *An Authentic Narrative of the Seminole War.* Providence. 1836. *Courtesy of the Library of Congress, Washington.*

309. "CHIEFS OF THE CREEK NATION & A GEORGIAN SQUATTER." Etching from Basil Hall, *Forty Etchings from Sketches Made in North America.* Edinburgh. 1829, no. XXVIII. *Courtesy of the New York Public Library.*

310. A. Zeno Shindler. "BILLY BOWLEGS." Photograph. 1858. *Courtesy of the Smithsonian Institution, Bureau of American Ethnology, Neg. 1175.*

311. Carl Wilmar. "BILLY BOWLEGS." Oil on canvas. 24 x 30 inches. 1861. *Courtesy of the City Art Museum of St. Louis.*

312. George Catlin. "CADDO INDIANS GATHERING WILD GRAPES." Oil on canvas. 14 x 10½ inches. *Courtesy of the Thomas Gilcrease Institute of American History and Art,* Tulsa.

313. Artist unknown. "SEMINOLE CHIEFS AND CONTENDING PARTIES." Oil on canvas. 52 x 38½ inches. *Courtesy of the Thomas Gilcrease Institute of American History and Art, Tulsa.*

Neagle and Others

CHOCTAW, CHICKASAW (MUSKHOGEAN), AND CHEROKEE (IROQUOIAN). 1840-1896. OKLAHOMA, ALABAMA, AND THE SOUTHEAST. In addition to the pictures below, there are doubtless others in private and museum collections, especially in Oklahoma. After 1860 photography rapidly replaced the need for hand produced portraits. Many portraits—paintings, drawings, and photographs—of members of the "Five Civilized Tribes" are contained in the various publications of the University of Oklahoma Press, including Muriel Wright, *A Guide to Indian Tribes of Oklahoma*.

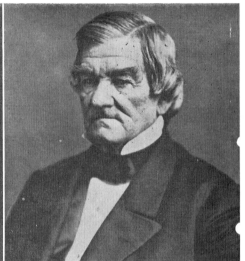

314. P. Romer. A CHOCTAW BELLE. Mobile. 1850. *Courtesy of the Washington and Lee University. Photograph by Frick Art Reference Library, New York, 2373.*

315. Edward Troye. CHEROKEE WOMAN. Undated probably between 1833 and 1874. *Courtesy of the Thomas Gilcrease Institute of American History and Art, Tulsa.*

316. A. Z. Shindler. JOHN ROSS. Cherokee. Photograph. Washington. 1858. *Courtesy of the Smithsonian Institution, Bureau of American Ethnology, Neg. 988-a(R).*

317. Samuel B. Waugh. THE JOHN AND MARY ROSS CHILDREN. Cherokee. 1843. *Courtesy of the Thomas Gilcrease Institute of American Histroy and Art, Tulsa.*

318. Samuel B. Waugh. MARY STAPLER ROSS. Oil on canvass. 36¼ x 30 inches. undated. *Collection of the Philbrook Art Center, Tulsa, Cat. P.O. A10. Photograph by Bob McCormack, Tulsa.*

319. John Neagle. JOHN ROSS. Cherokee. Oil on canvas. 36¼ x 29¾ inches. 1848. *Collection of the Philbrook Art Center, Tulsa, Cat. P. O. A9. Photograph by Bob McCormack, Tulsa.*

320. Artist unknown. PUSHMATA-HA. Choctaw. Crayon. 19 x 23 inches. *Courtesy of the Oklahoma Historical Society, Oklahoma City.*

321. Artist unknown. R. M. JONES. Choctaw. Oil. Oval, 26 x 30. ca. 1850? *Courtesy of the Oklahoma Historical Society, Oklahoma City.*

322. Artist unknown. L E M U E L COLBERT. Chickasaw. Crayon. 20 x 24 inches. *Courtesy of the Oklahoma Historical Society.*

323. Artist unknown. DAVID FOL-SOM. Choctaw. Oil on canvas. 30 x 36 inches. *Courtesy of the Oklahoma Historical Society, Oklahoma City.*

324. Artist u n k n o w n. GREEN-WOOD LEFLORE. Choctaw. Oil on canvas. 31 x 39 inches. *Courtesy of the Oklahoma Historical Society, Oklahoma City.*

325. Artist unknown. THOMPSON McKENNEY. Choctaw. Oil on canvas. 32 x 39 inches. *Courtesy of the Oklahoma Hisotrical Society, Oklahoma City.*

326. John Neagle. JOHN ROSS. Cherokee Oil on canvas. 36 x 42 inches. 1848? *Courtesy of the Oklahoma Historical Society, Oklahoma City. Photographs 320-328 by Mandell Matheson, Oklahoma City.*

327. John Neagle. MARY STAP-LER ROSS. oil on canvas. 36 x 42 inches. 1848? *Courtesy of the Oklahoma Historical Society, Oklahoma City. Photograph by Mandell Matheson, Oklahoma City.*

328. Self portrait. N A R C I S S A CHISHOLM OWEN. Cherokee. Oil on canvas. 1896. *Courtesy of the Oklahoma Historical Society, Oklahoma City. Photograph by Mandell Matheson, Oklahoma City.*

Stanley

CHEROKEE (IROQUOIAN) AND OTHERS. 1842-1844. IN-DIAN TERRITORY. OKLAHOMA. TEXAS. John Mix Stanley (1814-1872), an energetic American artist, went to the Arkansas Territory in 1842 in search of Indian subjects. By 1854 he had painted tribesmen and scenes throughout the west. He then attempted to sell the collection of some 150 paintings to the Smithsonian. When the purchase could not be financed, he left the pictures there, with the hope of an eventual trade. Most of them were destroyed in the Smithsonian fire of 1865.

329. John Mix Stanley. "CHEROKEE COUNCIL, TEXAS, March 20th, 1843. John M. Stanley." (note on back of canvas). Oil on canvas. 17 x 24 inches. Tawakoni Creek, Texas. *Courtesy of Pierce Mason Butler, Nashville.*

330. John Mix Stanley, LEWIS ANDERSON ROSS. Cherokee. Oil on canvas. 31¾ x 40½ inches. Park Hill. 1844. *Courtesy of the Thomas Gilcrease Institute of American History and Art, Tulsa.*

331. John Mix Stanley. ELIZABETH ROSS. Cherokee. Oil on canvas. 31½ x 39½ inches. Park Hill. 1844. *Courtesy of the Thomas Gilcrease Institute of American History and Art, Tulsa.*

332. John Mix Stanley. ELEANOR ROSS. Cherokee. Oil on canvas. 31¾ x 40½ inches. Park Hill. 1844. *Courtesy of the Thomas Gilcrease Institute of American History and Art, Tulsa.*

333. John Mix Stanley. "INTERNATIONAL INDIAN COUNCIL." Oil on canvas. June, 1843. Tahlequah, Indian Territory (Oklahoma). *Courtesy of the Smithsonian Institution, of the United States National Museum. Photograph by the Bureau of American Ethnology.*

Bernard and Others

CHOCTAW (MUSKHOGEAN) AND OTHER INDIANS. 1830-1850. LOUISIANA AND MISSISSIPPI. New Orleans as Charleston was a mecca for early American artists. Francisco Bernard is said to have been there from 1856-60 and in 1867; Alfred Boisseau, in 1845-46; and Leon Pomarede in 1830-32 and 1837-43. For other details about the life and work of these men, see G. C. Groce and D. H. Wallace, *The New-York Historical Society's Dictionary of Artists in America, 1564-1860.*

334. Francois Bernard. "CHOCTAW VILLAGE NEAR THE CHEFUNCTE." Oil painting. 48½ x 34½ inches. 1846? *Courtesy of the Peabody Museum, Harvard University, Bushnell Collection. Photograph by the Smithsonian Institution, Bureau of American Ethnology, Neg. 2860-zz-1.*

335. Alfred Boisseau. "LOUISIANA INDIANS WALKING ALONG A BAYOU." Oil on canvas. 24 x 40 inches. signed "A. L. Boisseau 1847." *Courtesy of the Delgado Museum of Art, New Orleans, W. E. Groves Collection.*

336. Leon Pomarede. INDIAN BURIAL. Oil on canvas. 27 x 34 inches. Undated. Several Indians are building a burial platform for a dead brave while women on the bluff watch. *Courtesy of W. E. Groves, New Orleans.*

Mollhaussen

CHOCTAW (MUSKOGEAN) AND SHAWNEE (ALGON-QUIAN) 1853. ARKANSAS RIVER AREA. INDIAN TER-RITORY. OKLAHOMA. Heinrich Balduin Möllhausen (1825-1905), German, was appointed "topographer or drafts-man" of an expedition led by Lt. A. W. Whipple, "Com-mander of the Southern Expedition for Determining the Line of Railway to the Pacific Ocean." He was also entrusted with the job of collecting natural history specimens. *(Diary, ix).* Many of his drawings and water colors are reproduced in Whipple's *Report* and in Möllhausen's *Diary.*

337. Heinrich B. Möllhausen. SHAWNEES. Pencil and water color. *Courtesy of the Oklahoma Historical Society, Oklahoma City, Whipple Collection.*

338. Heinrich B. Möllhausen. CHOCTAWS. Pencil and wa-ter color. *Courtesy of the Oklahoma Historical Society, Oklahoma City, Whipple Collection.*

339. "CREEK BOY. August 10th, 1853." From the *Journal of Lt. A. W. Whipple. Courtesy of the Oklahoma Historical Society, Oklahoma City, Whipple Collection.*

340. CHOCTAWS. Engravings after Henrich B. Möllhausen. 1853. From Lt A. W. Whipple, *Report of Explorations for a Railway Route, near the Thirty-Fifth Parallel of North Latitude, from the Mississippi River to the Pacific Ocean. 1953-4. 33rd Congress, 2d Session, Ex. Doc. No. 78, Vol. III, Washington, 1853-56. (The Indian Tribes, 1855, Chapter II, Fig. 12, p. 25. Courtesy of the Tennessee State Library and Archives, Nashville.*

341. CHOCTAWS. Engravings after Heinrich B. *Möllhausen, 1853. From Lt. A. W. Whipple, Report . . . (The Indian Tribes, Ch. II, Fig. 11, p. 24).*

342. SHAWNEES. Engraving after Heinrich B. Möllhausen. 1853. From Lt. A. W. Whipple, *Report . . . (The Indian Tribes, Chapter II, Fig. 13, p. 25).*

343. SHAWNEES. Engraving after Heinrich B. Möllhausen. 1853. Lt. A. W. Whipple, *Report . . . (The Indian Tribes, Ch. II, Fig. 14, p. 26).*

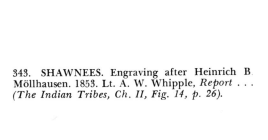

Notes On The Illustrations

1. "THE PROMONTORY OF FLORIDA, AT WHICH THE FRENCH TOUCHED; NAMED BY THEM THE FRENCH PROMONTORY. The French, on their first voyage to Florida, touched at a headland, not very high, as the coast in that vicinity is level, but heavily wooded with very lofty trees. This their commander named French Cape [Promontorium Gallicum] in honor of France. It is about thirty degrees from the equator. Coasting thence to the northward, they discovered a broad and beautiful river, at whose mouth they cast anchor in order to examine it more in detail next day. Laudonnière, in his second voyage, called this stream the River of Dolphins, because, when he touched there, a great many dolphins were seen in it. On landing on the shore of this river, our men saw many Indians, who came on purpose to give them a most kind and friendly reception, as their actions proved; for some of them gave their own skin-garments to the commander, and promised to point out to him their chief, who did not rise up, but remained sitting on boughs of laurel and palm which had been spread for him. He gave our commander a large skin, decorated all over with pictures of various kinds of wild animals drawn after the life."

In Plates and Notes 1-7 Le Moyne refers to explorations of the first French Huguenot colony in Spanish Florida in 1562. This short-lived attempt at settlement was promoted by Gaspard de Coligny, Huguenot leader, and directed by Jean Ribaut. The Charlesfort colony at Port Royal was the first of several attempts by France to establish a settlement in that area. The next expedition was lead by René de Laudonnière in 1564, and described in the narrative and pictures of Le Moyne. Laudonnière also produced a narrative of the expedition. Spain became incensed at French penetration of their claimed area, and in 1565 sent Pedro Menéndez de Avilés to destroy the colony. Le Moyne escaped the massacre, and found passage on a French vessel which sailed to England.

Little is known about the nature and media of his pictures of Florida. De Bry refers to them (1875 edition, p. 1) as "Pictures of Indians inhabiting the Province of Florida, first drawn on the spot, from life,..." In 1587 Richard Hakluyt refers to Le Moyne as a skillful artist, who produced drawings in colors. (Principal Navigations, MacLehose edition, New York, 1905, Vol. VIII, p. 440). Groce and Wallace, 1957, p. 392 described him as a watercolorist. See Note 8 for reference to water color believed to be an original by Le Moyne. There is no record of the location of any others.

The most complete source of information regarding De Bry, Voyages . . . America, Part I and Part II, is contained in Stefan Lorant, Editor, The New World, The First Pictures of America Made by John White and Jacques Le Moyne. Duell, Sloane, and Pearce, New York, 1946. A book entitled, Voyages en Virginie et en Floride, was produced in Paris in 1927. Charles de la Roncière edited La Floride Française in Paris in 1928. These contained reproductions after the De Bry engravings.

The titles and descriptions for Plates and Notes 1-42 have been quoted from the 1875 edition of the Narrative of Le Moyne, An Artist Who Accompanied the French Expedition to Florida under Laudonnière, 1564. Translated by Fred B. Perkins from the Latin of De Bry, with heliotypes of the engravings from the artist's original drawings. James R. Osgood and Company. Boston. Copyright, 1875, by William Appleton.

2. "THE FRENCH SAIL TO THE RIVER OF MAY. Re-embarking, they sailed to another place; and, before landing again, were received with salutations by another crowd of Indians, some of whom waded into the water up to their shoulders, offering the visitors little baskets full of maize and of white and red mulberries, while others offered to help them in going on shore. Having landed, they saw the chief, who was accompanied by two sons, and a company of Indians armed with bows and quivers full of arrows. After an exchange of salutations, our men went on into the woods, in hopes to discover many wonderful things. They found nothing, however, except trees bearing white and red mulberries, on the boughs of which were numerous silk-worms. They named this river the River of May, because they sighted it on the first day of that month."

3. "LEAVING THE RIVER OF MAY, THE FRENCH DISCOVER TWO OTHER RIVERS. A little afterwards they went on board again, hoisted anchors, and sailed farther on along the coast, until they entered a beautiful river, which the commander himself chose to explore in company with the chief of that vicinity and some of the natives, and which he named the Seine because it was very like the River Seine in France. It is about fourteen leagues from the River of May. Returning to the ships, they sailed still farther north; but, before going far, they discovered another fine river, and sent two boats to explore it. In it they discovered an island, whose chief was no less friendly than the others. This river they named the Aine. It is six miles from the Seine."

4. "SIX OTHER RIVERS DISCOVERED BY THE FRENCH. Sailing hence, about six miles farther on they discovered another river, which was called the Loire; and subsequently five others, named the Charente, Garonne, Gironde, Beautiful [Bellus], and Great, respectively. Having carefully explored all these, and having discovered along these nine rivers, within the space of less than sixty miles, many singular things, but still not being contented, they proceeded still farther north, until they arrived at the River Jordan, which is almost the most beautiful river of the whole of this northern region."

5. "THE FRENCH REACH PORT ROYAL. Resuming their voyage as before, they discovered a river which they called Bellevue [Conspectu bellum, 'beautiful to see'?]; and, after sailing three or four miles farther, they were informed that not far off was another river, surpassing all the rest in size and beauty. When they had reached this, they found it so magnificent and great a stream that they named it Port Royal. Here they took in sail, and came to anchor in ten fathoms. The commander, on landing with some soldiers, found the country very beautiful, as it was well wooded with oak, cedar, and other trees. As they went on through the woods, they saw Indian peacocks, or turkeys, flying past, and deer going by. The mouth of this river is three French leagues, or miles, wide, and is divided into two arms, one turning to the west, the other to the North. This latter is thought by some to connect with the Jordan; the other returns to the sea, as residents there have ascertained. These two branches are two full miles wide, and midway between them is an island whose point looks toward the mouth of the river. Shortly after, embarking again, they entered the arm making to the northward, in order to examine its advantages; and, after proceeding about twelve miles, they saw a company of Indians, who, on perceiving the boats, immediately took to flight, leaving a lynx's whelp which they were roasting; from which circumstance the place was called Lynx Point. On going still farther, they came to another branch of the river, coming in from the east, up which the commander determined to go, leaving the main channel."

6. "THE FRENCH COMMANDER ERECTS A COLUMN WITH THE ARMS OF THE KING OF FRANCE. The commander having, however, returned to his ships, and having remained on board one night, ordered into one of the boats a landmark carved in the form of a column, and having cut upon it the arms of the king of France, which was directed to be set up in some particularly pleasant spot. Such they found at a point about three miles to the west, where they discovered a small creek, which they entered, and, after following it for a time, found that it came

out into the main stream again, thus forming a small island. The commander directed the column to be erected on a small open mound in this place. After this they saw two deer of great size in comparison with any they had seen before, and which they could easily have killed with their arquebuses, had not the commander, admiring their large size, forbidden it. Before returning to the boat, they named this small island Libourne. Embarking again, they explored another island not far from the former; but finding upon it nothing except some very lofty cedars, larger than any they had yet seen in the country, they called it Cedar Island, and then returned to the ships. The small island on which the column was erected is marked F in the plate."

7. "THE FRENCH LEFT IN FORT CHARLES SUFFER FROM SCARCITY OF PROVISIONS. Not long after the departure of Ribaud from Florida, the men whom he left in Fort Charles (the work erected by him on an island on a stream entering the greater channel of Port Royal from the north) began to find their provisions fail them. After consulting upon the best way of meeting the difficulty, they concluded that the wisest plan was to apply to the chief Ouadé and to his brother Couëxis. Those who were sent on this business went in Indian canoes by the inland waters, and at a distance of some ten miles discovered a large and beautiful river of fresh water, in which they saw numerous crocodiles, much larger than those of the Nile. The banks of this stream were wooded with lofty cypresses. After a short delay here, they went on to the chief Ouadé; and, being received by him in the most friendly manner, they laid before him the object of their journey, and prayed him not to desert them in such a strait. Upon hearing this, the chief sent messengers to his brother Couëxis after maize and beans. The latter responded promptly; for next morning very early the messengers came back with the provisions, which the chief ordered on board the canoe. The French, very happy at this liberality of the chief's would have taken leave of him; but this he would not permit, keeping them with him, and entertaining them hospitably for that day. Next morning he showed them his fields of millet, or maize, and intimated that they should not want for food as long as that millet existed. Being now dismissed by the king, they returned by the way they had come."

8. "THE NATIVES OF FLORIDA WORSHIP THE COLUMN ERECTED BY THE COMMANDER ON HIS FIRST VOYAGE. When the French landed in Florida on their second voyage under Laudonnière, that leader went on shore with five and twenty arquebusiers, after obtaining a safe-conduct from the Indians, who had gathered in crowds to see them. The chief Athore, who lived four or five miles from the seashore, also came; and after an exchange of presents had been made, accompanied by demonstrations of all manner of kind feeling, the chief gave them to understand that he wished to show them something remarkable, and that he desired they would go with him for that purpose. To this consent was given; although, as the chief had with him a great number of his people, caution and circumspection were used. He then conducted them directly to the island where Ribaud had set up on a mound a stone column ornamented with the arms of the king of France. On approaching, they found that these Indians were worshipping this stone as an idol; and the chief himself, having saluted it with signs of reverence such as his subjects were in the habit of showing to himself, kissed it. His men followed his example, and we were invited to do the same. Before the monument there lay various offerings of the fruits, and edible or medicinal roots, growing thereabouts; vessels of perfumed oils; a bow, and arrows; and it was wreathed around from top to bottom with flowers of all sorts, and boughs of the trees esteemed choicest. After witnessing these ceremonies of these poor savages, our men returned to their companions, and set about choosing a place for erecting a fort. This chief, Athore, is very handsome, prudent, honorable, strong, and of very great stature, being more than half a foot taller than the tallest of our men; and his bearing was marked by a modest gravity, which had a strikingly majestic effect. He had married his mother, and had by her a number of sons and daughters, whom he

showed to us, striking his thigh as he did so. After this marriage, his father Saturioua lived with her no longer."

A water color of this scene, believed to be the original painting of Jacques le Moyne, is owned by James Hazen Hyde. It is pictured in black and white in Stefan Lorant, *The New World*, 1946, p. 32. The painting is reproduced in color in *Vogue* magazine, February 1, 1951, p. 189. The water color on vellum, 6 x 8½ inches, was discovered in a château near Paris in 1901. It is discussed in an article by E. T. Hamy, "Sur une Miniature de Jacques le Moyne de Morgues, représentant une Scène du voyage de Laudonnière en Florida (1564)." *Bulletin of the Académie des Inscriptions et Belles-Lettres*, January-February, 1901. A color reproduction of this painting was displayed as number 49 in an exhibition, "The Noble Savage," University Museum, Philadelphia, May 8—September 8, 1958.

9. "THE FRENCH SELECT A PLACE FOR BUILDING A FORT. After exploring many of the rivers in that country, it was finally decided that the River of May was the best one for an establishment, because millet and breadstuffs were most abundant there, besides the gold and silver that had been discovered there on the first voyage. They therefore sailed for that river; and, after ascending it to the neighborhood of a certain mountain, they selected a place more fit for the site of their fort than any previously observed. Next day, as soon as it was light, after offering prayers to God, and giving thanks for their prosperous coming into the province, they all went briskly to work; and, after a triangular outline had been measured out, they all began,—some to dig in the earth, some to make fascines of brushwood, some to put up the wall. Every man was briskly engaged with spade, saw, axe, or some other tool; and so diligent were they that the work went rapidly forward."

10. "PICTURE OF FORT CAROLINA. Thus was erected a triangular work, afterwards named Carolina. The base of the triangle, looking westward, was defended only by a small ditch, and a wall of sods nine feet high. The side next the river was built up with planks and fascines. On the southern side was a building after the fashion of a citadel, which was for a granary to hold their provisions. The whole was of fascines, except the upper part of the wall for two or three feet, which was of sods. In the middle of the fort was a roomy open space eighteen yards long, and as many wide. Midway on the southern side of this space were the soldiers' quarters; and on the north side was a building which was higher than it should have been, and was in consequence blown over by the wind a little afterwards. Experience thus taught us that in this country, where the winds are so furious, houses must be built low. There was also another open space, pretty large, one side of which was closed in by the granary above mentioned, while on another side stood the residence of Laudonnière, looking out upon the river, and with a piazza all round it. The principal door of this opened upon the larger open space; and the rear door, upon the river. At a safe distance from the works, an oven was erected; for, as the houses were roofed with palm-branches, they would very easily have caught fire."

11. "CEREMONIES PERFORMED BY SATURIOUA BEFORE GOING ON AN EXPEDITION AGAINST THE ENEMY. It is mentioned in the account of the second voyages that the French made a treaty of friendship with a powerful chief of the vicinity, named Saturioua, with agreement that they were to erect a fort in his territory, and were to be friends to his friends, and enemies to his enemies; and, further, that on occasion they should furnish him some arquebusiers. About three months afterwards, he sent messengers to Laudonnière to ask for the arquebusiers according to the treaty, as he was about to make war upon his enemies. Laudonnière, however, sent to him Capt. La Caille with some men, to inform him courteously that he could not just then supply any soldiers, for the reason that he hoped to be able to make peace between the parties. But the chief was indignant at this reply, as he could not now put off his expedition, having got his provisions ready, and summoned the neighboring chiefs to his aid; and he

therefore prepared to set out at once. He assembled his men, decorated, after the Indian manner, with feathers and other things, in a level place, the soldiers of Laudonnière being present; and the force sat down in a circle, the chief being in the middle. A fire was then lighted on his left, and two great vessels full of water were set on his right. Then the chief, after rolling his eyes as if excited by anger, uttering some sounds deep down in his throat, and making various gestures, all at once raised a horrid yell; and all his soldiers repeated this yell, striking their hips, and rattling their weapons. Then the chief, taking a wooden platter of water, turned toward the sun, and worshipped it; praying to it for a victory over the enemy, and that, as he should now scatter the water that he had dipped up in the wooden platter, so might their blood be poured out. Then he flung the water with a great cast up into the air; and, as it fell down upon his men, he added, 'As I have done with this water, so I pray that you may do with the blood of your enemies.' Then he poured the water in the other vase upon the fire, and said, 'So may you be able to extinguish your enemies, and bring back their scalps.' Then they all arose, and set off by land up the river, upon their expedition."

SATURIOUA

In John R. Swanton, *The Indians of the Southeastern United States*, 1946, Plate 42 (Bureau of American Ethnology Bulletin 137) is pictured a drawing entitled, "SATURIOUA RE DELLA FLORIDA NELL' AMERICA SETTERTIONALE IN ATTO DI ANDARE ALLA GUERRA."—"Saturioua King of Florida in North America in the act of going to war." It is a crayon drawing—black and red, 10 x 7 inches. This is in the Bushnell Collection, Peabody Museum, Harvard University, Neg. No. 16632. Spec. No. 41-72/446. The drawing is on loan to the National Park Service and displayed at Fort Caroline National Memorial, Route No. 1, Jacksonville, Florida. It is displayed with the following Museum label, "This charcoal drawing of Chief Saturiba is based on Le Moyne's observations at Fort Caroline. It is uncertain by whom or when it was drawn." It is said to have been purchased in 1925

by the late David I. Bushnell, Jr. for $105.64, from Messrs. Maggs, London. In Bushnell's article, "Drawing by Jacques le Moyne de Morgues of Saturioua, A Timucua Chief in Florida, 1564," *Smithsonian Miscellaneous Collections*, Vol. 81, No. 4, August 23, 1928 (Publication 2972) he expressed belief that it was the work of the artist, Jacques le Moyne. Since the drawing has been in the possession of the Peabody Museum, Harvard University, it has been examined by authorities in European drawings, and is not believed to be the original work of Le Moyne nor to have been produced as early as the 16th century. This opinion is corroborated by certain European authorities. (Correspondence in the file of Fort Caroline National Memorial).

Since there has been much discussion regarding this drawing, a picture of it is included here, *Courtesy of the Peabody Museum Harvard University.*

12. "OUTINA, GOING AT THE HEAD OF HIS ARMY AGAINST THE ENEMY, CONSULTS A SORCERER ON THE EVENT. Laudonnière, having received some of the men of the chief, Holata Utina, or Outina, living about forty miles south from the French fort, and who had been taken in a previous expedition by his enemy Saturioua, sent them back to their chief, upon which a solemn league was made, and mutual friendship promised. This treaty was made for the reason that the only road, whether by land or by the rivers, to the Apalatcy Mountains, in which gold, silver, and brass [as] are found, was through the dominions of this chief; and it was in his friendship, now of scarcely a year's standing, that the French trusted to obtain free access to those mountains. As this friendship, however, was as yet existing, he asked Laudonnière for some arquebusiers, as he wished to make war on an enemy; on which twenty-five were sent him, under D'Ottigny, Laudonnière's lieutenant. The chief received them with great delight, as he made sure of the victory through their assistance; for the fame of the arquebuses had penetrated throughout all that region, and had struck all with terror. The chief having therefore completed his preparations, the army marched. Their first day's journey was easy; the second very difficult, being through swamps thickly overgrown with thorns and brambles. Here the Indians were obliged to carry the French on their shoulders, which was the greater relief by reason of the extreme heats. At length they reached the enemy's territories, when the chief halted his force, and summoning an aged sorcerer, more than a hundred and twenty years old, directed him to report what was the state of affairs with the enemy. The sorcerer accordingly made ready a place in the middle of the army, and, seeing the shield which D'Ottigny's page was carrying, asked to take it. On receiving it, he laid it on the ground, and drew around it a circle, upon which he inscribed various characters and signs. Then he knelt down on the shield, and sat on his heels, so that no part of him touched the earth, and began to recite some unknown words in a low tone, and to make various gestures, as if engaged in a vehement discourse. This lasted for a quarter of an hour, when he began to assume an appearance so frightful that he was hardly like a human being; for he twisted his limbs so that the bones could be heard to snap out of place, and did many other unnatural things. After going through with all this, he came back all at once to his ordinary condition, but in a very fatigued state, and with an air as if astonished; and then, stepping out of his circle, he saluted the chief, and told him the number of the enemy, and where they were intending to meet him."

13. "OUTINA, WITH THE HELP OF THE FRENCH, GAINS A VICTORY OVER HIS ENEMY POTANOU. This report so terrified the chief that he began to consider not how to come up with the enemy, but how to get safe back again. But D'Ottigny, greatly vexed at the idea of making such exertions only to return without bringing anything to pass, threatened to consider him a base chief, and of no courage, if he should not risk an action; and, by force of reproaches and some threats too, brought him to order an attack. He, however, put the French in the advance, as they were quite willing to have him do; and indeed, unless they had sustained the whole brunt of the battle, killing very many of the enemy, and putting to flight the army of the chief Potanou, there is no question but Outina

would have been routed; for it became evident that the sorcerer had made a true report of the facts, and he must certainly have been possessed by a devil. Outina, however, quite contented with the flight of the enemy, recalled his men, and marched for home, to the great wrath of D'Ottigny, who wished to follow up the victory."

14. "ORDER OF MARCH OBSERVED BY OUTINA ON A MILITARY EXPEDITION. When Saturioua went to war, his men preserved no order, but went along one after another, just as it happened. On the contrary, his enemy Holata Outina, whose name, as I now remember, means 'king of many kings,' and who was much more powerful than he as regards both wealth, and number of his subjects, used to march with regular ranks, like an organized army; himself marching alone in the middle of the whole force, painted red. On the wings, or horns, of his order of march were his young men, the swiftest of whom, also painted red, acted as advanced guards and scouts for reconnoitring the enemy. These are able to follow up the traces of the enemy by scent, as dogs do wild beasts; and, when they come upon such traces, they immediately return to the army to report. And, as we make use of trumpets and drums in our armies to promulgate orders, so they have heralds, who by cries of certain sorts direct when to halt, or to advance, or to attack, or to perform any other military duty. After sunset they halt, and are never wont to give battle. For encamping, they are arranged in squads of ten each, the bravest men being put in squads by themselves. When the chief has chosen the place of encampment for the night, in open fields or woods, and after he has eaten, and is established by himself, the quartermasters place ten of these squads of the bravest men in a circle around him. About ten paces outside of this circle is placed another line of twenty squads; at twenty yards farther, another of forty squads; and so on, increasing the number and distance of these lines, according to the size of the army."

15. "HOW OUTINA'S MEN TREATED THE SLAIN OF THE ENEMY. At no time while the French were acting along with the great chief Holata Outina in his wars against his enemies, was there any combat which could be called a regular battle; but all their military operations consisted either in secret incursions, or in skirmishes as light troops, fresh men being constantly sent out in place of any who retired. Whichever side first slew an enemy, no matter how insignificant the person, claimed the victory, even though losing a greater number of men. In their skirmishes, any who fall are instantly dragged off by persons detailed for the purpose; who, with slips of reeds sharper than any steel blade, cut the skin of the head to the bone, from front to back, all the way round, and pull it off with the hair, more than a foot and a half long, still adhering, done up in a knot on the crown, and with that lower down around the forehead and back cut short into a ring about two fingers wide, like the rim of a hat. Then, if they have time, they dig a hole in the ground, and make a fire, kindling it with some which they keep burning in moss, done up in skins, and carry round with them at their belts; and then dry these scalps to a state as hard as parchment. They are accustomed, after a battle, to cut off with these reed knives the arms of the dead near the shoulders, and their legs near the hips, breaking the bones, when laid bare, with a club, and then to lay these fresh broken, and still running with blood, over the same fires to be dried. Then hanging them, and the scalps also, to the ends of their spears, they carry them off home in triumph. I used to be astonished at one habit of theirs,—for I was one of the party whom Laudonnière sent out under M. d'Ottigny,—which was, that they never left the field of battle without shooting an arrow as deep as they could into the arms of each of the corpses of the enemy, after mutilating them as above; an operation which was sometimes sufficiently dangerous, unless those engaged in it had an escort of soldiers."

16. "TROPHIES AND CEREMONIES AFTER A VICTORY. After returning from a military expedition, they assemble in a place set apart for the purpose, to which they bring the legs, arms, and scalps which they have taken from the enemy, and with solemn formalities fix them up on tall poles set in the ground in a row. Then they all, men and women, sit down on the ground in a circle before these members; while the sorcerer, holding a small image in his hand, goes through a form of cursing the enemy, uttering in a low voice, according to their manner, a thousand imprecations. At the side of the circle opposite to him, there are placed three men kneeling down, one of whom holds in both hands a club, with which he pounds on a flat stone, marking time to every word of the sorcerer. At each side of him, the other two hold in each hand the fruit of a certain plant, something like a gourd or pumpkin, which has been dried, opened at each end, its marrow and seeds taken out, and then mounted on a stick, and charged with small stones or seeds of some kind. These they rattle after the fashion of a bell, accompanying the words of the sorcerer with a sort of song after their manner. They have such a celebration as this every time they take any of the enemy."

17. "EMPLOYMENTS OF THE HERMAPHRODITES. Hermaphrodites, partaking of the nature of each sex, are quite common in these parts, and are considered odious by the Indians themselves, who, however, employ them, as they are strong, instead of beasts of burden. When a chief goes out to war, the hermaphrodites carry the provisions. When any Indian is dead of wounds or disease, two hermaphrodites take a couple of stout poles, fasten cross-pieces on them, and attach to these a mat woven of reeds. On this they place the deceased, with a skin under his head, a second bound around his body, a third around one thigh, a fourth around one leg. Why these are so used, I did not ascertain; but I imagine by way of ornament, as in some cases they do not go so far, but put the skin upon one leg only. Then they take thongs of hide, three or four fingers broad, fasten the ends to the ends of the poles, and put the middle over their heads, which are remarkably hard; and in this manner they carry the deceased to the place of burial. Persons having contagious diseases are also carried to places appointed for the purpose, on the shoulders of the hermaphrodites, who supply them with food, and take care of them, until they get quite well again."

18. "THE CHIEF APPLIED TO BY WOMEN WHOSE HUSBANDS HAVE DIED IN WAR OR BY DISEASE. The wives of such as have fallen in war, or died by disease, are accustomed to get together on some day which they find convenient for approaching the chief. They come before him with great weeping and outcry, sit down on their heels, hide their faces in their hands, and with much clamor and lamentation require of the chief vengeance for their dead husbands, the means of living during their widowhood, and permission to marry again at the end of the time appointed by law. The chief, sympathizing with them, assents; and they go home weeping and lamenting, so as to show the strength of their love for the deceased. After some days spent in this mourning, they proceed to the graves of their husbands, carrying the weapons and drinking-cups of the dead, and there they mourn for them again, and perform other feminine ceremonies."

19. "CEREMONIES OF WOMEN MOURNING FOR THEIR DECEASED HUSBANDS. After coming to the graves of their husbands, they cut off their hair below the ears, and scatter it upon the graves; and then cast upon them the weapons and drinking-shells of the deceased, as memorials of brave men. This done, they return home, but are not allowed to marry again until their hair has grown long enough to cover their shoulders. They let their nails grow long both on fingers and toes, cutting the former away, however, at the sides, so as to leave them very sharp, the men especially; and, when they take one of the enemy, they sink their nails deep in his forehead, and tear down the skin, so as to wound and blind him."

20. "MODE OF TREATING THE SICK. Their way of curing diseases is as follows: They put up a bench or platform of sufficient length and breadth for the patient, as seen in the plate, and lay the sick person upon it with his face up or down, according to the nature of his complaint;

and, cutting into the skin of the forehead with a sharp shell, they suck out blood with their mouths, and spit it into an earthen vessel or a gourd bottle. Women who are suckling boys, or who are with child, come and drink this blood, particularly if it is that of a strong young man; as it is expected to make their milk better, and to render the children who have the benefit of it bolder and more energetic. For those who are laid on their faces, they prepare fumigations by throwing certain seeds on hot coals; the smoke being to pass through the nose and mouth into all parts of the body, and thus to act as a vomit, or to overcome and expel the cause of the disease. They have a certain plant whose name has escaped me, which the Brazilians call *petum,* and the Spaniards *tapaco.* The leaves of this, carefully dried, they place in the wider part of a pipe; and setting them on fire, and putting the other end in their mouths, they inhale the smoke so strongly, that it comes out at their mouths and noses, and operates powerfully to expel the humors. In particular, they are extremely subject to the venereal disease, for curing which they have remedies of their own, supplied by nature."

21. "MODE OF TILLING AND PLANTING. The Indians cultivate the earth diligently; and the men know how to make a kind of hoes from fishes' bones, which they fit to wooden handles, and with these they prepare the land well enough, as the soil is light. When the ground is sufficiently broken up and levelled, the women come with beans and millet, or maize. Some go first with a stick, and make holes, in which the others place the beans, or grains of maize. After planting they leave the fields alone, as the winter in that country, situated between the west and the north, is pretty cold for about three months, being from the 24th of December to the 15th of March; and during that time, as they go naked, they shelter themselves in the woods. When the winter is over, they return to their homes to wait for their crops to ripen. After gathering in their harvest, they store the whole of it for the year's use, not employing any part of it in trade, unless, perhaps, some barter is made for some little household article."

22. "INDUSTRY OF THE FLORIDIANS IN DEPOSITING THEIR CROPS IN THE PUBLIC GRANARY. There are in that region a great many islands, producing abundance of various kinds of fruits, which they gather twice a year, and carry home in canoes, and store up in roomy low granaries built of stones and earth, and roofed thickly with palm-branches and a kind of soft earth fit for the purpose. These granaries are usually erected near some mountain, or on the bank of some river, so as to be out of the sun's rays, in order that the contents may keep better. Here they also store up any other provisions which they may wish to preserve, and the remainder of their stores; and they go and get them as need may require, without any apprehensions of being defrauded. Indeed, it is to be wished, that, among the Christians, avarice prevailed no more than among them, and tormented no more the minds of men."

23. "BRINGING IN WILD ANIMALS, FISH, AND OTHER STORES. At a set time every year they gather in all sorts of wild animals, fish, and even crocodiles; these are then put in baskets, and loaded upon a sufficient number of the curly-haired hermaphrodites above mentioned, who carry them on their shoulders to the storehouse. This supply, however, they do not resort to unless in case of the last necessity. In such event, in order to preclude any dissension, full notice is given to all interested; for they live in the utmost harmony among themselves. The chief, however, is at liberty to take whatever of this supply he may choose."

24. "MODE OF DRYING FISH, WILD ANIMALS, AND OTHER PROVISIONS. In order to keep these animals longer, they are in the habit of preparing them as follows: They set up in the earth four stout forked stakes; and on these they lay others, so as to form a sort of grating. On this they lay their game, and then build a fire underneath, so as to harden them in the smoke. In this process they use a great deal of care to have the drying perfectly performed, to prevent the meat from spoiling, as the picture shows. I suppose this stock to be laid in for their winter's supply in the woods, as at that time we could never obtain

the least provision from them. For the like reason their granaries, as was related, are placed close under some rock or cliff, near a river, and not far from some deep forest, so that when necessary they can carry a supply in canoes."

25. "HUNTING DEER. The Indians have a way of hunting deer which we never saw before. They manage to put on the skins of the largest which have before been taken, in such a manner, with the heads on their own heads, so that they can see out through the eyes as through a mask. Thus accoutred, they can approach close to the deer without frightening them. They take advantage of the time when the animals come to drink at the river, and, having their bow and arrows all ready, easily shoot them, as they are very plentiful in those regions. It is usual, however, to protect the left arm with the bark of the branch of a tree, to keep it from being grazed by the bow-string,— a practice which they have learned naturally enough. They know how to prepare deer-skins, not with iron instruments, but with shells, in a surprisingly excellent manner; indeed, I do not believe that any European could do it as well."

26. "KILLING CROCODILES (PROBABLY ALLIGATORS). Their way of attacking crocodiles is as follows: They put up, near a river, a little hut full of cracks and holes, and in this they station a watchman, so that he can see the crocodiles, and hear them, a good way off; for, when driven by hunger, they come out of the rivers, and crawl about on the islands after prey, and, if they find none, they make such a frightful noise that it can be heard for half a mile. Then the watchman calls the rest of the watch, who are in readiness; and, taking a portion, ten or twelve feet long, of the stem of a tree, they go out to find the monster, who is crawling along with his mouth wide open, all ready to catch one of them if he can; and with the greatest quickness they push the pole, small end first, as deep as possible down his throat, so that the roughness and irregularity of the bark may hold it from being got out again. Then they turn the crocodile over on his back, and with clubs and arrows pound and pierce his belly, which is softer; for his back, especially if he is an old one, is impenetrable, being protected by hard scales. This is their way of hunting crocodiles; by which they are, nevertheless, so much annoyed that they have to keep up a regular watch against them both day and night, as we should do against the most dangerous enemy."

27. "FLORIDIANS CROSSING OVER TO AN ISLAND TO TAKE THEIR PLEASURE. That country abounds in most delightful islands, as the first pictures of our series show. The rivers are not deep; but the water, which comes not higher than to the breast, is very clear and pure. When they desire to make a little pleasure excursion with their wives and children, to one of these islands, they cross over by swimming, in which they are very skilful; or, if they have young children, by wading. The mother can carry three children at a time, the smallest on one shoulder, and holding it by one arm, the other two holding on to her under her arms; while in her other hand she holds up a basket full of fruit or other provisions for the occasion. When there is any fear of the enemy, the men take their bows and arrows; and, to keep them from being wet, they attach the quiver to the hair of the head, and hold up in one hand a bow all ready strung, and an arrow, for instant defence if necessary: as in the picture."

28. "PREPARATIONS FOR A FEAST. At the time of year when they are in the habit of feasting each other, they employ cooks, who are chosen on purpose for the business. These, first of all, take a great round earthen vessel (which they know how to make and to burn so that water can be boiled in it as well as in our kettles), and place it over a large wood-fire, which one of them drives with a fan very effectively, holding it in the hand. The head cook now puts the things to be cooked into the great pot; others put water for washing into a hole in the ground; another brings water in a utensil that serves for a bucket; another pounds on a stone the aromatics that are to be used for seasoning; while the women are picking over or preparing the viands. Although they have great festivities, after their manner, yet they are very temperate in eating, and, in con-

sequence, they live to a great age; for one of their inferior chiefs affirmed to me that he was three hundred years old, and that his father, whom he pointed out to me, was fifty years older; indeed, this last personage, I confess, looked like nothing but the bones of a man covered with a skin. Such facts might well make us Christians ashamed, who are so immoderate in indulgence both in eating and drinking, who shorten our own lives thereby, and who richly deserve to be put under the authority of these savages and of brute beasts, to be taught sobriety."

29. "PROCEEDINGS OF THE FLORIDIANS IN DELIBERATING ON IMPORTANT AFFAIRS. The chief and his nobles are accustomed during certain days of the year to meet early every morning for this express purpose in a public place, in which a long bench is constructed, having at the middle of it a projecting part laid with nine round trunks of trees, for the chief's seat. On this he sits by himself, for distinction's sake; and here the rest come to salute him, one at a time, the oldest first, by lifting both hands twice to the height of the head, and saying, 'Ha, he, ya, ha, ha.' To this the rest answer, 'Ha, ha.' Each, as he completes his salutation, takes his seat on the bench. If any question of importance is to be discussed, the chief calls upon his *laüas* (that is, his priests) and upon the elders, one at a time, to deliver their opinions. They decide upon nothing until they have held a number of councils over it, and they deliberate very sagely before deciding. Meanwhile the chief orders the women to boil some *casina;* which is a drink prepared from the leaves of a certain root, and which they afterwards pass through a strainer. The chief and his councillors being now seated in their places, one stands before him, and, spreading forth his hands wide open, asks a blessing upon the chief and the others who are to drink. Then the cupbearer brings the hot drink in a capacious shell, first to the chief, and then, as the chief directs, to the rest in their order, in the same shell. They esteem this drink so highly, that no one is allowed to drink it in council unless he has proved himself a brave warrior. Moreover, this drink has the quality of at once throwing into a sweat whoever drinks it. On this account those who cannot keep it down, but whose stomachs reject it, are not intrusted with any difficult commission, or any military responsibility, being considered unfit, for they often have to go three or four days without food; but one who can drink this liquor can go for twenty-four hours afterwards without eating or drinking. In military expeditions, also, the only supplies which the hermaphrodites carry consist of gourd bottles or wooden vessels full of this drink. It strengthens and nourishes the body, and yet does not fly to the head; as we have observed on occasion of these feasts of theirs."

30. "CONSTRUCTION OF FORTIFIED TOWNS AMONG THE FLORIDIANS. The Indians are accustomed to build their fortified towns as follows: A position is selected near the channel of some swift stream. They level it as even as possible, and then dig a ditch in a circle around the site, in which they set thick round pales, close together, to twice the height of a man; and they carry this paling some ways past the beginning of it, spiral-wise, to make a narrow entrance admitting not more than two persons abreast. The course of the stream is also diverted to this entrance; and at each end of it they are accustomed to erect a small round building, each full of cracks and holes, and built, considering their means, with much elegance. In these they station as sentinels men who can smell the traces of an enemy at a great distance, and who, as soon as they perceive such traces, set off to discover them. As soon as they find them, they set up a cry which summons those within the town to the defence, armed with bows and arrows and clubs. The chief's dwelling stands in the middle of the town, and is partly underground, in consequence of the sun's heat. Around this are the houses of the principal men, all lightly roofed with palm-branches, as they are occupied only nine months in the year; the other three, as has been related, being spent in the woods. When they come back, they occupy their houses again; and, if they find that the enemy has burnt them down, they build others of similar materials. Thus magnificent are the palaces of the Indians."

31. "HOW THEY SET ON FIRE AN ENEMY'S TOWN. For the enemy, eager for revenge, sometimes will creep up by night in the utmost silence, and reconnoitre to see if the watch be asleep. If they find every thing silent, they approach the rear of the town, set fire to some dry moss from trees, which they prepare in a particular manner, and fasten to the heads of their arrows. They then fire these into the town, so as to ignite the roofs of the houses, which are made of palm-branches thoroughly dried with the summer heats. As soon as they see that the roofs are burning, they make off as fast as possible, before they are discovered, and they move so swiftly that it is a hard matter to overtake them; and meanwhile also the fire is giving the people in the town enough to do to save themselves from it, and get it under. Such are the stratagems used in war by the Indians for firing the enemy's towns; but the damage done is trifling, as it amounts only to the labor required for putting up new houses."

32. "HOW SENTINELS ARE PUNISHED FOR SLEEPING ON THEIR POSTS. But, when the burning of a town has happened in consequence of the negligence of the watch, the penalty is as follows: The chief takes his place alone on his bench, those next to him in authority being seated on another long bench curved in a half circle; and the executioner orders the culprit to kneel down before the chief. He then sets his left foot on the delinquent's back; and, taking in both hands a club of ebony or some other hard wood, worked to an edge at the sides, he strikes him on the head with it, so severely as almost to split the skull open. The same penalty is inflicted for some other crime reckoned capital among them; for we saw two persons punished in this same way."

33. "HOW THEY DECLARE WAR. A chief who declares war against his enemy does not send a herald to do it, but orders some arrows, having locks of hair fastened at the notches, to be stuck up along the public ways; as we observed when, after taking the chief Outina prisoner, we carried him around to the towns under his authority, to make them furnish us provisions."

34. "FIRST-BORN CHILDREN SACRIFICED TO THE CHIEF WITH SOLEMN CEREMONIES. Their custom is to offer up the first-born son to the chief. When the day for the sacrifice is notified to the chief, he proceeds to a place set apart for the purpose, where there is a bench for him, on which he takes his seat. In the middle of the area before him is a wooden stump two feet high, and as many thick, before which the mother sits on her heels, with her face covered in her hands, lamenting the loss of her child. The principal one of her female relatives or friends now offers the child to the chief in worship, after which the women who have accompanied the mother form a circle, and dance around with demonstrations of joy, but without joining hands. She who holds the child goes and dances in the middle, singing some praises of the chief. Meanwhile, six Indians, chosen for the purpose, take their stand apart in a certain place in the open area; and midway among them the sacrificing officer, who is decorated with a sort of magnificence, and holds a club. The ceremonies being through, the sacrificer takes the child, and slays it in honor of the chief, before them all, upon the wooden stump. This offering was on one occasion performed in our presence."

35. "SOLEMNITIES AT CONSECRATING THE SKIN OF A STAG TO THE SUN. The subjects of the chief Outina were accustomed every year, a little before their spring, that is, in the end of February, to take the skin of the largest stag they could get, keeping the horns on it; to stuff it full of all the choicest sorts of roots that grow among them, and to hang long wreaths or garlands of the best fruits on the horns, neck, and other parts of the body. Thus decorated, they carried it, with music and songs, to a very large and splendid level space, where they set it up on a very high tree, with the head and breast toward the sunrise. They then offered prayers to the sun, that he would cause to grow on their lands good things such as those offered him. The chief, with his sorcerer, stands nearest the

tree, and offers the prayer; the common people, placed at a distance, make responses. Then the chief and all the rest, saluting the sun, depart, leaving the deer's hide there until the next year. This ceremony they repeat annually."

36. "THE YOUTH AT THEIR EXERCISES. Their youth are trained in running, and a prize is offered for him who can run longest without stopping; and they frequently practice with the bow. They also play a game of ball, as follows: in the middle of an open space is set up a tree some eight or nine fathoms high, with a square frame woven of twigs on the top; this is to be hit with the ball, and he who strikes it first gets a prize. They are also fond of amusing themselves with hunting and fishing."

37. "THE DISPLAY WITH WHICH A QUEEN ELECT IS BROUGHT TO THE KING. When a king chooses to take a wife, he directs the tallest and handsomest of the daughters of the chief men to be selected. Then a seat is made on two stout poles, and covered with the skin of some rare sort of animal, while it is set off with a structure of boughs, bending over forward so as to shade the head of the sitter. The queen elect having been placed on this, four strong men take up the poles, and support them on their shoulders; each carrying in one hand a forked wooden stick to support the pole at halting. Two more walk at the sides; each carrying on a staff a round screen elegantly made, to protect the queen from the sun's rays. Others go before, blowing upon trumpets made of bark, which are smaller above, and larger at the farther end, and having only the two orifices, one at each end. They are hung with small oval balls of gold, silver, and brass, for the sake of a finer combination of sounds. Behind follow the most beautiful girls that can be found, elegantly decorated with necklaces and armlets of pearls, each carrying in her hand a basket full of choice fruits; and belted below the navel, and down to the thighs, with the moss of certain trees, to cover their nakedness. After them come the body-guards."

38. "SOLEMNITIES AT THE RECEPTION OF THE QUEEN BY THE KING. With this display the queen is brought to the king in a place arranged for the purpose, where a good-sized platform is built up of round logs, having on either side a long bench where the chief men are seated. The king sits on the platform on the right-hand side. The queen, who is placed on the left, is congratulated by him on her accession, and told why he chose her for his first wife. She, with a certain modest majesty, and holding her fan in her hand, answers with as good a grace as she can. Then the young women form a circle without joining hands, and with a costume differing from the usual one; for their hair is tied at the back of the neck, and then left to flow over the shoulders and back; and they wear a broad girdle below the navel, having in front something like a purse, which hangs down so as to cover their nudity. To the rest of this girdle are hung ovals of gold and silver, coming down upon the thighs, so as to tinkle when they dance, while at the same time they chant the praises of the king and queen. In this dance they all raise and lower their hands together. All the men and women have the ends of their ears pierced, and pass through them small oblong fish-bladders, which when inflated shine like pearls, and which, being dyed red, look like a light-colored carbuncle. It is wonderful that men so savage should be capable of such tasteful inventions."

39. "THE KING AND QUEEN TAKING A WALK FOR THEIR AMUSEMENT. Sometimes the king likes to take a walk in the evening in a neighboring wood, alone with his principal wife, wearing a deer's hide so elegantly prepared, and painted of various colors, so that nothing more beautifully finished can be seen anywhere. Two young men walk at his sides, carrying fans to make a breeze for him; while a third, ornamented with little gold and silver balls hanging to his belt, goes behind, and holds up the deer's hide, so that it shall not drag on the ground. The queen and her handmaids are adorned with belts hung on the shoulders or around the body, made of a kind of moss that grows on some trees; with slender filaments which are at-

tached to each other, after the fashion of links of a chain, of a bluish-green color, and so beautiful in texture that it might be mistaken for filaments of silk. The trees laden with this moss are beautiful to see; for it sometimes hangs down from the highest boughs of a very tall tree to the ground. While hunting once with some of my fellow-soldiers in the woods near King Saturioua's residence, I saw him and his queen thus decorated.

"The reader should be informed that all these chiefs and their wives ornament their skin with punctures arranged so as to make certain designs, as the following pictures show. Doing this sometimes makes them sick for seven or eight days. They rub the punctured places with a certain herb, which leaves an indelible color. For the sake of further ornament and magnificence, they let the nails of their fingers and toes grow, scraping them down at the sides with a certain shell, so that they are left very sharp. They are also in the habit of painting the skin around their mouths of a blue-color."

40. "CEREMONIES AT THE DEATH OF A CHIEF OR OF PRIESTS. When a chief in that province dies, he is buried with great solemnities; his drinking-cup is placed on the grave, and many arrows are planted in the earth about the mound itself. His subjects mourn for him three whole days and nights, without taking any food. All the other chiefs, his friends, mourn in like manner; and both men and women, in testimony of their love for him, cut off more than half their hair. Besides this, for six months afterwards certain chosen women three times every day, at dawn, noon, and twilight, mourn for the deceased king with a great howling. And all his household stuff is put into his house, which is set on fire, and the whole burned up together.

"In like manner, when their priests die, they are buried in their own houses; which are then set on fire, and burned up with all their furniture."

41. "MODE OF COLLECTING GOLD IN STREAMS RUNNING FROM THE APALATCY MOUNTAINS. A great way from the place where our fort was built, are great mountains, called in the Indian language Apalatcy; in which, as the map shows, arise three great rivers, in the sands of which are found much gold, silver, and brass, mixed together. Accordingly, the natives dig ditches in these streams, into which the sand brought down by the current falls by gravity. Then they collect it out, and carry it away to a place by itself, and after a time collect again what continues to fall in. They then convey it in canoes down the great river which we named the River of May, and which empties into the sea. The Spaniards have been able to use for their advantage the wealth thus obtained."

42. "MURDER OF PIERRE GAMBRE, A FRENCHMAN,
"I have spoken in my Brief Account of one Pierre Gambré, a Frenchman, who obtained a license from Laudonnière for carrying goods, and trading, throughout the province; and who was successful enough not only to accumulate considerable means, but also to marry into the family of a certain chief of the country. Being seized with an earnest desire of returning to see his friends at the fort, he urged his new relative until he got permission to go, but on condition of returning within a fixed number of months; and a canoe was provided for him besides, and two Indians to convey him. The goods which he had obtained were stowed in the boat; and his Indian companions murdered him while on the journey, while he was stooping over to make a fire. This was done partly in revenge, as he had, while acting in the chief's absence in his stead, beaten one of them with his fists; and partly out of greediness for the riches which the soldier had with him in the boat. These they took, and fled; and the facts were unknown for a long time.

"This picture, not to interrupt the series of those preceding it, is put last; nor would it have been inserted at all, had not the author of the Brief Account remembered the circumstances."

43. THE ARRIVAL OF THE ENGLIFHEMEN IN VIRGINA. The sea coasts of Virginia arre full of Ilands, wher by the entrance into the mayne lad is hard to finde.

For although they bee separated with diuers and sundrie large Diuision, which seeme to yeeld conuenient entrance, yet to our great perill we proued that they wear shallowe, and full of dangerous flatts, and could neuer perce opp into the mayne land, vntill wee made trialls in many places with or small pinness. At lengthe wee fownd an entrance vppon our mens diligent serche therof. Affter that wee had passed opp, and sayled ther in for a short space we discouered a mightye riuer fallinge downe in to the sownde ouer against those Ilands, which neuerthelesse wee could not saile opp any thinge far by Reason of the shallewnes, the mouth ther of beinge annoyed with sands driuen in with the tyde therfore saylinge further, wee came vnto a Good bigg yland, the Inhabitants therof as soone as they saw vs began to make a great and horrible crye, as people which neuer befoer had seene men apparelled like vs, and camme a way makinge out crys like wild beasts or men out of their wyts. But beenge gentlye called backe, wee offred them of our wares, as glasses, kniues, babies (Babies or babes, i.e. dolls.), and other trifles, which wee thougt they deligted in. Soe they stood still, and perceuinge our Good will and courtesie came fawninge vppon vs, and bade us welcome. Then they brougt vs to their village in the iland called, Roanoac, and vnto their Weroans or Prince, which entertained vs with Reasonable curtesie, althoug they wear amased at the first sight of vs. Suche was our arriuall into the parte of the world, which we call Virginia, the stature of bodye of wich people, theyr attire, and maneer of lyuinge, their feasts, and banketts, I will particullerlye declare vnto yow."

The titles and descriptions for Plates and Notes 43-64 have been quoted from the 1893 edition of *Hariot's Narrative of the First Plantation of Virginia in 1585.* . . . Including the Trve Pictures and Fashions of the People . . . Diligentlye collected and drawne by Ihon White . . . who was sent thither speciallye and for the same purpose by the said Sir Walter Raleigh. . . . Reprinted from the Edition of 1590 with De Bry's Engravings. Translated out of Latin into English by Richard Hacklvit. The "old English" spelling differs in position of letters as well as in characters. The letter "f" is used for "s;" "y" for "i;" and "i" for "j." The spelling in the narrative is very inconsistent, probably due to typographical errors in the 1893 edition.

The first of De Bry's "Grands et petits Voyages" featured the narrative of Hariot and engravings after John White's water colors. Though Le Moyne depicted an earlier expedition—1564—Hakluyt persuaded De Bry to publish the Virginia manuscript and pictures first.

For his publication, *A Briefe and True Report of the New Found Land of Virginia,* De Bry produced 23 engravings after White. One, a map—"The Carte of all the coast of Virginia" is not reproduced here. None of the several dozen water colors of the flora and fauna of the area were reproduced singly; however, they probably served as information used in producing realistic backgrounds for the portraits.

De Bry (1528-1598) was a Flemish engraver and goldsmith. He was born in Liege. He later moved to Frankfurt. With the publication of the 1590 edition, he began a series of travel books which after his death was continued by his family. He published 6 of the series, and they pushed the vision of his "Voyages" to several dozen books by 1634. De Bry's engravings after White in 1590 and Le Moyne in 1591 were the earliest pictures of native life in the now Southeastern United States. See also Stefan Lorant, 1946, and David I. Bushnell, "John White; The First English Artist to Visit America, 1585." *The Virginia Magazine,* v. 35, 1927, 419-30; v. 36, 1928, 17-26 and 124-134. See also, Lawrence Binyon, *Catalogue of Drawings by British Artists and Artists of Foreign Origin Working in Great Britain,* v. 4, 1907, 326-337.

44. "A WEROAN OR GREAT LORDE OF VIRGINIA. The Princes of Virginia are attyred in suche manner as is expressed in this figure. They weare the haire of their heades long and bynde opp the ende of the same in a knot vnder their eares. Yet they cutt the topp of their heades from the forehead to the nape of the necke in manner of a cokscombe, stickinge a faier longe fether of some berd att the Begininge of the creste vppon their foreheads, and another short one on bothe seides about their eares. They

hange at their eares ether thicke pearles, or somwhat els, as the clawe of some great birde, as cometh in to their fansye. Moreouer They ether pownes, or paynt their forehead, cheeks, chynne, bodye, armes, and leggs, yet in another sorte then the inhabitants of Florida. They weare a chaine about their necks of pearles or beades of copper, wich they muche esteeme, and ther of wear they also braselets on their armes. Vnder their brests about their bellyes appeir certayne spotts, whear they vse to lett them selues bloode, when they are sicke. They hange before them the skinne of some beaste verye feinelye dresset in suche sorte, that the tayle hangeth downe behynde. They carye a quiuer made of small rushes holding their bowe readie bent in one hand, and an arrowe in the other, redie to defend themselues. In this manner they goe to warr, or to their solemne feasts and banquetts. They take muche pleasure in huntinge of deer wher of ther is great store in the contrye, for yt is fruitfull, pleasant, and full of Goodly woods. Yt hathe also store of riuers full of diuers sorts of fishe. When they go to battel they paynt their bodyes in the most terible manner that thei can deuise."

45. "ONE OF THE CHIEFF LADYES OF SECOTA. The woemen of Secotam are of Reasonable good proportion. In their goinge they carrye their hands danglinge downe, and air dadil in a deer skinne verye excelletlye wel dressed, hanginge downe fro their nauell vnto the mydds of their thighes, which also couereth their hynder parts. The reste of their bodies are all bare. The forr parte of their haire is cutt shorte, the rest is not ouer Longe, thinne, and softe, and falling downe about their shoulders: They weare a Wreath about their heads. Their foreheads, cheeks, chynne, armes and leggs are pownced. About their necks they wear a chaine, ether pricked or paynted. They haue small eyes, plaine and flatt noses, narrow foreheads, and broade mowths. For the most parte they hange at their eares chaynes of longe Pearles, and of some smootht bones. Yet their nayles are not longe, as the woemen of Florida. They are also delighted with walkinge in to the fields, and beside the riuers, to see the huntinge of deers and catchinge of fische."

46. "ONE OF THE RELIGEOUS MEN IN THE TOWNE OF SECOTA. The Priests of the aforesaid Towne of Secota are well stricken in yeers, and as yt seemeth of more experience then the comon sorte. They weare their heare cutt like a creste, on the topps of thier heades as other doe, but the rest are cutt shorte, sauinge those which growe aboue their foreheads in manner of a perriwigge. They also haue somwhat hanginge in their ears. They weare a shorte clocke made of fine hares skinns quilted with the hayre outwarde. The rest of their bodie is naked. They are notable enchaunters, and for their pleasure they frequent the riuers, to kill with their bowes, and catche wilde ducks, swannes, and other fowles."

47. "A YOUNGE GENTILL WOEMAN DOUGHTER OF SECOTA. Virgins of good parentage are apparelled altogether like the woemen of Secota aboue mentionned, sauing that they weare hanginge abowt their necks in steede of a chaine certaine thicke, and rownde pearles, with little beades of copper, or polished bones betweene them. They pounce their foreheads, cheeckes, armes and legs. Their haire is cutt with two ridges aboue their foreheads, the rest is trussed opp on a knott behinde, they haue broade mowthes, reasonable fair black eyes: they lay their hands often vppon their Shoulders, and couer their brests in token of maydenlike modestye. The rest of their bodyes are naked, as in the picture is to bee seene. They deligt also in seeinge fishe taken in the riuers."

48. "A CHEIFF LORDE OF ROANOAC. The cheefe men of the yland and towne of Roanoac weare the haire of their crounes of theyr heades cutt like a cokes combe, as the others doe. The rest they wear longe as woemen and truss them opp in a knott in the nape of their necks. They hange pearles stringe vppon a threed att their eares, and weare bracelets on their armes of pearles, or small beades of copper or of smoothe bone called minsal, nether paintinge nor powncinge

of them selues, but in token of authoritye, and honor, they wear a chaine of great pearles, or copper beades or smoothe bones abowt their necks, and a plate of copper hinge vppon a stringe, from the nauel vnto the midds of their thighes. They couer themselues before and behynde as the woemen doe with a deers skynne handsomley dressed, and fringed. More ouer they fold their armes together as they walke, or as they talke one with another in signe of wisdome. The yle of Roanoac is verye pleisant, and hath plaintie of fishe by reason of the Water that enuironeth the same."

49. "A CHEIFF LADYE OF POMEIOOC. About 20. milles from that Iland, neere the lake of Paquippe, ther is another towne called Pomeioock hard by the sea. The apparell of the cheefe ladyes of that towne differeth but litle from the attyre of those which lyue in Roanoac. For they weare their haire trussed opp in a knott, as the maiden doe which we spake of before, and haue their skinnes pownced in the same manner, yet they wear a chaine of great pearles, or beades of copper, or smoothe bones 5. or 6. fold about their necks, bearinge one arme in the same, in the other hand they carye a gourde full of some kinde of pleasant liquor. They tye deers skinne doubled about them crochinge hygher about their breasts, which hange downe before almost to their knees, and are almost altogither naked behinde. Commonlye their yonge daugters of 7. or 8. yeares olde do wait vpon them wearinge abowt them a girdle of skinne, which hangeth downe behinde, and is drawen vnder neath betwene their thighes, and bownde aboue their nauel with mosse of trees betwene that and their skinnes to couer their priuities withall. After they be once past 10. yeares of age, they wear deer skinnes as the older sorte do. They are greatlye Diligted with puppetts, and babes which wear brought oute of England."

50. "AN AGED MANNE IN HIS WINTER GARMENT. The aged men of Pommeioocke are couered with a large skinne which is tyed vppon their shoulders on one side and hangeth downe beneath their knees wearinge their other arme naked out of the skinne, that they maye bee at more libertie. Those skynnes are Dressed with the hair on, and lyned with other furred skinnes. The yonnge men suffer noe hairr at all to growe vppon their faces but assoone as they growe they put them away, but when they are come to yeeres they suffer them to growe although to say truthe they come opp very thinne. They also weare their haire bownde op behynde, and, haue a creste on their heads like the others. The contrye abowt this plase is soe fruit full and good, that England is not to bee compared to yt."

51. "THEIR MANNER OF CAREYNGE THER CHILDREN AND ATYERE OF THE CHEIFFE LADYES OF THE TOWNE OF DAFAMONQUEPEUC. In the towne of Dasemonquepeuc distant from Roanoac 4. or 5. miles, the woemen are attired, and pownced, in suche sorte as the woemen of Roanoac are, yet they weare noe wreathes vppon their heads, nether haue they their thighes painted with small pricks. They haue a strange manner of bearing their children, and quite contrarie to ours. For our woemen carrie their children in their armes before their brests, but they taking their sonne by the right hand, bear him on their backs, holdinge the left thighe in their lefte arme after a strange, and conuesnall (probably a typographical error for "vnuseuall.") fashion, as in the picture is to bee seene."

52. "THE CONIUERER. They haue comonlye coniurers or iuglers which vse strange gestures, and often contrarie to nature in their enchantments: For they be verye familiar with deuils, of whome they enquier what their enemys doe, or other suche thinges. They shaue all their heads sauinge their creste which they weare as other doe, and fasten a small black birde, aboue one of their ears as a badge of their office. They weare nothinge but a skinne which hangeth downe from their gyrdle, and couereth their priuityes. They weare a bagg by their side as is expressed in the figure. The Inhabitants giue great credit vnto their speeche, which oftentymes they finde to bee true."

53. "THE MANNER OF MAKINGE THEIR BOATES. The manner of makinge their boates in Virginia is verye

wonderfull. For wheras they want Instruments of yron, or other like vnto ours, yet they knowe howe to make them as handsomelye, to saile with whear they liste in their Riuers, and to fishe withall, as ours. First they choose some longe, and thicke tree, according to the bignes of the boate which they would frame, and make a fyre on the grownd abowt the Roote therof, kindlinge the same by little, and little with drie mosse of trees, and chipps of woode that the flame should not mounte opp to highe, and burne to muche of the lengte of the tree. When yt is almost burnt thorough, and readye to fall they make a new fyre, which they suffer to burne ventill the tree fall of yts owne accord. Then burninge of the topp, and bowghs of the tree in suche wyse that the bodie of the same may Retayne his iust lengthe, they raise yt vppon potes laid ouer cross wise vppon forked posts, at suche a reasonable heighte as they may handsomlye worke vppon yt. Then take they of the barke with certayne shells: they reserue the innermost parte of the lennke (probably a typographical effort for "barke") for the nethermost parte of the boate. On the other side they make a fyre according to the lengthe of the bodye of the tree, sauinge at both the ends. That which they thinke is sufficientlye burned they quenche and scrape away with shells, and makinge a new fyre they burne yt agayne, and soe they continne somtymes burninge and sometymes scrapinge, vntill the boate haue sufficient bothowmes. Thus God indueth thise sauage people with sufficient reason to make thinges necessarie to serue their turnes."

John White did not produce a picture of this subject.

54. "THEIR MANNER OF FISHYNGE IN VIRGINIA. They haue likewise a notable way to catche fishe in their Riuers, for whear as they lacke both yron, and steele, they fasten vnto their Reedes or longe Rodds, the hollowe tayle of a certaine fishe like to a sea crabb in steede of a poynte, wherwith by nighte or day they stricke fishes, and take them opp into their boates. They also know how to vse the prickles, and pricks of other fishes. They also make weares, with settinge opp reedes or twiggs in the water, which they soe plant one with another, that they growe still narrower, and narrower, as appeareth by this figure. Ther was neuer seene amonge vs soe cunninge a way to take fish withall, wherof sondrie sortes as they fownde in their Riuers vnlike vnto ours, which are also of a verye good taste. Dowbtless yt is a pleasant sighte to see the people, somtymes wadinge, and goinge somtymes sailinge in those Riuers, which are shallowe and not deepe, free from all care of heapinge opp Riches for their posterite, content with their state, and liuinge frendlye together of those thinges which god of his bountye hath giuen vnto them, yet without giuinge hym any thankes according to his desarte.

"So sauage is this people, and depriued of the true knowledge of god. For they haue none other then is mentionned before in this worke."

55. "THE BROVVYLLINGE OF THEIR FIFHE OUER THE FLAME. After they haue taken store of fishe, they gett them vnto a place fitt to dress yt. Ther they sticke vpp in the grownde 4. stakes in a square roome, and lay 4 potes vppon them, and others ouer thwart the same like vnto an hurdle, of sufficient heigthe, and layinge their fishe vppon this hurdle, they make a frye vnderneathe to broile the same, not after the manner of the people of Florida, which doe but schorte, (Scorche?) and harden their meate in the smoke onlye to Reserue the same duringe all the winter. For this people reseruinge nothinge for store, thei do broile, and spend away all att once and when they haue further neede, they roste or seethe fresh, as wee shall see heraffter. And when as the hurdle can not holde all the fishes, they hange the Rest by the fyrres on sticks sett vpp in the grounde a gainst the fyre, and than they finishe the rest of their cookerye. They take good heede that they bee not burntt. When the first are broyled they lay others on, that weare newlye broughte, continuinge the dressinge of their meate in this sorte, vntill they thincke they haue sufficient."

John White painted the fish on the frame. De Bry added the men.

104

56. "THEIR FEETHEYNGE OF THEIR MEATE IN EARTHEN POTTES. Their woemen know how to make earthen vessells with special Cunninge and that so large and fine, that our potters with lhoye (theyr?) wheles can make noe better: ant then Remoue them from place to place as easelye as we can doe our brassen kettles. After they haue set them vppon an heape of erthe to stay them from fallinge, they putt wood vnder which being kyndled one of them taketh great care that the fyre burne equallye Rounde abowt. They or their woemen fill the vessel with water, and then putt they in fruite, flesh, and fish, and lett all boyle together like a galliemaufrye, which the Spaniarde call, olla podrida. Then they putte yt out into disches, and sett before the companye, and then they make good cheere together. Yet are they moderate in their eatinge wherby they auoide sicknes. I would to god wee would followe their exemple. For wee should bee free from many kyndes of diseasyes which wee fall into by sumptwous and vnseasonable banketts, continuallye deuisinge new sawces, and prouocation of gluttonnye to satisfie our vnsatiable appetite."

John White painted the vessel over the fire. De Bry added the woman and man.

57. "THEIR FITTING AT MEATE. Their manner of feeding is in this wise. They lay a matt made of bents one the grownde and sett their meate on the mids therof, and then sit downe Rownde, the men vppon one side, and the woemen on the other. Their meate is Mayz sodden, in suche sorte as I described yt in the former treatise of verye good taste, deers flesche or of some other beaste, and fishe, They are verye sober in their eatinge, and drinkinge, and consequentlye verye longe liued because they doe not oppress nature."

58. "THEIR MANNER OF PRAINGE VVITH RATTELS ABOWT THE FYER. Vvhen they haue escaped any great danger by sea or lande, or be returned from the warr in token of Ioye they make a great fyer abowt which the men, and woemen sitt together, holdinge a certaine fruite in their hands like vnto a rownde pompion or a gourde, which after they haue taken out the fruits, and the seedes, then fill with small stons or certayne bigg kernells to make the more noise, and fasten that vppon a sticke, and singinge after their manner, they make merrie: as my selfe obserued and noted downe at my beinge amonge them. For it is a strange custome, and worth the obseruation."

59. "THEIR DANFES VVHICH THEY VFE ATT THEIR HYGHE FEAFTES. At a Certayne tyme of the yere they make a great, and solemne feaste wherunto their neighbours of the townes adioininge repayre from all parts, euery man attyred in the most strange fashion they can deuise hauinge certayne marks on the backs to declare of what place they bee. The place where they meet is a broade playne, abowt the which are planted in the grownde certayne posts carued with heads like to the faces of Nonnes couered with theyr vayles. Then beeing sett in order they dance, singe, and vse the strangest gestures that they can possiblye deuise. Three of the fayrest Virgins, of the companie are in the mydds, which imbrassinge one another doe as yt wear turne abowt in their dancing. All this is donne after the sunne is sett for auoydinge of heate. When they are weerye of dancinge. they goe oute of the circle, and come in vntill their dances be ended, and they goe to make merrye as is expressed in the 16. figure."

60. "THE TOVVNE OF POMEIOOC. The townes of this contrie are in a maner like vnto those which are in Florida, yet are they not soe strong nor yet preserued with soe great care. They are compassed abowt with poles starcke faste in the grownd, but they are not verye stronge. The entrance is verye narrowe as may be seene by this picture, which is made accordinge to the forme of the towne of Pomeiooc. Ther are but few howses therin, saue those which belonge to the kinge and his nobles. On the one side is their tempel separated from the other howses, and marked with the letter A. yt is builded rownde, and couered with skynne matts, and as yt wear compassed abowt with cortynes without windowes, and hath noe lighte but by the doore. On the other side is the kings lodginge marked with the letter B. Their dwellinges are builded with certaine potes fastened together, and couered with matts which they turne op as high as they thinke good, and soe receue in the lighte and other. Some are also couered with boughes of trees, as euery man lusteth or liketh best. They keepe their feasts and make good cheer together in the midds of the towne as yt is described in the 17. Figure. When the towne standeth fare from the water they digg a great ponde noted with the letter C wherhence they fetche as muche water as they neede."

61. "THE TOVVNE OF SECOTA. Their townes that are not inclosed with poles are commonlye fayrer then suche as are inclosed, as appereth in this figure which liuelye expresseth the towne of Secotam. For the howses are Scattered heer and ther, and they haue gardein expressed by the letter E. wherin groweth Tobacco which the inhabitants call Vppowoc. They haue also groaues wherein thei take deer, and fields wherin they sowe their corne. In their corne fields they builde as yt weare a scaffolde wher on they sett a cottage like to a rownde chaire, signiffied by F. wherin they place one to watche, for there are suche number of fowles, and beasts, that vnless they keepe the better watche, they would soone deuoure all their corne. For which cause the watcheman maketh continual cryes and noyse. They sowe their corne with a certaine distance noted by H. other wise one stalke would choke the growthe of another and the corne would not come vnto his rypenes G. For the leaues therof are large, like vnto the leaues of great reedes. They haue also a seuerall broade plotte C. whear they meete with their neighbours, to celebrate their cheefe solemne feastes as the 18. picture doth declare: and a place D. whear after they haue ended their feaste they make merrie togither. Ouer against this place they haue a rownd plott B. wher they assemble themselues to make their solemne prayers. Not far from which place ther is a lardge buildinge A. wherin are the tombes of their kings and princes, as will appere by the 22. figure likewise they haue garden notted bey the letter I. wherin they vse to sowe pompions. Also a place marked with K. wherin the make a fyre att their solemne feasts, and hard without the towne a riuer L. from whence they fetche their water. This people therfore voyde of all couetousnes lyue cherfullye and att their harts ease. Butt they solemnise their feasts in the night, and therfore they keepe verye great fyres to auoyde darkenes, and to testifie their Ioye."

62. "THE TOMBE OF THEIR WEROVVANS OR CHEIFF LORDES. They builde a Scaffolde 9. or 10. foote highe as is expressed in this figure vnder the tombs of their Weroans, or cheefe lordes which they couer with matts, and lai the dead corpses of their weroans theruppon in manner followinge, first the bowells are taken forthe. Then layinge downe the skinne, they cutt all the flesh cleane from the bones, which they drye in the sonne, and well dryed they inclose in Matts, and place at their feete. Then their bones (remaininge still fastened together with the ligaments whole and vncorrupted) are couered agayne with leather, and their carcase fashioned as yf their flesh wear not taken away. They lapp eache corps in his owne skinne after the same is thus handled, and lay yt in his order by the corpses of the other cheef lordes. By the dead bodies they sett their Idol Kiwasa, wherof we spake in the former chapter: For they are persuaded that the same doth kepe the dead bodyes of their cheefe lordes that nothinge may hurt them. Moreouer vnder the foresaid scaffolde some one of their preists hath his lodginge, which Mumbleth his prayers nighte and day, and hath charge of the corpses. For his bedd he hath two deares skinnes spredd on the grownde, yf the wether bee cold hee maketh a fyre to warme by withall. Thes poore soules are thus instructed by nature to reuerence their princes euen after their death."

63. "THER IDOL KIVVAFA. The people of this cuntrie haue an Idol, which they call Kiwasa: yt is carued of woode in lengthe 4. foote whose heade is like the heades of the people of Florida, the face is of a flesh colour, the brest white, the rest is all blacke, the thighes are also spottet with whitte. He hath a chayne abowt his necke of white

beades, betweene which are other Rownde beades of copper which they esteeme more then golde or siluer. This Idol is placed in the temple of the towne of Secotam, as the keper of the kings dead corpses. Somtyme they haue two of thes idoles in theyr churches, and somtine 3. but neuer aboue, which they place in a darke corner wher they shew terrible. Thes poore soules haue none other knowledge of god although I thinke them verye Desirous to know the truthe. For when as wee kneeled downe on our knees to make our prayers vnto god, they went abowt to imitate vs, and when they saw we moued our lipps, they also dyd the like. Wherfore that is verye like that they might easelye be brougt to the knowledge of the gospel. God of his mercie grant them this grace."

64. "THE MARCKES OF FUNDRYE OF THE CHEIF MENE OF VIRGINIA. The inhabitants of all the cuntrie for the most parte haue marks rased on their backs, wherby yt may be knowen what Princes subiects they bee, or of what place they haue their originall. For which cause we haue set downe those marks in this figure, and haue annexed the names of the places, that they might more easelye be discerned. Which industrie hath god indued them withal although they be verye simple, and rude. And to confesse a truthe, I cannot remember that euer I saw a better or quietter people then they.
"The marks which I obserued amonge them, are heere put downe in order folowinge.
"The marke which is expressed by A. belongeth to Wingino, the cheefe lorde of Roanoac.
"That which hath B. is the marke of Wingino his sisters husbande.
"Those which be noted with the letters, of C. and D. belonge vnto diverse chefe lordes in Secotam.
"Those which haue the letters E. F. G. are certaine cheefe men of Pomeiooc, and Aquascogoc."

65. John White. "THE MANNER OF THEIR ATTIRE AND PAINTING THEM SELUES WHEN THEY GOE TO THEIR GENERALL HUNTINGS, OR AT THEIRE SOLEMNE FEASTS." Reg. # LB 13. ECM 48. 1906.5. 9.1 (12). Neg. # 5254. *BM*. See # 44.

66. John White. "THE WYFE OF AN HEROWAN OF SECOTAN." Reg. # LB 19. ECM 37. 1906.5.9.1 (18). Neg. # 5260. *BM*. See # 45.

67. John White. "ONE OF THEIR RELIGIOUS MEN." Reg. # LB 15. ECM 42. 1906.5.9.1. (14). Neg. # 5256. *BM*. See # 46.

68. John White. "ONE OF THE WYUES OF WYNGYNO." Reg. # LB 18. ECM 47, 1906.5.9.1 (17). Neg. # 5259. *BM*. See # 47.

69. John White. "CHEIFE HEROWAN." Reg. # LB 22. ECM 46. 1906.5.9.1 (21). Neg. # 5263. *BM*. See # 48.

70. John White. "A CHEIFE HEROWANS WYFE OF POMEOC AND HER DAUGHTER OF THE AGE OF .8. or .10. YEARES." Reg. # LB 16. ECM 33. 1906.5.9.1 (13). Neg. # 5257. *BM*. See # 49.

71. John White. "THE AGED MAN IN HIS WYNTER GARMENT." Reg. # LB 20. ECM 34. 1906.5.9.1 (19). Neg. # 5261. *BM*. See # 50.

72. John White. "THE WYFE OF AN HEROWAN OF POMEIOOC." Reg. # LB 14. ECM 35. 1906.5.9.1 (15). Neg. # 5255. *BM*. See # 51.

73. John White. "THE FLYER." Reg. # LB 17. ECM 49. 1906.5.9.1 (16) . Neg. # 5258. *BM*. See # 52.

74. John White. "THE MANNER OF THEIR FISHING." Reg. # LB 5. ECM 43. 1906.5.9.1 (?). Neg. # 5246. *BM*. See # 54.

75. John White. "THEIRE SITTING AT MEATE." Reg. # LB 21. ECM 41. 1906.5.9.1 (20). Neg # 5262. *BM*. See # 57.

76. John White. "CEREMONY OF SITTING ROUND A FIRE." Reg. # LB 10. ECM 40. 1906.5.9.1 (11). Neg. # 5251. *BM*. See # 58.

77. John White. RELIGIOUS DANCE. Reg. # LB 9. ECM 49. 1906.5.9.1 (16). Neg. # 5250. *BM*. See # 59.

78. John White. "SECOTON. (Right) Their rype corne. Their greene corne. Corne newly sprong. A Ceremony in their prayers with strange iestures and songs and dansing abowt posts carued on the topps lyke mens faces. (Center) Their sitting at meate. (Left) The place of Solemne prayer. The howse wherin the Tombe of their Herounds standeth." Reg. # LB 6. ECM 36. 1906.5.9.1 (7). Neg. # 5247. *BM*. See # 61.

79. John White. "THE TOMBE OF THEIR CHEROUNES OR CHEIFE PERSONAGES, their flesh clene taken of from the bones saue the skynn and heare of theire heads, wth flesh is dried and enfolded in matts laide at theire feete. Their bones also being made dry ar couered wth deare skynns not altering their forme or proportion. With theire Kywash, which is an Image of woode keeping the deade." Reg. # LB 8. ECM 38. 1906.5.9.1 (9). Neg. # 5249. *BM*. See # 62.

80. John White. "THE TOWNE OF POMEIOCK AND TRUE FORME OF THEIR HOWSES, couered and enclosed some wth matts, and some wth barcks of trees. All compassed abowt wth smale poles stock thick together in stedd of a wall." Reg. # LB 7. ECM 32. 1906.5.9.1 (8). Neg. # 5248. *BM*. See # 60.

81. John White. "OF FLORIDA." Reg. # LB 24. ECM 62. 1906.5.9.1. (23). Neg. # 5265. *BM*. The source of John White's information or inspiration for painting the two Florida Indians is not known.

82. John White. "OF FLORIDA." Reg. # LB 23. ECM 61. 1906.5.9.1 (22). Neg. # 5264. *BM*.

83. "CAPTAIN JOHN SMITH'S MAP OF VIRGINIA. 1607." Published in London, 1612. The description with the picture from the Bur. of Am. Ethn. states: "This negative was taken from *Contributions from the Museum of the American Indian, Heye Foundation*, Vol. II, No. 4, 1915-16, Plate 1, which in turn was taken from the Arber edition of Smith's *Works*. Smith's original 'Mappe of the Bay and Rivers' was sent by him to the Council in London about November, 1608, as the result of his explorations in Chesapeake Bay in the previous summer (—Arber, p. 42)." Note that the map is decorated with drawings of Indians. In the upper left hand corner is a sketch of Powhatan with the title "Powhatan held this state and fashion when Capt. Smith was delivered to him prisoner. 1607." On the right it states "The Sasques-ahanougs are a gyant like people & thus atyred." On this map he locates the Indian villages and points out the "Kings howses." In this volume we have not included the many maps which accompany the early accounts of travel, trade, settlement, and exploration. Many of them record the location of Indian villages, tribes, and trails. Some also include in their margins, pictures of scenes and individuals. A number of rare maps, manuscripts, and pictures are referred to in *The Mirror of the Indian*, John Carter Brown Library, Brown University, Providence, R. I., 1958. See also, Walter T. Merserve, "English Works of Seventeenth-Century Indians," *American Quarterly*, 8 (1956), pp. 264-276.

84. Artist unknown. POCAHONTAS. The "Booton" portrait. Carolyn Thomas Foreman, *Indians Abroad*, Chapter II, "Pocahontas, Maid of Virginia," p. 26, states that this portrait was owned by The Reverend Mr. Whitwell Elwin, Booton Rectory, Norfolk, England, that his family was related to the Rolfe family, and that this portrait is thought to have been painted by an Italian artist. Regarding Pocahontas, W. F. Hodge, Bur. Am. Ethn. Bull. 30, Pt. 1, p. 269 writes:
Pocahontas was ". . . the daughter of Powhatan, chief of a group of Virginian tribes, 1595-1617. Her real name was Matoaka (Matowaka), ... The sole Algonquian root from

which the name can be derived is *metaw* 'to play,' 'to amuse one's self;' . . . .

". . . Pocahontas . . . was decoyed on board the ship of Capt. Argall in the Potomac, carried off to Jamestown (1712), and afterward taken to Werawocomoco, Powhatan's chief place of residence, where a sort of peace was effected and the ransom of Pocahontas agreed upon. While among the Englishmen, however, Pocahontas had become acquainted with John Rolfe, 'an honest gentleman, and of good behavior.' These two fell in love, . . . and in Apr. 1613, they were duly married, Pocahontas having been previously converted to Christianity and baptized under the name of 'the Lady Rebecca.' This alliance was of great advantage to the colonists, for Powhatan kept peace with them until his death. In 1616, Mr. and Mrs. Rolfe, with her brother-in-law Uttamatomac and several other Indians, accompanied Sir Thomas Dale to England, where, . . . Mrs. Rolfe was received as a 'princess.' In Mar. 1617, while on board ship at Gravesend ready to start for America with her husband, she fell ill of smallpox, and died about the 22nd year of her life. . . . She left behind her one son, Thomas Rolfe, who was educated by his uncle, Henry Rolfe, in England. Thomas Rolfe afterward went to Virginia, where he acquired wealth and distinction, leaving at his death an only daughter, from whom was descended, on the mother's side, John Randolph of Roanoke (1773-1833).

"Starchey, the first secretary of the colony, gives some details (*Hist. Trav. Va. Brit.*, 1849) regarding the early life and marriage of Pocahontas to an Indian chief, named Kocoum, previous to her union with Rolfe."

The story written by Capt. Smith, that he was saved from death by a plea of Pocahontas to Powhatan, has been questioned by a number of historians.

For an interesting account of Pocahontas and her trip to England, see Carolyn Thomas Foreman, *Indians Abroad, 1493-1938*, pp. 22-28. Many articles have been written regarding Pocahontas, among them, that of Louise P. Kellogg, "Pocahontas and Jamestown." *Wisconsin Magazine of History*, vol. 25, Sept. 1941, pp. 38-42. The Wisconsin Historical Society owns a copy of a portrait of Pocahontas painted by Robert M. Sully, ca. 1832, from his original which is now owned by the Virginia Historical Society. That Society also owns a portrait of Pocahontas by Thomas Sully. They were referred to by the Society as "purely imaginary." (correspondence June, 1958). They are described by A. W. Weddell, *Portraiture in the Virginia Historical Society,* Richmond, 1945. See also, Plate 158 and the description of the McKenney and Hall lithograph.

85. Simon de Passe. (Simon vrn de Vass). "MATAOKA (POCAHONTAS)." Line Engraving. 6¾ x 4½ inches. London. 1616. British Museum, Reg. No. 1863.5.9.625. Carolyn Thomas Foreman, *Indians Abroad*, pp. 25-26 mentions this engraving and states that the engraving pictured her as dignified and modest. (not shown herein).

86. Wencelaus Hollar. INDIAN OF VIRGINIA, MALE ("Vnus Americanus ex Virginia. Aetat: 23 (Age 23) W. Hollar ad viuam delia: et fecit, (made from Life) 1645").

87. Marquette et Joliet. "PAYS ET PEUPLES DE L'AMERIQUE DU NORD DECOUVERTS EN 1673 PAR MARQUETTE ET JOLIET." Carte, illustrée, en bas, d'une scène avec des Indiens récoltant des plantes au bord de l'eau. Bibliothèqve Nationale, Cabinet des Estampes. Paris, France. Vx 113, pet. fol. Cl. 55 - C. 10291. (not shown herein).

88. Christopher von Graffenried. "CHRISTOPHER V. GRAFFENRIED (1661-1743) AND THE ENGLISH SURVEYOR LAWSON AND THEIR NEGRO-SERVANT AT THE RED INDIAN TRIBUNAL IN CATECHNA (N. C.), 1711. This scene is discussed in "De Graffenried's Manuscript. . . ." *The Colonial Records of North Carolina*, Vol. I— 1662 to 1712. Raleigh, 1886. In this De Graffenried (Graffenrid) gives an interesting account of the founding of "Newbern" (N. C.). In speaking of the Indian wars he several times mentions the causes, "These poor Indians, insulted in many ways by a few rough Carolinians, more barbarous and inhuman than the Savages themselves, could not stand such treatment any longer, and began to think of their safety and

of vengeance, what they did very secretly." (p. 922).

On a short exploration trip up the Neus River, Graffenried and Lawson were captured by the Indians. After questioning at their village, the prisoners were released, but before leaving: "The next morning we were again examined, and we returned the same answer; but one Cor Thom being present, whom Mr. Lawson reprimanded for sundry things which had happened, gave a very unfavorable turn to our affairs. After the Council had broke up and the major part of the Indians had gone off, Mr. Lawson and myself were talking to-gether on indifferent subjects an Indian who understood a little English informed the remaining Indians that we had spoken very disrespectfully of them, which however was totally groundless. Whereupon three or four of them fell on us in a furious manner, took us by the arms and forced us to set down on the ground before the whole of them that were then collected. They instantly took off our wigs and threw them into the fire and we were at once condemned to death. . . On the day following we were taken to the great place of execution, where we were again tied and compelled to sit on the ground, being stripped of our surtouts. Before us a large fire was kindled, whilst some of them acted the part of conjurors, and others made a ring around us which they strewed with flowers. Behind us lay my innocent negro, who was also bound, and in this miserable situation we remained that day and the subsequent night. On the morning of the next day at which we were to die, a large multitude was collected to see the execution. . . ." (extract from a letter to Edward Hyde, Esq. Governor of North Carolina, pp. 991-92).

In the text of his manuscript he describes the "Indian Ceremonies of Execution." (pp. 930-933).

". . . the elder 'Greats' came back and took us to the execution-ground, binding our hands and feet: they did the same to my bigger negro. Then began our sad tragedy, ...

"In the centre of that great place, we were seated on the ground, the Surveyor-general and myself, bound and undressed, with bare heads; behind me, was the bigger one of my negroes, and in front of us, a great fire; near it, was the conjuror or High Priest (an old grizzled Indian; the priests are generally magicians,—and even conjure up the Devil); he made two white rounds,—whether of flour or white sand I do not know,—just in front of us, there was a wolf's skin, and a little further an Indian Savage standing, in the most dreadful and horrible position to be imagined; he did not move from the spot, with a knife in one hand, and an axe in the other,—it was apparently the executioner. Further still, on the other side of the fire, there was a great mob of Indian rabble, consisting of young men, women, and children, who danced with frightful contortions. In the centre of the circle was the Priest or Conjuror, who made his threatenings and exorcisms, when there was a pause in the dance; there were, at the four angles, officers armed with guns, who stimulated the dancers by stamping with their feet, and when a dance came to an end, they fired their guns.

"In some part of the circle, two Indian savages were seated on the ground and beat a small drum; they sung a mournful tune, rather fit to provoke tears and anger than joy. After they were tired of dancing, they all ran into the woods with dreadful outcry and howling, and soon came back with their faces painted in black, red, and white. Some of them had their hair flying, greased all over and sprinkled with minute cotton and small white feathers, and some arrayed in all kinds of furs. In short, they were dressed in such frightful way, that they looked rather like a set of Devils than like any other creatures; yes indeed, never was the Devil represented with a more frightful appearance than these savages running and dancing as they came forth from out the woods, drew up at the old place once more, and danced around the fire.

"Meanwhile, two lines of armed Indians stood behind us as guards, and never moved from their post, till everything was over. Behind this guard the Council of war sat on the ground in a circle, and were busy with consultation. Towards evening, the mob left off dancing, in order to bring wood from the forest, and to keep up the fires in different places;— especially, they made one far in the woods, which lasted all night, and so great that I thought the all forest to be in fire. I leave you to think, my most honored Lord, what a fearful and sad sight that was to me. I was wholly resolved to die, and accordingly I offered up my fervent prayers during the whole day and night. . . .

"Really, the sun was nearly set, when the Council assembled once more, probably to make an end of that fatal, frightful, and mournful ceremony; I turned round some little, though I was bound, knowing that one of them knew English pretty well, and I made a short discourse showing my innocence and insinuating that, if they would not spare me, the great and powerful Queen of England would avenge my blood, as I had brought that colony in those countries by her orders, not to do them any wrong but to live on good terms with them. I further stated whatever I thought fit besides, to induce them to some mitigation, offering them my services, if I were liberated. After I had done speaking, I remarked that one of the notables (who had seemed already disposed to do me some good,— who had even brought me to eat once,—and who was a relation to King Taylor, from whom I had bought the land where New Bern now stands), that that notable spoke earnestly, apparently in my favour, as it came out. Then it was forthwith resolved, to send a few members to their neighbors, *the villages of the Tuscaroros*, and to a certain King Tom Blunt, in high repute among them. . . .

"I spent the whole night in great anguish, awaiting my fate, (always bound in the same place), in continuous prayers and sighs. Meanwhile I also examined my poor negro, exhorting him in the best way I knew, and he gave me more satisfaction than I expected,—but I left Surveyor-General L. offer his own prayers, as being a man of understanding, and not over-religious. Towards 3 or 4 in the morning, the delegates came back from their mission and brought an answer, but very secretly. One of them came to me to unbind me; not knowing what this meant, I submitted to the will of the Allmighty, rose, and followed him as a poor lamb to the slaughter. Alas! I was much astonished when the Indians, a few steps from the former place, whispered into my ear, in a gibberish intermingled with English, that I had nothing to fear, that they would not kill me, but that Lawson would die, what affected me much. About twenty steps away from the place where I had been bound, the Indian led me to the cabins or dens, but I had no appetite. All at once, came quite a crowd of Indians around me, and did unanimously show much pleasure at my liberation. This very same man brought me back to the old place, but a little further, where the Council was assembled, and they congratulated me in their way, and smiled at me.

"I was however forbidden to speak the least word to Mr. Lawson, ... They also liberated my negro, but I never saw him since then. . . .

". . . they executed that unfortunate Lawson; as to his death, I know nothing certain; some Indians told me, that he was threatened to have his throat cut, with the razor which was found in his pocket,—what also acknowledged the small negro, who was not executed,—but some said he was hung, some said he was burnt. The Indians kept that execution very secret. . . .

"The day after Surveyor-General Lawson's execution, the notables of the village came to me, making me acquainted with their design to make war in North Carolina, and that they were especially embittered against the people on the Rivers Pamptego, New, Trent, and Cor sound, and that they had accordingly good reasons not to let me go, till they would have ended their expeditions. . . ."

De Graffenried describes his life among the Tuscaroras, the treaty of peace with them, and the nature of their warfare with the North Carolina colonists.

89. Francis Louis Michel. "DREY AMERICANS." This drawing and an explanation of it are found in the "Report of the Journey of Francis Louis Michel from Berne, Switzerland, to Virginia, October 2, 1701-December 1, 1702.(1)," translated and edited by Prof. Wm. J. Hinke, Ph.D., and originally published in *The Virginia Magazine of History and Biography*, Vol. XXIV, January, 1916, No. 1, p. 130. (From the manuscript in The Bern Library). A longer description of the Indians appears on pages 129-134. *Quoted by permission from the Virginia Magazine of History and Biography.*

"As mentioned above the representatives and principal men of four different tribes, about forty in number, appeared on the appointed day. . . . (p. 129).

"Those who are still alive, are four different nations. (footnote 23: The same statement is found in Jones, *Present State of Virginia*, 1724, p. 18: . . . .) In summer they stay in the forests here and there for the sake of hunting, but the permanent homes of one of the nations are at the Potomac River, (footnotes 24-27: Indian settlement at Potomac, Rappahannock, &c. See, 'The Powhatan Confederacy Past and Present.' by James Mooney, in the *American Anthropologist*, January-March 1907.), several hundred miles inland or in the wilderness. Another nation dwells at the Rabahanac River, (25) far up in the country, the third not far from Manigkinton, (26) the fourth along the ocean, between Virginia and Carolina (27). Those who were present at the proclamation brought with them as much as they could carry of all kinds of wild animal skins, prepared or fresh. They prepare them entirely white. They also brought a large number of baskets, carried on the arms, of different colors, made very artistically. The material is a kind of root (footnote 28: According to Beverley, *History*, 1725, Book III, pp. 7, 62, the Indians made their baskets of silk grass.) They weave into them all kinds of animals, flowers and other strange things, very beautifully. Everything that they bring is bought to send it as a present to England. They also make tobacco pipes, very beautifully cut out and formed. Their hats are small, round above and well closed, as the drawing shows.

"They have no clothes, except what they get through trade with the English (footnote 29: This does not agree with Beverley, *History*, 1725, Book III, pp. 3-7, who describes at length the summer and winter clothes of the Indians.) They wear them when they have to go to the Christians, which happens once a year, at the annual muster of the troops, in order to show them the power (of the English). Their loins and feet are then covered with a little piece of skin. They are well formed brown people, of ordinary size, but a little smaller then we. They have small fierce eyes set deep in their heads, black hair, hanging down upon their shoulders, most of them, however, have it cut short, except the women, who wear long, black hair. When they are summoned, their king or queen, as also their princes and nobles (but with some difference) wear crowns of bark, (footnote 30: This crown is also described by Beverley, ed. 1725, part III, p. 2: 'The people of condition of both sexes wear a sort of coronet on their Heads, from 4 to 6 inches broad, open at the top and composed of Peak or Beads, or else both interwoven together, and worked into Figures, made by a nice mixture of the Colours. Sometimes they wear a Wreath of Dyed Furs.' Plate 3 facing p. 5 of Beverley's account shows such a coronet.) a little more than a buckle wide, round and open above, with white and brown stripes, half an inch long, set in beautifully in spiral form, so that no bark is visible. The women, especially the queen and her three servants, were overhung with such things, strung on big and small threads or something similar, in place of chains. (footnote 31: Michel refers evidently to what Beverley, *History*, 1725, III, 58f calls 'wampon peak.' These, he says, 'they wear instead of Medals before or behind their Neck, and use the Peak, Runtees and Pipes for Coronets, Bracelets, Belts or long Strings, hanging down before their Breast, or else they lace their Garments with them.') . . . . (p. 131).

"There were also some who had a narrow spangle drawn through their nose. Its meaning is unknown to me. Some had also a tuft of strange feathers under their ears, in some cases larger than in others (footnote 34: Beverley, *History*, III, 4, speaks only of one feather stuck into the knot of hair behind the ear.) I think it indicates those who are the best hunters. They were ridiculously dressed. One had a shirt on with a crown on his head, another a coat and neither trousers, stockings nor shoes. Others had a skin or red cover around them. In their homes they are naked, as I have seen one at Manigkinton, who came back from hunting. He had nothing but his rifle, knife and powder horn, except a linen rag which covered his sexual parts a little, and a deer skin (moccasin) protecting his feet, that the thorns might not hurt him. . . ." (Michel also describes their food, dancing, religion, medium of exchange—shells, and his trade with them). (excerpts from pp. 129-134).

Lassus. NOUVELLE ORLEANS, 1726

90. Lassus. NOUVELLE ORLEANS. ". . . est un grand dessin, à la plume rehaussé de couleurs représentant la Nouvelle Orléans. Sur le fleuve figure une piroque chargée d'indiens. Celle ci- doit mesurer ciny centimètres et les petits personnages n'ont guère plus de neuf millimètres chacun. Examinés à la loupe, ils peuvent cependant présenter un intéret ethnographique non tant par leurs traits, forcément réduit, que par la forme de la piroque, les coiffures, une espèce de totem à l'avant du bateau." Collection of the Ministère de la France d'Outre-Mer, Paris, Archives Coloniales, Depot des Fortifications, N° 71. 1726.

91-97 have been omitted from Plates Section, because all the pictures had not been received at the time the book went to press. These are as follows:

LE ROY DE LA FLORIDE

91. "LE ROY DE LA FLORIDE." Line engraving. 9¼ x 6¼ inches. "A Paris chez P. Bertrand Rue St. Jacques a la pomme d'or. proche St. Seuerin." Not dated? A mustache on an Indian is probably a fanciful representation. *Photograph*

Courtesy of the New York Public Library. It is also in the print files of the British Museum.

92. "'CHARLES FORT EN FLORIDE,' gravure hollandaise, chez Van der Aa (extrait de la 'Galerie du Monde') "V x 113, pet. fol. Cl. 55 - C. 10287. Collection of the Bibliothèqve Nationale, Cabinet des Estampes, Paris—Jean Vallery-Radot, Conservateur en Chef.

93. "'VIRGINIE ET FLORIDE,' carte illustrée de quelques types d'Indiens, avec vue de plantations." Vx 113, pet. fol. Cl. 55 - C. 10292. Collection of the Bibliothèqve Nationale, Cabinet des Estampes, Paris.

94. "LABOURAGE, TENTES ET NAVIRES DES FLORIDIANS." Vx 113, pet. fol. Cl. 55. B. 15.165. Collection of the Bibliothèqve Nationale, Cabinet des Estampes, Paris.

95. "SASQUESANAHOK. VILLAGE PALISSADE EN VIRGINIE." Vx 114, pet. fol. Cl. 47 - A. 1682. Collection of the Bibliothèqve Nationale, Cabinet des Estampes, Paris.

96. "CABAN DE CONSEILLE." Council house of the Alibamus. Bureau of American Ethnology, Neg. 1169-b-1. "Reproduced 42nd Ann. Rept., B.A.E., Fig. 5, with caption: 'One of the beds in the Alabama Square Ground as it appeared in the early part of the eighteenth century. From a contemporary sketch. Medicine pots and spoons to right, on ground; gourd rattles to left; flag over the center pole; notched pole or atásá at either end and another pair some distance in from either end; a pole carrying a scalp at the top of each intermediate post; two full-length cane seats below. Near the left end, under the front of roof, are written the words 'Caban de Conseille.' (From an article entitled 'Documents concernant l'Histoire des Indians,' by the Baron Marc de Villiers, in the Journal de la Société des Américanistes de Paris, n. s. vol. xiv, 1922, p. 136.)' Also reproduced by Swanton, B. A. E. Bull. 137, Pl. 59 (1), with the attribution, 'From a sketch in the French archives reproduced by du Terrage.'? (This may be in error, since it is not in bibliography Bull. 137, or it may refer to a print instead of manuscript or book)? Note that of the 3 objects designated by Swanton as gourd rattles, the middle one is probably a conch shell dipper."

CABAN DE CONSEILLE. ALIBAMUS

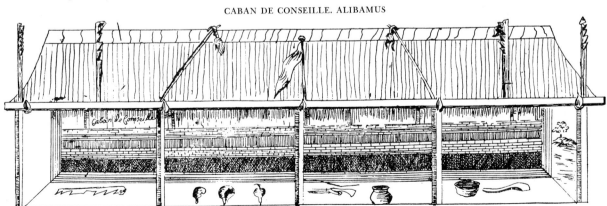

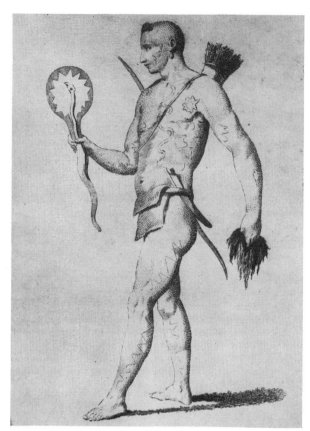

INDIAN OF THE NORTHWEST OF LOUISIANA

97. "AN INDIAN INHABITING THE COUNTRY, Nth WEST OF LOUISIANA, IN 1741." Engraving, black and white. Unsigned. Picture area 3⅝ x 6⅜ inches. Below, "Sauvage du Nord Ouest de la Louisiane." And, "196." "This is a handsome engraving of a brave nearly nude with decorations (tattoo or scarification) on torso, arms, and legs; he is carrying in his left hand a scalp and in his right some sort of totem or fetish. A quiver is slung over his left shoul-

der." *Collection of the Howard-Tilton Memorial Library, Tulane University Library, New Orleans, Louisiana.* **Another print in this collection which probably depicts 18th century warriors of Louisiana is entitled: "Guerriers de la Louisiane marchant à l'ennemi." It is an engraving with colored washes (probably later), and is undated and unsigned. 5⅝ x 4¼ inches. Above the pictorial area: "Amérique Septentrionale."** *Collection of the Howard-Tilton Memorial Library, Tulane University Library, New Orleans, Louisiana.*

98. "MORTUARY RITES OVER THE TATTOOED-SERPENT." (Caption, Swanton, BAE Bull. 43, Pl. 4b. and BAE Bull 137, Pl. 63). This illustration differs from the text since it shows eight instead of six bearers of the litter. It is believed that the woodcuts were probably after drawings by Du Pratz. In addition to the French edition in 1758, there have been three in English—a two-volume edition in 1763; a one-volume edition in 1774 (without illustrations; the latter had two maps); a one-volume edition about 1947 by J. S. W. Harmanson, Publisher, New Orleans (contained all illustrations of the 1758 edition and two maps of 1774 edition). In Chapter III, Section IV, 1774 edition. Du Pratz describes, "Temples, Tombs, Burials, and Other Religious Ceremonies. . . ." He describes in detail the mortuary ceremony surrounding the death of the "Stung Serpent," and concludes (1947 edition, pp. 337-339):

"Soon after the natives began the dance of death, and prepared for the funeral of the Stung Serpent. Orders were given to put none to death on that occasion, but those who were in the hut of the deceased. A child however had been strangled already by its father and mother, which ransomed their lives upon the death of the Great Sun, and raised them from the rank of Stinkards to that of Nobles. Those who were appointed to die were conducted twice a day, and placed in two rows before the temple, where they acted over the scene of their death, each accompanied by eight of their own relations who were to be their executioners, and by that office exempted themselves from dying upon the death of any of the Suns, and likewise raised themselves to the dignity of men of rank. . . .

"On the day of the interment, the wife of the deceased made a very moving speech to the French who were present, recommending her children, to whom she also addressed herself, to their friendship, and advising perpetual union between the two nations. Soon after the master of ceremonies appeared in a red-feathered crown, which half encircled his head, having a red staff in his hand in the form of a cross, at the end of which hung a garland of black feathers. All

WARRIORS OF LOUISIANA

the upper part of his body was painted red, excepting his arms, and from his girdle to his knees hung a fringe of feathers, the rows of which were alternately white and red. When he came before the hut of the deceased, he saluted him with a great *hoo,* and then began the cry of death, in which he was followed by the whole people. Immediately after the Stung Serpent was brought out on his bed of state, and was placed on a litter, which six of the guardians of the temple bore on their shoulders. The procession then began, the master of ceremonies walking first, and after him the oldest warrior, holding in one hand the pole with the rings of canes, and in the other the pipe of war, a mark of the dignity of the deceased. Next followed the corpse, after which came those who were to die at the interment. The whole procession went three times round the hut of the deceased, and then those who carried the corpse proceeded in a circular kind of march, every turn intersecting the former, until they came to the temple. At every turn the dead child was thrown by its parents before bearers of the corpse, that they might walk over it; and when the corpse was placed in the temple the victims were immediately strangled. The Stung Serpent and his two wives were buried in the same grave within the temple; the other victims were interred in different parts, and after the ceremony they burnt, according to custom, the hut of the deceased."

99. "THE CEREMONY OF THE CALUMET WHEN PEACE WAS CONCLUDED BETWEEN THE CHITIMACHA INDIANS AND THE FRENCH, 1718." Caption, Swanton, BAE Bull. 43, Pl. 4 c). In Chapter III, Section VII, 1774 edition (1947 edition, pp. 351-352):
". . . . When one nation intends to make war upon another in all the forms, they hold a council of war, which is composed of the oldest and bravest warriors. . . . There is always some pretence for declaring war; and this pretence, whether true or false, is explained by the war-chief, who omits no circumstance that may excite his nation to take up arms. . . .

"If it is resolved to demand from the other nation the reason of the hostilities committed by them, they name one of their bravest and most eloquent warriors, as a second to their speech-maker or chancellor, who is to carry the pipe of peace, and address that nation. These two are accompanied by a troop of the bravest warriors, so that the embassy has the appearance of a warlike expedition; and, if satisfaction is not given, sometimes ends in one. The ambassadors carry no presents with them, to show that they do not intend to supplicate or beg a peace; they take with them only the pipe of peace, as a proof that they come as friends. The embassy is always well received, entertained in the best manner, and kept as long as possible; and if the other nation is not inclined to begin a war, they make very large presents to the ambassadors, and all their retinue, to make up for the losses which their nation complains of."

100. "NATIVE IN SUMMER." (Caption, Swanton, BAE Bull. 137, Pl. 69-1). In Chaper III, Section V, 1774 edition (1947 edition, p. 341). Regarding clothing Du Pratz states:
"The skins of the beasts which they killed in hunting naturally presented themselves for their covering; but they must be dressed however before they could be properly used. After much practice they at length discovered that the brain of any animal suffices to dress its skin. To sew those skins they use the tendons of animals beat and split into threads, and to pierce the skins they apply the bone of a heron's leg, sharpened like an awl."

101. "WINTER CLOTHING OF A NATCHEZ MAN." (Repr. Swanton, BAE Bull. 43, Pl. 26 and Bull. 137, Pl. 70-1). See note 100.

102. "GENERAL DANCE OF THE NATCHEZ INDIANS." (Repr. Swanton, BAE Bull. 43, Pl. 4a and Bull. 137, Pl. 105). Du Pratz describes the dance culminating the solemn festival of the "Great Corn" in September, (Chapter III, Section 1, 1774 edition and pp. 322-324, 1947 edition).
"This great solemnity is concluded with a general dance by torch-light. Upwards of two hundred torches of dried canes, each of the thickness of a child, are lighted round the place, where the men and women often continue dancing

till daylight; and the following is the disposition of their dance. A man places himself on the ground with a pot covered with a deer-skin, in the manner of a drum, to beat time to the dances; round him the women form themselves into a circle, not joining hands, but at some distance from each other; and they are inclosed by the men in another circle, who have in each hand a chichicois, or calabash, with a stick thrust through it to serve for a handle. When the dance begins, the women move round the men in the center, from left to right, and the men contrariwise from right to left, and they sometimes narrow and sometimes widen their circle. In this manner the dance continues without intermission the whole night, new performers successively taking the place of those who are wearied and fatiqued."

103. "A WOMAN AND HER DAUGHTER." (Repr. Swanton, BAE Bull. 137, Pl. 69-2).

104. "THE MANNER IN WHICH THE GREAT SUN WAS CARRIED TO THE HARVEST FESTIVAL OF THE NATCHEZ." (Repr. Swanton, BAE Bull. 43, Pl. 3a and Bull. 137, Pl. 75).

105. "PLAN OF A FORT AND PRISONER IN THE FRAME FOR EXECUTION." (Repr. Swanton, BAE Bull. 137, Pl. 83). Du Pratz Chapter III, Section VII, describes the torture of a prisoner. (1947 edition, pp. 354-355).
"The women and children whom they take prisoners are made slaves. But if they take a man prisoner the joy is universal, and the glory of their nation is at its height. The warriors, when they draw near to their own villages after an expedition, raise the cry of war three times successively; and if they have a man prisoner with them, immediately go and look for three poles to torture him upon; which, however weary or hungry they be, must be provided before they take any refreshment. When they have provided those poles, and tied the prisoner to them, they may then go and take some victuals. The poles are about ten feet long; two of them are planted upright in the ground at a proper distance, and the other is cut through in the middle, and the two pieces are fastened cross-ways to the other two, so that they form a square about five feet every way. The prisoner being first scalped by the person who took him, is tied to this square, his hands to the upper part, and his feet to the lower, in such a manner that he forms the figure of a St. Andrew's cross. The young men in the mean time having prepared several bundles of canes, set fire to them; and several of the warriors taking those flaming canes, burn the prisoner in different parts of his body, while others burn him in other parts with their tobacco-pipes. The patience of prisoners in those miserable circumstances is altogether astonishing. No cries or lamentations proceed from them; and some have been known to suffer tortures, and sing for three days and nights without intermission. Sometimes it happens that a young woman who has lost her husband in the war, asks the prisoner to supply the room of the deceased, and her request is immediately granted."

106. "INDIANS OF THE NORTHWEST OF LOUISIANA LEAVING IN WINTER WITH THEIR FAMILY FOR A HUNT." (Naturels du Nord Qui Vont en chaisse D'Hyver Aves Leur Famille). Described in French by Du Pratz, Vol. 3, pp. 163-164, of meeting with a group of 'Canzés' (Kansa tribe).

107. "DEER HUNT." (Described by Du Pratz, Vol. 2, pp. 69-73 (in French); trans. in Swanton, BAE Bull. 43, p. 70-71). Several Southeastern travelers and explorers have mentioned group hunting. It was described in Florida by Gabriel Diaz Vara Caldron "17th Century Letter." *Smithsonian Misc. Coll.* Vol. XCV, No. 16. 1937.

108. "BISON HUNT." (Desc. by Du Pratz, Vol. 2, pp. 67-78 (in French); trans. in Swanton, BAE Bull. 43. p. 71. Chapter III, Section I, Du Pratz mentions the Bison hunt (1947, edition, p. 324):
"The ninth moon (November) is that of the Buffalo; and it is then they go to hunt that animal. Having discovered whereabouts the herd feeds, they go out in a body to hunt them. Young and old, girls and married women, except those who are with child, are all of the party, for

there is generally work for them all. Some nations are a little later in going out to this hunting, that they may find the cows fatter, and the herds more numerous."

109. "CHIEFS . . . FROM CAROLINA." This engraving has been reproduced many times. The New York Public Library and the De Renne Collection, University of Georgia Libraries, Athens, own 1730 prints. The text beneath the engraving includes the names and a description:

"The above Indian Kings or Chiefs were brought over from Carolina by Sir Alexander Coming Bart. (being the Chiefs of the Cherokee Indians) to enter into Articles of Friendship and Commerce with his Majesty. As soon as they arriv'd they were conducted to Windsor, & were present at the Installation of Prince William & the Ld. Chesterfield. The Pomp and Splendour of the Court, and ye Grandeur, not only of the Ceremony as well of the Place was what Struck them with infinite Surprize and Wonder. They were handsomely entertained at his Majesty's Charge, & Cloath'd with these habits out of ye Royal Wardrobe. When the Court left Windsor they were brought to Town and proper Lodgings & Attendance provided for them near Covent-Garden. They were entertain'd at all ye Publick Diversion of the Town, and carried to all Places of Note & Curiosity. They were remarkably strict in their Probity and Morality. Their Behaviour easy and courteous; and their Gratitude to his Majesty was often express'd in a publick Manner, for ye many Favours they receiv'd.—On Monday Sept. 7, 1730. Articles of Friendship and Commerce were accordingly propos'd to them by ye Lds. Commissioners for Trade and Plantations, wch, were agreed on Two Days after, viz. on ye 9.th at Whitehall, and Sign'd on ye Part of their Lordships by Alured Popple Esq. upon wth. Ketagusta after a Short Speech, in Complement to his Majesty, Concluded by laying down his Feathers upon ye Table & said; This is our Way of Talking, wch is ye same Thing to us, as yr Letters in ye Book are to you; and to you, BELOVED MEN, we deliver these Feathers in Confirmation of all that we have said."

This agreement took place nine years after South Carolina's Governor Nicholson called Cherokee chiefs to a Charles Town trade conference in 1721, to soothe the abuses of traders and to strengthen control in the area. Again in 1730 the Indians pledged themselves to loyalty to England, exclusive trade privileges, and to open certain areas to forts, traders, and settlers. Six years later the French sent Christian Priber, Jesuit Priest, to counter the English—Cherokee courtship. He settled at Tellico, adopted Indian dress and customs, and created good will for France until he was captured by English traders three years later. Tension between the British and French in this area mounted, and culminated in the skirmishes which resulted from the continental conflict between France and England—the Seven Year's War in the 1750's.

110. "TOMO-CHI-CHI AND OTHER YAMACRAWS PRESENTED TO THE TRUSTEES OF THE COLONY OF GEORGIA." Oglethorpe is in the center in a black suit and the 8 Indians are near. An interpreter accompanied the party to England, and at the meeting with the Trustees, they discussed trade, licensing of traders, missionaries, firearms and prohibition of rum. In 1733 Oglethorpe founded the colony of Georgia as a buffer between South Carolina and Spanish Florida. He gained the friendship of the Indians in the area around Savannah, and in 1734 took to England a delegation headed by Tomochichi, which included his wife, his nephew, and five warriors. Though dignified in conduct, their native attire provoked comment . They were entertained in England for four months. After the Indians returned to Georgia they sent to the Trustees a painted buffalo hide symbolizing their appreciation. (Foreman, 1943, p. 60). For a careful discussion of the trip see, Foreman, 1943, pp. 56-64. It is also mentioned in Alice G. B. Lockwood, "Gardens of Colony and State," 1934, p. 271.

111. "THE REVEREND CHARLES WESLEY, THE POET OF METHODISM, PREACHING TO THE AMERICAN INDIANS IN 1736." According to the date on the engraving this was not produced at the time of Wesley's trip, and the costumes of the Indians are probably to some extent fanciful.

When Tomochichi met the Trustees in 1734 he asked for missionaries to be sent to the Indians (Foreman, 1943, p. 59). Charles and John Wesley went to Georgia in 1735, and spent several years preaching to the colonists and Indians.

112. "TOMO CHACHI MICO OR KING OF YAMACRAW AND TOOANAHOWI HIS NEPHEW, SON OF THE MICO OF THE ETCHITAS." (Hitchitis) Other copies of this print are located in the New York Public Library and the De Renne Collection, University of Georgia Libraries, Athens. Frederick Webb Hodge, *Handbook of American Indians North of Mexico*, Bureau of American Ethnology, Bulletin 30, Part 2, 1910, p. 776 writes:

"Tomochichi (spelled also Bocachee, Temochichi, Thamachaychee, Thomochichi, Tomachachi, Tomeychee, etc., and said by Gatschet to mean 'the one who causes to fly up'?). A Creek chief, noted in the early history of Georgia. He was originally of Apalachukla, a Lower Creek town on Chattahoochee r. in Alabama, and his name appears in behalf of this settlement in a treaty between the Creeks and the Carolina government in 1721. Shortly afterward, for some unknown reason, he was outlawed from his people and withdrew with a few followers to Savannah r., where, by permission of South Carolina, he established himself in a new town called Yamacraw (q. v.), at the present Savannah, Ga. On the foundation of the Georgia colony by Oglethorpe in 1733, Tomochichi assumed a friendly attitude toward the newcomers and was instrumental in bringing about a treaty of alliance between that colony and the Lower Creeks in that year. At the same time a reconciliation was effected between himself and his tribe, and he was given permission to collect his friends from the various Lower Creek towns to take up their residence with him at Yamacraw. In the next year, 1734, with his wife, nephew, and several others, he accompanied Oglethorpe to England, where his well-known portrait was painted. He continued to be helpful to the colonists after his return until his death, which occurred in his own town, Oct. 5, 1739, he being then perhaps 75 years of age. He was given a public funeral at Savannah, where a monument to his memory was erected in 1899 by the Colonial Dames of America." In addition to the Faber engraving of the painting by Verelst, another was made by Kleinschmidt, of Augsburg, Germany, for a publication in 1735. Hodge states that the original painting hung in the Georgia Office, London, for many years, but he gives no information as to its presence now. (Swanton, BAE, Bull. 137, p. 210 is of the opinion that the Yamacraw may have been part of the Yamassee). (BAE Neg. from print in British Museum).

113. A. de Batz. "CHOCTAW SAVAGES PAINTED AS WARRIORS, CARRYING SCALPS. (Choctaw Warriors, Natchez Chief)." Bushnell, 1927, pp. 11-12, Pl. 5, describes this:

"The massacre of the French by the Natchez occurred late in the year 1729. A large number of Choctaw warriors soon joined the remaining French and late in January, 1730, Le Sueur reached the scene of devastation accompanied by a force of some hundred Choctaw. The warriors sketched by DeBatz may have been some of that wild group.

"Two young children are shown playing a game.

"The seated figure, on the right, evidently represents a Natchez chief, wearing a crown of feathers as described by DuPratz. Early in the spring of 1725 the great Natchez chief Stung Serpent died at the principal Natchez village. When prepared for burial the body was viewed by French officers. DuPratz then wrote: 'we found him on his bed of state, dressed in his finest cloaths, his face painted with vermilion, shod as if for a journey, with his feather-crown on his head.' And when describing the dress of the Natchez he again mentioned the feather-crown in these words: 'The chief ornament of the sovereigns is their crown of feathers; this crown is composed of a black bonnet of net work, which is fastened to a red diadem about two inches broad. The diadem is embroidered with white kernel-stones, and surmounted with white feathers, which in the forepart are about eight inches long, and half as much behind. This crown or feather hat makes a very pleasing appearance.'" Signed, A. Debatz T.

Regarding De Batz, Bushnell states: ". . . . The few

drawings known to exist prove him to have been a careful observer and to have been interested in the manners and customs of the Indians. His sketches are crude but graphic.

114. A. de Batz. "DRAWINGS OF THE SAVAGES OF SEVERAL NATIONS. New Orleans. 1735." Bushnell, 1927, pp. 9-10, Pl. 4, explains:

"During the year 1735 the French took many Illinois Indians to Lower Louisiana, probably to New Orleans, to assist in the war against the Chickasaw. From the interesting drawing made at that time it is evident that not only warriors but women and children made the long journey down the Mississippi. In the sketch the chief, on the extreme left, is shown with his right hand resting on the head of a Whooping Crane, *Grus americana*, which may indicate that the bird had been domesticated. This would agree with a statement by Lawson, who, when referring to the Congaree of North Carolina, wrote: 'they take storks and cranes before then can fly and breed them as tame and familiar as dung-hill fowls.'

"The Fox woman was evidently a captive taken by the Illinois in their then recent war with that tribe.

"The Atakapa is represented holding a calumet in his right hand and a small pipe in the left, with a quiver filled with arrows on his back, but no bow.

"The sketch was probably intended to represent the bank of the Mississippi, and at the bottom appears the words: 'Balbahachas. Missysipy ou fleuve St. Louis.' DuPratz described the Mississippi and mentioned the various names by which it was then known, and continued: 'Other *Indians*, especially those lower down the river, call it *Balbancha;* and at last the *French* have given it the name of *St. Louis.*'"

115. A. de Batz. "SAVAGE ADORNED AS WARRIOR, HAVING TAKEN THREE SCALPS." Bushnell, 1927, pp. 5-6, Pl. 2, states:

"The spring of 1731 found the Natchez scattered and wandering as a result of the destruction of their villages during the wars of the preceding years. Soon they appealed to the French for a pardon, and asked that they might settle near the Tunica; permission was granted them to erect a village not less than two leagues from that of the Tunica, but they were to come unarmed. Later a large number of Natchez arrived at the Tunica village where they were received and given food, and Charlevoix related how the Tunica and their new guests 'danced till after midnight, after which the Tunica retired to their cabins, thinking that of course the Natchez would also go to rest. But soon after—that is to say, one hour before day, for it was the 14th day of June (1731)—the Natchez . . . fell upon all the cabins and slaughtered all whom they surprised asleep. The head chief ran up at the noise and first killed four Natchez; but, overborne by numbers, he was slain with some twelve of his warriors. His war chief, undismayed by this loss or the flight of most of his braves, rallied a dozen, with whom he regained the head chief's cabin; he even succeeded in recalling the rest, and after fighting for five days and nights almost without intermission remained master of his village.' The name of the Tunica chief killed in this encounter and whose wife and child escaped was Cahura-Joligo, and evidently Brideles Boeuf, or Buffalo Tamer, was his successor. Buffalo Tamer may have been the war chief mentioned by Charlevoix."

The description on the picture states:

" 'Savage adorned as a Warrior, having taken three scalps, that is to say having killed three Natchez men. A. Buffalo Tamer Chief of the Tunica, he takes the place of his predecessor whom the Natchez killed in the month of June last. B. Woman chief widow of the defunct. E. Jacob son of the defunct. H. Scalps ornamenting the staff likewise drawn from nature on the spot. Redrawn at New Orleans the 22 June 1732. DeBatz.' "

116. A. de Batz. "A SAVAGE IN WINTER DRESS." Bushnell, 1927, pp. 13-14, Pl. 6 states:

"Buffalo skins, dressed so as to allow them to become soft and pliable and without removing the hair, were used by the Indians throughout the Mississippi Valley to protect them from the cold of winter. Such robes were often deco-

rated on the inner side by designs painted in several colors. This sketch shows a robe decorated with a simple design in red and black.

"The drawing has not been identified but is believed to have been made to represent an Indian belonging to one of the tribes living at that time in the vicinity of New Orleans. The figure suggests the sketch of the 'Atakapas' shown in Plate 4, and it may have been intended to portray one of that tribe in winter dress."

117. A. de Batz. "TEMPLE, AND CABIN OF THE CHIEF. ACOLAPISSA. 1732." Bushnell, 1927, pp. 3-4, Pl. 1, describes this:

"Two centuries and more ago, when the French entered Lower Louisiana, many tribes occupied the region near or bordering the Mississippi. The scattered native villages differed in size and importance but may not have varied greatly in general appearance. One custom was followed in common for as DuPratz then wrote: 'All the people of Louisiana have temples, which are more or less well cared for according to the ability of the nation.' Some were quite simple in form and resembled the habitations in the nearby or surrounding villages, others were more elaborate and of greater size, and such was the temple which stood in the village of the Acolapissa during the spring of 1732. This settlement was probably a short distance up the Mississippi from the site of the earlier village of the same tribe which was visited by Charlevoix just 10 years before when he described it as 'the finest in all Louisiana.' Three carved and painted figures of birds, probably quite similar to those so clearly shown in the sketch of the Acolapissa temple, are mentioned as having surmounted like structures which had formerly stood in the villages of the Taensa and Natchez. These and other temples in Lower Louisiana served as burial places for the chiefs of the tribes.

"The cabin of the Acolapissa chief, as given in the sketch, was probably a typical habitation of the region and time, but among some tribes rectangular cabins were also erected."

UPPER. " 'Temple of the Savages, constructed of posts in the ground, covered with mats of cane, and roofed with same, ending in three (stakes) of Wood, $3\frac{1}{2}$ feet long, 18 inches (wide) and 4 inches thick, crudely colored and (sculptured). The 3 pyramids (are of) reed-work trimmed with pointed canes (to) prevent one climbing to the 3 figures, the body and tail of which represent turkeys and the head of the eagle, which seemed to us the most like it.' "

CENTER. " 'Cabin of the Chief, of posts in the ground plastered with clay or earth mortar, also covered with mats. n.ª The temple is 22 feet long and 14 feet wide; it serves as the sepulcher for the chiefs of the nation. All the Cabins of the savages are of similar construction, all being round, this one is 18 feet in diameter.' "

LOWER. " 'Surveyed and sketched at the Village of the Acolapissa the fifteenth of April of the present year. Redrawn at New Orleans the twenty-second of June 1732. De-Batz.' "

118. A. de Batz. "TREE NEAR SITE OF THE NATCHEZ TEMPLE. 1732." Bushnell, 1927, pp. 7-8, Pl. 3, describes this:

"This tree, considered a great rarity by the French and evidently regarded with awe by the Natchez who 'held it in great veneration,' is believed to have been an Osage orange, *Toxylon pomiferum*.

"The tree probably stood near the temple and not far from the Village of Valleur, therefore in the immediate vicinity of the severe fighting between the French and Natchez during the later part of February, 1730. The French were intrenched near or surrounding the temple while the Natchez held the village, having constructed what the French termed Fort de la Valeur. The great Natchez temple was destroyed at that time, on or about February 23, 1730."

" 'Unknown Tree. This Tree is now standing among the Natchez. The Savages preserved it and held it in great Veneration, taking from it some branches or twigs to cast into the Sacred fire which they maintained perpetually in their Temple which was built near the said Tree. The French burned and destroyed this Temple in February 1730. According to the report of the most ancient of this Colony this Tree is the unique and only one in this Province. A. Branch covered with Leaves of the natural size and Color. B. Flower of pale White color. C. The starting point of the leaf, a scar remains when the leaf falls, which forms a Bud and it may be seen how many leaves it produced. The Tree is always Green. Sketched from nature at the village of Valleur the 13 of May later Redrawn at New Orleans the 22 June 1732. DeBatz. 25 feet high.' "

119. "THE THREE CHEROKEES. CAME OVER FROM THE HEAD OF THE RIVER SAVANNA TO LONDON, 1762. 1: Their Interpreter that was Poisoned. 2: Outacite or Man-Killer, who sets up the War Whoop, as (Woach Woach ha ha hoch Waoch) with his Wampum. 3: Austenaco or King, a great Warrior who has his calumet or Pipe, by taking a Whiff of which, is their most sacred emblem of Peace. 4: Uschesees ye Great Hunter, or Scalpper, as the Character of a Warrior depends on the Number of Scalps, he has them without Number."

Although Lt. Timberlake took the Indians to England at the request of the Governor of Virginia they were a great expense to him. Foreman (1943, pp. 65-81) discusses this trip of Cherokees to England. Sir Joshua Reynolds and Francis Parsons are reported to have made single and group pictures of the Indians. A Parson's portrait of Cunne Shote is shown on Plate 120. Foreman (1943, pp. 69-70) discusses the various references to portraits of these Indians. In a *Biographical Dictionary of Printers and Engravers* is a reference to the work of Parsons, 'Portrait group of Indian chiefs who visited England in 1763'. Engraved by McArdell. In July, 1762, the *St. James Chronicle* reported that Sir Joshua Reynolds was producing portraits of the Indians. This group may have been engraved after his work. A copy of this print is found in the British Museum, the New York Public Library, the University of Georgia Libraries, and possibly many other Americana collections.

120. Francis Parsons. "CUNNE SHOTE." The Stalking Turkey, nephew of Old Hop, who was head chief of the Overhill towns. A print engraved after this which has become well known is that of "Js. McArdell fecit. Sold at the Golden Head, in Queen's Square, Ormond Street, Pr. 2 s.6d." SI:BAE Neg. 997, is from a copy of this portrait, now in the Bushnell Collection, Peabody Museum, Harvard University.

121. "OUTACITE, Chief of the Cherokees." From Samuel G. Drake, *Biography and history of the Indians of North America*, 1837. The Bureau of American Ethnology states that the print shown is "the same subj. as N. M. Neg. 44,318-A." The New York Public Library owns another print of this in which the head is facing in the opposite direction and the caption is in a different type face. Drake uses this picture in Book IV, opp. p. 32 as an illustration of "Wootassitaw," a Cherokee chief in 1723? It appears likely that he was in error. Foreman, (1943, p. 75) refers to an advertisement July 31, 1762, in the *Public Advertiser* which states that "an elegant Head of Outacite, King of the Cherokees, drawn from Life, and engraved by a masterly Hand" (sold by Fletcher and company . . . .) would be published in the Court Magazine, No. XI. The British Museum refers to an engraving by this title as being after Reynolds.

122. "AUSTENACO, GREAT WARRIOR." Foreman (1943, p. 81) refers to the fact that in July, 1762, the British Magazine, published a copper-plate engraving of the King. All of these prints are available in the British Museum, and careful research there would doubtless unravel the mystery which surrounds their identity. No information is available regarding the location of the originals; such could probably be uncovered or traced in England. (Engraving from Royal Magazine after Reynolds.)

123. "CUNNE SHOTE." Full length portrait with scalping knife in right hand. 11 x 8⅝ inches. A.P.D.R. A Paris chez Duflos, rue St. Victor. Circa 1780? A full-length engraving is shown in Thomas Jefferys, *A Collection of the Dresses of Different Nations*, Vol. 4, London, 1757? It is entitled, the "Habit of Cunne Shote, a Cherokee Chief."

124. "MICO CHLUCCO THE LONG WARIOR OR KING OF THE SIMINOLES." Frontispiece from William Bartram,

Travels Through North and South Carolina, Georgia, East and West Florida, the Cherokee Country, the Extensive Territories of the Muscogulges or Creek Confederacy, and the Country of the Chactaws. Philadelphia, 1791. A slightly different engraving was made by Holloway Sculp. for the 1792, London edition. The attachment of the feathers to the staff was not shown in the latter. They erroneously appear to be a cape. The 1958 edition, edited by Francis Harper and published by the Yale University Press includes the 1791 engraving. A negative of this is owned by the Library of Congress, 15844.

125. "ANCIENT INDIAN MONUMENTS, CONSISTING OF PUBLIC BUILDINGS, AREAS, VESTIGES OF TOWNS, ETC. . . . ." From William Bartram, "Observations on the Creek and Cherokee Indians, 1789," with Prefatory and Supplementary Notes by E. G. Squier. *Transactions of the American Ethnological Society*, Vol. III, Part I, New York, 1853. There is no record of the original manuscript. The Historical Society of Pennsylvania owns a copy of the manuscript produced by John Howard Payne. It contains seven drawing as does the 1853 edition. Figure 7, "the mode of lighting the new fire, amongst the Mexicans" is not shown here.

Figure 1. "Villa of the Chief of the Town of the Apalachians." (pp. 37-38).

"All that a man earns by his labor or industry belongs to himself; he has the use and disposal of it according to the custom and usages of the people. He may clear, settle, and plant as much land as he pleases, and wherever he will within the boundaries of his tribe. There are, however, very few instances amongst the Creeks, of farms or private plantations out of sight of the town. I was at one belonging to a chief of the town of the Apalachians, about six miles from the town, on or near the banks of the river: I went to pay him a visit with an old trader, my fellow pilgrim, in consequence of an invitation to breakfast with him. He is called the *Bosten* or Boatswain by the traders. As a prince, he received us with politeness and most perfect good breeding. His villa was beautifully situated and well constructed. It was composed of three oblong uniform frame buildings, and a fourth, four-square, fronting the principal house or common hall, after this manner, encompassing one area. The hall was his lodging-house, large and commodious; the two wings were, one a cook-house, the other a skin or warehouse; and the large square one was a vast open *pavilion*, supporting a canopy of cedar roof by two rows of columns or pillars, one within the other. Between each range of pillars was a platform, or what the traders call cabins, a sort of sofa raised about two feet above the common ground, and ascended by two steps; this was covered with checkered mats of courious manufacture, woven of splints of canes dyed of different colors; the middle was a four-square stage or platform, raised nine inches or a foot higher than the cabins or sofas, and also covered with mats. In this delightful airy place we were received, and entertained by this prince.

Figure 2. "Plan of the Ancient Chunky-Yard." (pp. 51-53).

"The subjoined plan (fig. 2) will illustrate the form and character of these yards. *A*, the great area, surrounded by terraces or banks. *B*, a circular eminence, at one end of the yard, commonly nine or ten feet higher than the ground round about. Upon this mound stands the great *rotunda*, *Hot House*, or *Winter Council House*, of the present Creeks. It was probably designed and used by the ancients who constructed it, for the same purpose. *C*, a square terrace or eminence, about the same height with the circular one just described, occupying a position at the other end of the yard. Upon this stands the *Public Square*. The banks inclosing the yard are indicated by the letters *b,b,b,b; c* indicates the 'Chunk-Pole,' and *d,d*, the 'Slave-Posts.'

"Sometimes the square, instead of being open at the ends, as shown in the plan, is closed upon all sides by the banks. In the lately built, or new Creek towns, they do not raise a mound for the foundation of their Rotundas or Public Squares. The yard, however, is retained, and the public buildings occupy nearly the same position in respect to it. They also retain the central obelisk and the slave-posts.

Figure 3. "The Public Square and Arrangement of Public Buildings." (pp: 53-54).

"The Public Square of the Creeks consists of four buildings of equal size, placed one upon each side of a quadrangular court. The principal or Council House is divided transversely into three equal apartments, separated from each other by a low clay wall. This building is also divided longitudinally into two nearly equal parts; the foremost or front is an open piazza, where are seats for the council. The middle apartment is for the king (mico), the great war chief, second head man, and other venerable and worthy chiefs and warriors. The two others are for the warriors and citizens generally. The back apartment of this house is quite close and dark, and without entrances, except three very low arched holes or doors for admitting the priests. Here are deposited all the most valuable public things, as the eagle's tail or national standard, the sacred calumet, the drums, and all the apparatus of the priests. None but the priests having the care of these articles are admitted; and it is said to be certain death for any other person to enter.

"Fronting this is another building, called the 'Banqueting House;' and the edifices upon either hand are halls to accommodate the people on public occasions, as feasts, festivals, etc. The three buildings last mentioned are very much alike, and differ from the Council House only in not having the close back apartment.

"This (Fig. 3) is the most common plan or arrangement of the Chunky-Yard, Public Square, and Rotunda of the *modern* Creek towns. A, the Public Square or area. B, the Rotunda; a, the door opening towards the square; the three circular lines show the two rows of seats, sofas, or cabins; the punctures show the pillars or columns which support the building; c, the great central pillar, or column, surrounded by the spiral fire, which gives light to the house.

"C, part of the Chunky-Yard.

Figure 4 and 5. "Creek towns and Dwellings." (pp. 54-57).

"The general position of the Chunk-Yard and Public Buildings of the Creeks, in respect to the dwellings of the Indians themselves, is shown in the following engraved plan:

"A is the Rotunda; B, the Public Square; C, the grand area or Chunky-Yard. The habitations of the people are placed with considerable regularity in streets or ranges, as indicated in the plan.

"The dwellings of the Upper Creeks consist of little squares, or rather of four dwelling-houses inclosing a square area, exactly on the plan of the Public Square. *(See fig. 1)*. Every family, however, has not four of these houses; some have but three, others not more than two, and some but one, according to the circumstances of the individual, or the number of his family. Those who have four buildings have a particular use for each building. One serves as a cook-room and winter lodging-house, another as a summer lodging-house and hall for receiving visitors, and a third for a granary or provision house, etc. The last is commonly two stories high, and divided into two apartments, transversely, the lower story of one end being a potato house, for keeping such roots and fruits as require to be kept close, or defended from cold in winter. The chamber over it is the *council*. At the other end of this building, both upper and lower stories are open on their sides: the lower story serves for a shed for their saddles, pack-saddles, and gears, and other lumber; the loft over it is a very spacious, airy, pleasant pavilion, where the chief of the family reposes in the hot seasons, and receives his guests, etc. The fourth house (which completes the square) is a skin or ware-house, if the proprietor is a wealthy man, and engaged in trade or traffic, where he keeps his deer-skins, furs, merchandise, etc., and treats his customers. Smaller or less wealthy families make one, two, or three houses serve all their purposes as well as they can.

"The Lower Creeks or Seminoles are not so regular or ingenious in their building, either public or private. They have neither the Chunky-Yard nor Rotunda, and the Public Square is an imperfect one, having but two or three houses at furthest. Indeed they do not require it; as their towns are small, and consequently their councils just sufficient for the government or regulation of the town or little tribe: for in all great and public matters they are influenced by the Nation, or Upper Creeks.

"Their private habitations consist generally of two buildings: one a large oblong house, which serves for a cook-room, eating-house, and lodging-rooms, in three apartments under one roof; the other not quite so large, which is situated eight or ten yards distant, one end opposite the principal house. This is two stories high, of the same construction, and serving the same purpose with the granary or provision house of the Upper Creeks.

"The Cherokees, too, differ greatly from the Muscogulges, in respect to their buildings. They have neither the Square nor the Chunky-Yard. Their Summer Council House is a spacious open loft or pavilion, on the top of a very large oblong building; and the Rotunda, or great Hot or Town House, is the Council House in cold seasons.

"Their private houses or habitations consist of one large oblong-square log building, divided transversely into several apartments; and a round hot-house stands a little distance off, for a winter lodging-house.

Figure 6. "Ancient Remains." (pp. 57-58).

"In the Cherokee country, all over Carolina, and the Northern and Eastern parts of Georgia, wherever the ruins of ancient Indian towns appear, we see always beside these remains one vast, conical-pointed mound. To mounds of this kind I refer when I speak of *pyramidal mounds*. To the south and west of the Altamaha, I observed none of these in any part of the Muscogulge country, but always flat or square structures. The vast mounds upon the St. John's, Alachua, and Musquito rivers, differ from those amongst the Cherokee with respect to their adjuncts and appendages, particularly in respect to the great highway or avenue, sunk below the common level of the earth, extending from them, and terminating either in a vast savanna or natural plain, or an artificial pond or lake. A remarkable example occurs at Mount Royal, from whence opens a glorious view of Lake George and its environs.

"Fig. 6, is a perspective plan of this great mound and its avenues, the latter leading off to an expansive savanna or natural meadow. A, the mound, about forty feet in perpendicular height; B, the highway leading from the mound in a straight line to the pond C, about half a mile distant. What may have been the motive for making this pond I cannot

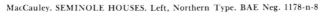

MacCauley. SEMINOLE HOUSES. Left, Northern Type. BAE Neg. 1178-n-8

115

conjecture, since they are situated close to the banks of the river San Juan. It could not, therefore, be for the conveniency of water. Perhaps they raised the mound with the earth taken out of the pond. The sketch of the mound also illustrates the character of the mounds in the Cherokee country; but the last have not the highway or avenue, and are always accompanied by vast square terraces, placed upon one side or the other. On the other hand, we never see the square terraces accompanying the high mounds of East Florida."

Clay MacCauley, "The Seminole Indians of Florida," *Bureau of American Ethnology, 5th Annual Report* (1883-84) 1887, pp. 469-531 gives many drawings illustrating Seminole Indians and surroundings. Among these are several pictures of houses—BAE Negs. 1178-n-8 and 1178-n-8:1. Other pictures of Seminole buildings (two houses, a corn crib, and sugarcane mill) are shown in "R. H. Pratt's Report on the Seminole in 1879," presented and annotated by William C. Sturtevant; *The Florida Anthropologist*, Vol. IX, March, 1956, No. 1, frontispiece and p. 11. See also Seth Eastman, "The Village of Sam Jones, or Arpeika, a Hitchiti Seminole Chief in Florida, "Bushnell Collection, Peabody Museum, Harvard University.

126. "CHOCTAW BURIALS." Repr. Bushnell, BAE Bull. 71, Pl. 12. Swanton, BAE Bull, 137, Pl. 89. In addition to the pictures shown in 126-130, one of the details in the frontispiece (Romans, 1775) is an Indian holding a pipe with a feather-decorated stem.

127. "PICTOGRAPHS." Left. ". . . found at a Choctaw place called 'Hoopah Ullah (i. e.) the noisy owl,' but was made by a Creek war party" (Swanton, BAE Bull. 137, p. 734). Romans writes:

"It means that ten of that nation of the Stag family came in three canoes into their enemies country, that six of the party near this place, which was at *Oopah Ullah*, a brook so called on the road to the Choctaws, had met two men, and two women with a dog, that they lay in ambush for them, killed them, and that they all went home with the four scalps; the scalp in the stag's foot implies the honour of the action to the whole family." (Romans, 1775, p. 102).

Right. "Pictograph found by Romans near the Pascagoula River in Choctaw country. Made by Choctaw." He explains that it

". . . means that an expedition by seventy men, led by seven principal warriors, and eight of inferior rank, had in an action killed nine of their enemies, of which they brought the scalps, and that the place where it was marked was the first publick place in their territories where they arrived with the scalps." (Romans, 1775, p. 102).

128-130. "CHARACTERITIC. . . . (Indian heads). Romans, 1775, gives many interesting descriptions of Creek, Choctaw, and Chickasaw Indians which are more vivid than his drawings. (Number 128 is reproduced in Swanton, BAE Bull. 137, Pl. 13-2).

131. "A LOG HABITATION, 1791." After Tidball. Note the difference in this log house and those engraved by De Bry after Le Moyne. Horizontally placed logs show the influence of the Europeans. For more information about Tidball, see, Robert Taft, *Artists and Illustrators of the Old West, 1850-1900*, New York, 1953.

132. John Trumbull. "HOPOTHLE MICO, OR THE TALASSEE KING OF THE CREEKS." An engraving of this original drawing can be found in John Trumbull, *Autobiography*, . . . , New York, 1841, Pl. 21. It is reproduced in Swanton, BAE Bull. 137, Pl. 32:2 (HOP-HITHLI MICO). BAE Neg. 1169-L-4.

John Trumbull, a portrait painter and soldier of the American Revolution, was neither a student of Indian life nor a painter of Indian subjects. His life's work was ". . . painting a series of pictures, in commemoration of the prin-

cipal events of the Revolution, ..." His production of the five pencil sketches of Creek Indians in 1790 was accidental. The Indians were attending a conference in New York, which had been called by President Washington to discuss land cessions. In July, 1790, John Trumbull was commissioned by the City of New York to paint a portrait of the President. In Trumbull's *Autobiography* (1841, pp. 164-165) he describes this picture, and the occasion of his meeting and sketching the Creek Indians. Engravings of the five sketches are pictured in Trumbull's book. He writes regarding the incident:

"In May, I went to Philadelphia, where I obtained some portraits for my great work, and a number of subscribers. I returned in July to New York, where I was requested to paint for the corporation a full length portrait of the President. I represented him in full uniform, standing by a white horse, leaning his arm upon the saddle; in the background, a view of Broadway in ruins, as it then was, the old fort at the termination; British ships and boats leaving the shore, with the last of the officers and troops of the evacuating army, and Staten Island in the distance. The picture is now in the common council room of the city hall. Every part of the detail of the dress, horse, furniture, &c., as well as the scenery, was accurately copied from the real objects.

"At this time, a numerous deputation from the Creek nation of Indians was in New York, and when this painting was finished, the President was curious to see the effect it would produce on their untutored minds. He therefore directed me to place the picture in an advantageous light, facing the door of entrance of the room where it was, and having invited several of the principal chiefs to dine with him, he, after dinner, proposed to them a walk. He was dressed in full uniform, and lead the way to the painting-room, and when the door was thrown open, they started at seeing another 'Great Father' standing in the room. One was certainly with them, and they were for a time mute with astonishment. At length one of the chiefs advanced towards the picture, and slowly stretched out his hand to touch it, and was still more astonished to feel, instead of a round object, a flat surface, cold to the touch. He started back with an exclamation of astonishment—'Ugh!' Another then approached, and placing one hand on the surface and the other behind, was still more astounded to perceive that his hands almost met. I had been desirous of obtaining portraits of some of these principal men, who possessed a dignity of manner, form, countenance and expression, worthy of Roman senators, but after this I found it impracticable; they had received the impression, that there must be magic in an art which could render a smooth flat surface so like to a real man; I however succeeded in obtaining drawings of several by stealth."

133. John Trumbull. "TUSKATCHE MICO, OR THE BIRDTAIL KING OF THE CUSITAHS." An engraving of this original drawing can be found in Trumbull, *Autobiography*, Pl. 22. It is reproduced in Swanton, BAE Bull. 137, Pl. 32:1 ("Properly Fus-hatchee Miko . . . of the Kasihta). BAE Neg. 1169-L-5. (The two original pencil sketches owned by the Yale University Library and pictured herein are in an interleaved copy of the 1905 edition of Trumbull's *Autobiography in the Benjamin Franklin Collection*).

134. "STIMAFUTCHKI, OR GOOD-HUMOUR OF THE COOSADES (KOASATI), CREEKS." (original lost?). The engraving is reproduced in Swanton, BAE Bull. 137, Pl. 26.

135. John Trumbull. "JOHN . . ." The engraving of this original appears in Trumbull, *Autobiography*, Pl. 18. Engraving is reproduced in Swanton, BAE Bull 137, Pl. 33:2 (caption transposed with 33:1), BAE Neg. 1169-L-1.

136. "HYSAC, OR THE WOMAN'S MAN." (original lost?) The five engravings from Trumbull, *Autobiography* were produced by Daggett, Hinman & Co., 1841. They are excellent likenesses of the drawings. Only two are reproduced here, because three of the originals are used. All the engravings are reproduced in Swanton, BAE Bull 137, Pls. 26, 32, and 33.

137. Charles B. King. DAVID VANN. The Gilcrease Institute states: "This is the oil painting that served as the original for the engraving in *A History of the North American Indians* by McKinney and Hall, Vol. III, p. 112, titled 'David Vann a Cherokee Chief.'" See Pl. 160.

WILL ROGERS

Mrs. Paula M. Love, Curator, the Will Rogers Memorial Commission (Museum) wrote (correspondence, July 1958):

"The portrait of David Vann, who was a great-uncle of Will Rogers, is listed in McKenney and Hall as a Cherokee Chief, but he was not a chief. He was a very prominent man in the Cherokee nation, and at one time was Treasurer of the Cherokee nation in the years 1838, 1843, 1847 and 1851. He was elected Superintendent, Saline District, Tahlequah, Indian Territory, November 4, 1849; and a delegate to Washington 1843, and 1849.

"It was Joseph Vann, who was a chief, and he was a cousin of David. David's sister Sallie Vann married Robert Rogers and they were the paternal grandparents of Will Rogers." Because Will Rogers was of Cherokee lineage, as a descendant of the Vann family, and was a great American, we present his picture here, *Courtesy of the Will Rogers Memorial Commission, Claremore. Photograph by Hopkins Photographic Company, Tulsa.*

This portrait of Will Rogers (1879-1935) was painted by Count Arnaldo Tamburini, Royal Court Artist of Italy. A description of the painting is given by the Will Rogers Memorial Commission:

"Count Tamburini was in Pasadena, California, commissioned by Mr. Morrie Morrison to make paintings of the Morrison family. He visited the Riviera Polo Field and in sketching the players, became much interested in Will Rogers. These sketches were followed up by a visit to the Rogers' home and an original painting of Will Rogers was made and completed before Will Rogers left for Alaska (1935).

"After Will Rogers' death Mr. Morrison acquired the painting from Count Tamburini and in conjunction with Mrs. Rogers and Mr. Frank Phillips, who was anticipating the purchase of the painting several changes were made in it.

"The painting remained for several months at the Rogers' home in Santa Monica, California. Later it was sent to Woolaroc Museum at Bartlesville, Oklahoma, where it remained from the middle of 1936-1939. In 1939 or 1940 Mr.

Morrison moved the painting to the Petroleum Club—in the Adolphus Hotel, Dallas, where it was until approximately 1951, at which time the painting went on exhibit at the Will Rogers State Park in Santa Monica, California. It was purchased by the Will Rogers Memorial Commission to hang in the Will Rogers Memorial, Claremore, Oklahoma, on January 14, 1953, and is here today, the property of the Will Rogers Memorial.

"The painting is approximately 2' 11" x 3' 6", including frame. It is of Will Rogers in flying costume, three-quarter face, looking to the left. The colors are in light brown with a blue sky background. Painting is life-size.

"The men on the Will Rogers Memorial Commission who were personal friends of Will Rogers feel it is the best one they have ever seen and that is the reason they purchased it. It hangs over the mantel in the north gallery where anyone entering from the main doors is able to see it. It is considered a very good likeness of the man."

138. Charles B. King. TULCEE MATHLA. (UM, 38427). See Pl. 174. This portrait was number 21 in the University Museum's "Special Exhibition of the American Indian," *The Noble Savage,* 8 May-8 September, 1958, Philadelphia.

The paintings of Charles Bird King are listed by tribe in John C. Ewers, "Charles Bird King, Painter of Indian Visitors to the Nation's Capital," *Smithsonian Report, 1953,* pp. 463-473 (Publication 4168) 1954, pp. 469-472. He shows eight plates and discusses the life and work of Charles Bird King. Excerpts from this are below:

"Among the many artists who depicted the North American Indians in the days before the development of photography, Charles Bird King enjoyed a unique and rather paradoxical distinction. . . . It is doubtful if King ever saw an Indian village. Yet he painted from life portraits of Indian leaders from more than a score of tribes. Except for those intrepid paintbrush pioneers, George Catlin and John Mix Stanley, who traveled extensively amid the dangers and inconveniences of the Indian country, no other artist of the precamera period painted a larger or more varied series of Indian portraits.

"Charles Bird King was born in Newport, R. I., in 1785. He showed an early interest in painting that was encouraged by some of the best artists of his day. Samuel King of Newport, instructor of Allston and Malbone, was his first teacher. Later (probably from 1800 to 1805) he studied under Edward Savage in New York. Thereafter, he spent 7 years in London, where he roomed with Thomas Sully and had the advantage of Benjamin West's instruction. In 1812 he returned to this country. For 4 years he worked at his easel in Philadelphia with little success. In 1816 he moved to Washington, D. C. Here he remained until his death on March 18, 1862: (p. 463).

"Here, at the seat of government, King achieved a reputation as a painter of portraits, of socially and politically prominent persons of his time. Among his sitters were John C. Calhoun, Henry Clay, and John Howard Payne, famed writer of "Home Sweet Home." King built a studio and gallery on the east side of Twelfth Street between E and F Streets NW. Probably, many, if not all, of his Indian portraits were executed there. (pp. 463-464).

"The first Indians known to have been painted by King were members of a delegation of 16 leaders from the Pawnee, Omaha, Kansa, Oto, and Missouri Tribes of the Great Plains who arrived in Washingotn on November 29, 1821, in care of Maj. Benjamin O'Fallon, United States Indian agent. . . . It was probably Thomas L. McKenney, United States Superintendent of Indian Trade, who encouraged King to paint portraits of several members of this delegation. . . . Probably these were among the Indian portraits that hung on the walls of McKenney's office in Georgetown. . . . (p. 464).

"When Thomas L. McKenney was placed in charge of the Bureau of Indian Affairs under the War Department in March 1824, he took vigorous steps to enlarge the Government collection of Indian portraits. Secretary of War James Barbour in 1832 credited McKenney with conceiving 'the expediency of preserving the likenesses of some of the most distinguished among this most extraordinary race of people. Believing, as I did, that this race was about to become extinct, and that a faithful resemblance of the most remarkable among them would be full of interest in aftertimes, I cordially approved of the measure. This duty was assigned to Mr. King, of Washington, an artist of acknowledged reputation; he executed it with fidelity and success, by producing the most exact resemblances, including the costume of each." Thomas L. McKenney stated (1828) that King was paid for his Indian portraits at the rate of $20 for 'each head and about half the body.' (Hodge, 1916, pp. 190-191).

"There was no dearth of Indian delegations trekking to Washington during the decades of the 1820's and 1830's. Some groups of Indians from beyond the Mississippi were brought to Washington primarily to impress tribal leaders with the numbers of Whites, with the power and good intentions of the United States Government and to encourage Indian loyalty and good behavior. Others came to do business with the Government in matters involving cessions of Indian lands. In 1825, President Monroe recommended to the Congress a plan for the resettlement of Indian tribes then living east of the Mississippi on lands west of that great river, in order to permit the expansion of white settlement in the South and Midwest. In those days the United States recognized the Indian tribes as independent nations. To effect their removal from their traditional agricultural lands and hunting grounds, legal treaties had to be negotiated. Other treaties had to be made with tribes of Plains Indians to secure portions of their hunting grounds upon which the eastern Indians could be resettled. These treaties required prolonged and complicated negotiations between representatives of the Government and leaders of the Indian tribes involved. During the years 1824-38 no fewer than 18 Indian treaties were signed in the city of Washington. Each ceremony was attended by a delegation of chiefs and headmen of the tribe or tribes concerned. Other tribes sent delegations to Washington to discuss land cessions which were later formally negotiated by treaties signed in the field.

"King painted portraits of many members of these delegations when they came to Washington during the periods 1821-22 and 1824-37. During the years 1826-27, when Indian visitors to the capital were few, King copied for the Government collection at least 26 portraits of Indians of the western Great Lakes (most of them Ojibwa), executed in the field by the less able artist, James Otto Lewis. In 1837, when the number of Indian visitors to Washington was unusually large, George Cooke, friend and pupil of King, was called in to paint some of their portraits. In the 16-year period 1821-37 King painted from life Cherokee, Choctaw, Creek, Seminole, and Uchi Indian leaders from the South; Ojibwa, Potawatomi, Menomimi, Sac, Fox, and Seneca from the Great Lakes region; Iowa, Kansa, Omaha, Oto, and Pawnee from the central Great Plains; Eastern, Yankton, and Yanktonai Dakota, and a lone Assiniboin from the far Northwest. . . .

"The great majority of King's original Indian portraits were executed for the Government collection. Frances Trollope, that indefatigable recorder of American customs, saw this collection in Washington in 1832, and wrote: 'The bureau for Indian affairs contains a room of great interest; the walls are entirely covered with original portraits of all the chiefs who from time to time, have come to negotiate with the great father, as they call the President. These portraits are by Mr. King, and it cannot be doubted, are excellent likenesses, as are all the portraits I have ever seen from the hands of that gentlemen.' (Trollope, 1832, vol. 1, pp. 314-315).

"This collection was transferred to the National Institute in 1841 and exhibited in the old Patent Office building. Curator John Varden counted 'One Hundred and Thirty Indian Portraits Taken by Charles King and Others' in this collection September 1, 1852. In 1858 the collection was transferred to the Smithsonian Institution. *A Catalogue of Indian Paintings Belonging to the Government Collection* (by William J. Rhees) in 1859 lists 147 items. Of this number 82 are attributed to Charles Bird King, 15 are attributed to other artists, while the names of the painters of the remaining portraits are not given. Some, possibly many, of the paintings in the last group should be attributed to King. (Rhees, 1859, pp. 55-58.) The collection remained on exhibition in the art gallery of the Smithsonian building until most of the art collection was destroyed by fire, January 15, 1865.

"It is fortunate that Charles Bird King painted replicas of a number of the Indian portraits he had created for the Government collection. Some subjects he copied more than once. Two replicas of The Eagle of Delight, (Oto) for example, have been preserved. Careful study of these portraits indicates that the two paintings differ somewhat in detail. This suggests that King's replicas may not be meticulous duplicates of the originals.

"King's originals also were copied by other artists. In the early 1830's Henry Inman copied in oil a majority of the Indian paintings in the Government collection. These copies are now preserved in the Peabody Museum of Harvard University. From Inman's copies colored lithographs were prepared for McKenney and Hall's *History of the Indian Tribes of North America*, published by Key and Biddle of Philadelphia, 1836-44. These large, handsome, 19¼ by 13¼ inch plates are now collector's items. In the form of these lithographic reproductions many of King's Indian portraits have survived.

"Contemporaries of Charles Bird King made no rash claims for his artistic genius. Nevertheless, they had respect for his technical skill. Thomas Sully, who roomed with King in London, termed him 'the most industrious person I ever met' and the possessor of 'much mechanical skill.' Dunlap decried King's use of a mechanical gadget to measure the proportions of his sitter's features and appendages Tuckerman thought King's paintings were 'not remarkable for artistic superiority, but often curious and valuable likenesses, especially the Indian portraits.' (Dunlap, 1834, vol. 2, pp. 261-262; Tuckerman, 1867, p. 68.) (p. 467). . . .

". . . King achieved varying degrees of success in portraying the likenesses of his sitters. Perhaps he was most successful in profile and three-quarter-view portraits. He was not uniformly successful in the more difficult front-view poses." (p. 468).

139. Charles B. King. PUSHMATAHA. (1764-1824). The portraits owned by the Redwood Library and Athenaeum are on permanent loan to the Newport Historical Society. See Pl. 157. Ewers (1954, p. 466) writes regarding this portrait:

". . . Of outstanding historical significance is King's portrait of Pushmataha, the great Choctaw leader and consistent friend of the Whites. Pushmataha sat for King on his visit to Washington in 1824. He died in Washington on December 24 in that year, and was buried in the Congressional Cemetery. . . .

"Of the extant collections, the largest is the series of 21 paintings given or bequeathed by King to the Redwood Library and Athenaeum in his home town of Newport, R. I." *Photograph by the Smithsonian Institution, Bureau of American Ethnology*, Neg. 1092-B.

140. Charles B. King. MISTIPPEE. Son of Yoholo Micco. See Pl. 145. *Photograph by the Smithsonian Institution, Bureau of American Ethnology*, Neg. 1150.

141. Charles B. King. MAJOR TIMPOOCHEE BARNARD. See Pl. 156. See biographical sketch, BAE Bull 30. This picture was number 23 in the University Museum's exhibition, *The Noble Savage*, Philadelphia, May 8-September 8, 1958. *Photograph by Smithsonian Institution, Bureau of American Ethnology*, 1179.

142. Baroness Anne-Marguerite-Henriette Hyde de Neuville. CHEROKEE. According to G. C. Groce and D. H. Wallace, *The New-York Historical Society's Dictionary of Artists in America, 1564-1860*, Yale University Press, 1957, p. 337, the Baroness (c. 1779-1849) and her husband were exiles in America from 1807 until about 1814. They lived in New York and New Jersey and traveled also in Connecticut, Pennsylvania, and Tennessee. On these travels she made watercolor and pencil sketches. They lived in France from 1814-1816 when they returned for four years while the Baron served as his government's Minister to the United States. Many of her drawings are located in the New-York Historical Society and the New York Public Library.

143. Washington Allston. "WILLIAM McINTOSH. CREEK INDIAN, BORN AT KAWITA (COWETA) RUSSELL CO., ALABAMA. ("Chief of the Coweta Indians and The Lower Creeks." Title in BAE Bull. 137, Pl. 35-2). This portrait was

first discovered by Peter A. Brannon (now Director of the Alabama Department of Archives and History) in a bar in Columbus, Ga. He wrote that there is a record of a large portrait of William McIntosh which hung in the house of Chilly McIntosh (his son). According to Brannon, the painting was given by C. McIntosh in payment of a debt and from him passed to the owner of the bar where Brannon discovered it around 1900. In 1922 he finally succeeded in buying it for Alabama Department of Archives and History. He wrote that the artist, Washington Allston, was identified by the Boston Museum partly through the initials "WA" on the painting. Brannon said that a pen sketch from this portrait is in White, "Historical Collections of Georgia." *Photograph by Scott Photographic Services, Montgomery.* (See Peter A. Brannon, "McIntosh Portrait," *Montgomery Advertiser,* Nov. 3, 1935).

144. "McINTOSH. A Creek Chief." William McIntosh. McKenney and Hall, vol. I, No. 34. opp. p. 129, 1842. There is no portrait by C. B. King (Ewers, p. 469) listed. In a footnote by Frederick Webb Hodge (McKenney and Hall, 1933 edition, p. 272) he states in Note 14: "The portrait of Chilly (son of William McIntosh, who is pictured here) was painted by J. M. Stanley in June 1843, but was burned in the Smithsonian fire of 1865. Stanley says of him (*Portraits of North American Indians,* Washington, 1852, page 14): 'He speaks English fluently, and has seen much of civilized life, having spent much time at Washington transacting business with heads of Departments in behalf of his people. He is among the first men of his nation.'" *Quoted by permission from John Grant, Publisher, Edinburgh, Scotland.* Dr. A. J. Waring, Savannah, owns a copy of an oil painting of "Chilly McIntosh." He states: ". . . I have reason to believe that it is a good likeness. . . It is unsigned and was painted in identically the costume and pose of his father's picture which at that time was hanging in the Indian gallery." (Correspondence).

William McIntosh was slain in 1825, so his portrait would have had to been produced before that time.

A biography of William McIntosh is found in McKenney and Hall, Vol. 1, 1842, pp. 129-133; Frederick Webb Hodge, *Handbook of American Indians North of Mexico.* Smithsonian Institution, Bureau of American Ethnology, Bulletin 30, 1907-1910, Part I, p. 782; and in Thomas M. Owen, *History of Alabama and Dictionary of Alabama Biography,* Vol. II, under the section regarding Indians. Several dozen short biographies of Indian leaders of the area are contained therein. They were reprinted in The *Alabama Historical Quarterly,* Vol. 13, Nos. 1, 2, 3, and 4, 1951: William McIntosh-pp. 37-45. Other sources of information are: *American State Papers, Military Affairs. American State Papers, Indian Affairs.* Pickett, *History of Alabama.* White, *Historical Collections of Georgia,* 1855. The several histories of the life of Andrew Jackson. Halbert and Ball, *Creek War,* 1895. *The Colonial Records of Georgia.* Woodward, *Reminiscenes of the Creek or Muscogee Indians.* Claiborne, *Mississippi. Hawkins' Sketch of Creek Country.* The various Southeastern Archives have biographical information. Also see *Dictionary of American Biography* and *National Cyclopedia of American Biography.*

Though there have been many articles and references to these Indians since McKenney and Hall, their biographical publications remain the most complete early work on this subject. The three volume reprint of McKenney and Hall, published by John Grant, Edinburgh (31 George IV. Bridge), 1933-34, edited by Frederick Webb Hodge and David I Bushnell, Jr., contains their footnotes, modifying and clarifying various points in the McKenney and Hall narrative; Hodge and Bushnell also identify the photographs as to probable date and artist; Rhees (1859) *Catalogue* number; and Inman copy number (Harvard University).

The original McKenney and Hall volumes are known as: Thomas L. McKenney and James Hall. *History of the Indian Tribes of North America, with biographical sketches and anecdotes of the principal chiefs. Embellished with one hundred and twenty portraits, from the Indian Gallery in the Department of War, at Washington. By Thomas L. M'Kenney . . . and James Hall, Esq. . . .*
Vol. 1. Philadelphia: Frederick W. Greenough, 23 Minor Street. 1838 (BAE Lib. Cat. No. 574.)
Vol. 2. Philadelphia: Daniel Rice and James G. Clark, 132 Arch St. 1842. (BAE Lib. Cat. No. 575.)

Vol. 3. Philadelphia: Daniel Rice and James G. Clark, 132 Arch St., 1844. (BAE Lib. Cat. No. 576.)

The photographs herewith were supplied by the Bureau of American Ethnology and are from the folio of illustrations in: Thomas L. McKenney and James Hall, *History of the Indian Tribes of North America, with biographical sketches and anecdotes of the principal chiefs. Embellished with one hundred and twenty portraits, copied from the Indian Gallery, recently destroyed by fire, in the Smithsonian Institute at Washington. By Thomas L. M'Kenney, late of the Indian Department, Washington. Complete in one folio volume of illustrations, and two imperial volumes of biographies and general history. Philadelphia: D. Rice & Co., 508 Minor Street. no date.* 3 vols.—1 folio and two imperial volumes of text. (Probably 1872). (BAE Library Catalog No. 30271). There are slight variations in some of the engravings in different editions. In the 1934 edition, in the long introduction F. W. Hodge discusses not only the various volumes issued, but the lives of the authors and artists. Hodge states that Hall tried to get Catlin to include pictures in the volumes, but Catlin refused. (p. xxxii). Frederick W. Hodge and David I. Bushnell, Jr. (the John Grant Edition of 1934) added explanation footnotes to the original McKenney and Hall biographies. Below are indicated dates which Hodge believed the paintings to have been made. (C. B. King).

145-155. CREEK INDIANS. 145. Mistippee, M. & H. Vol. 1. (p. 1825). Son of Yaholo-Micco. 146. Menewa. M & H. Vol. II Leader in the Battle of Horseshoe Bend. Hodge, Bull. 30, p. 841. 147 Legadie. M & H. Vol. III (no bibliog.). 148. Tustennuggee Emathla. M & H. Vol. III (no bibliog.) "Wea-Mathla" "A Creek Chief, Jim Boy." (P. 1826) (also, Stanley, 1843). 149. Se-loc-ta. "Creek Chief" Vol. II (P. 1825) 150. Yoholo-Micco. Chief. Vol. II. Hodge, Bull. 30, p. 998. (P. 1825-26). 151. Opothle Yoholo. Vol. II. "'Creek Chief" (P. King, 1825; Stanley, 1843). 152. Apauly-Tustennuggee, Creek Chief. Vol. III (no bibliog.) 153. "Oche-Finceco, Half-breed Creek." Vol. III (no bibliog.). 154. "Nah-et-luc-hopie. Muskogee Chief." Vol. III (no biblio.). 155. "Paddy Carr. Creek Interpreter." Vol. II. (P. 1826).

156. TIMPOOCHEE BARNARD. M & H Vol II. (P. 1825) Hodge, BAE Bull. p. 752 describes him: "A Yuchi chief, son of Timothy Barnard, a Scotchman, and a Yuchi woman, who first became generally known when, in 1814, he took part with the American forces against the hostile Creeks."

157. PUSH-MA-TA-HA. M & H Vol. I. (P. 1824). Hodge, Bull. 30 pp. 329-330 writes: "A noted Choctaw, of unknown ancestry, born on the E. bank of Noxuba cr. in Noxubee Co., Miss., in 1764; died at Washington, D. C. Dec. 24, 1824. Before he was 20 years of age he distinguished himself in an expedition against the Osage, w. of the Mississippi. . . . When Tecumseh visited the Choctaw in 1811 to persuade them to join in an uprising against the Americans, Pushmataha strongly opposed the movement. . . . In 1813, with about 150 Choctaw warriors he joined Gen. Claiborne and distinguished himself in the attack and defeat of the Creeks under Weatherford at Kantchati, or Holy Ground, on the Alabama r., Ala. . . . Pushmataha signed the treaties of Nov. 16, 1805; Oct. 24, 1816; and Oct. 18, 1820. In 1824 he went to Washington to negotiate another treaty in behalf of his tribe. Following a brief visit to Lafayette, then at the capital, Pushmataha became ill and died within 24 hours. In accordance with his request he was buried with military honors, a procession of 2,000 persons, military and civilian, accompanied by (General) Jackson, . . ." See also, Gideon Lincecum, "Life of Apushimata Ha," *Mississippi Hist. Soc., Pub. 9 (Oxford, 1906), pp. 415-485.*

158. POCAHONTAS. In Vol. III, McKenney explains that this was engraved after a portrait by Robert Sully, which painting was produced after an old portrait, the scraps of which were owned by man in Virginia, whose ancestor had brought the portrait from England. (M & H, 1934, ix-xii). The portrait is probably more fanciful than fact. See Pl. 84.

159-161. CHEROKEE INDIANS. 159. Spring Frog. Chief. (Tooan Tuh). M. & H. Vol. II. Hodge, Bull. 30, p. 784. 160.

David Vann. M & H Vol. III (no bibliography). 161. Tah-chee. 'Dutch.' M & H Vol. I. Hodge, Bull. 30, p. 670.

162. SE-QUO-YAH. George Guess. M & H Vol. I. (p. 1828). Hodge Bull. 30, pp. 510-511 writes: "Inventor of the Cherokee alphabet, born in the Cherokee town of Taskigi, Tenn., about 1760; died near San Fernando, Tamaulipas, Mexico, in Aug. 1843. He was the son of a white man and a Cherokee woman of mixed blood, daughter of a chief in Echota. . . . Sequoya grew up in the tribe, quite unacquainted with English or civilized arts, becoming a hunter and trader in furs. He was also a craftsman in silverwork, an ingenious natural mechanic, and his inventive powers had scope for development in consequence of an accident that befell him in hunting and rendered him a cripple for life. The importance of the arts of writing and printing as instruments and weapons of civilization began to impress him in 1809, and he studied, undismayed by the discouragement and ridicule of his fellows, to elaborate a system of writing suitable to the Cherokee language. In 1821 he submitted his syllabary to the chief men of the nation, and on their approval the Cherokee of all ages set about to learn it with such zeal that after a few months thousands were able to read and write their language. Sequoya, in 1822, visited Arkansas to introduce writing in the Western division of the Cherokee, among whom he took up his permanent abode in 1823. . . ." See also Grant Foreman, *Sequoyah*, University of Oklahoma Press, 1938. A statue of Sequoyah, by Vinnie Ream Hoxie is in the United States Capitol, Washington.

163. JOHN RIDGE. "Cherokee Interpreter. Son of Major Ridge." M & H Vol. II. (P. 1825).

164. JOHN ROSS. Chief. M & H Vol. III (no bibliog.) Hodge Bull. 30, pp. 396-397 writes: "Chief of the Cherokee; born in Rossville, Ga., Oct. 3, 1790; died in Washington, D. C., Aug. 1, 1866. He was the son of an immigrant from Scotland by a Cherokee wife who was herself three-quarters white. . . . He went to school in Kingston, Tenn. In 1809 he was sent on a mission to the Cherokee in Arkansas by the Indian agent, and thenceforward till the close of his life he remained in public service to his nation. At the battle of the Horseshoe, and in other operations of the Cherokee contingent against the Creeks in 1813-14, he was adjutant of the Cherokee regiment. He was chosen a member of the national committee of the Cherokee Council in 1817, and drafted the reply to the U. S. commisisoners who were sent to negotiate the exchange of the Cherokee lands for others w. of the Mississippi. In the contest against removal his talents found play and recognition. As president of the na-itonal committee from 1819 till 1826 he was instrumental in the introduction of school and mechanical training, and led in the development of the civilized autonomous government embodied in the republican constitution adopted in 1827. From 1828 till the removal to Indian Ter. in 1839 he was principal chief of the Cherokee Nation, and headed the various national delegations that visited Washington. . . . After arrival in Indian Ter., he was chosen chief of the United Cherokee Nation, and held that office until his death, although during the dissensions caused by the Civil War the Federal authorities temporarily deposed him." See, Rachel C. Eaton, *John Ross and the Cherokee Indians*, Menasha, 1914. Catlin (1842, Vol. 2) contains a line reproduction of Ross.

165. MAJOR RIDGE. Chief. M & H Vol. I.

166-170. SHAWNEE. 166. Tenskwautawa, M & H Vol. I (Lewis, Detroit, 1823?). Hodge Bull. 30, p. 729. A picture of "Tens-qua-ta-way," Shawnee prophet appeared in James Otto Lewis, *The Aboriginal Portfolio*, Philadelphia, 1836, Vol. 2, p. 70 (17⅞ x 11 inches). With the caption, "Painted for Gov. Lewis Cass by J. O. Lewis at Detroit 1823. Lehman & Duval Lithrs. 167. Kishkalwa, M & H Vol. I. (P. 1825). 168. Quatawapea, or Colonel Lewis. Chief. M & H Vol. I (Lewis ?) 169. Paytakootha, "Flying Clouds." Warrior. M & H Vol. I. 170. Catahecassa. "Black Hoof." M & H Vol. I. Hodge Bull. 30, p. 212. (J. H. French, Winchester, Clark Co., Kentucky, owns "three fine pictures" of Catahecassa printed in Philadelphia).

Lewis. TENS-QUA-TA-WA

171-180. SEMINOLE. 171. Yahajo. M & H Vol. II (P. 1826). 172. Micanopy. M & H Vol. II. Hodge Bull 30, p. 860. 173. Osceola. M & H Vol. II. Hodge Bull 30, p. 159. 174. Tukoseemathla. M & H Vol. III(no bibliog.). 175. Chittee Yoholo. M & H Vol. II. 176. Tulcee-Mathla. M & H III(no bibliog). 177. Foke-luste-hajo. M & H Vol. II. 178. Neamathla. M & H Vol. II. Hodge Bull. 30, p. 48-49. 179. Itacho-Tustinnuggee. M & H Vol III(no bibliog.). 180 Billy-Bowlegs, undated volume—1872? (after a photograph).

181. Charles A. Lesueur. "INDIAN CABANNE." Leland No. 179 gives the location as "near Memphis." The originals shown in Plates 181-187 are approximately 8 x 6 inches. Correspondence regarding these was address to André Maury, Conservateur, Museum of Natural History, 130 Rue Anatole-France, Le Havre, France, which museum owns the originals. The photographs were from Ateliers, V. Genetier, 7, Rue Guy de la Brosse, Paris V, France. Other information regarding the artist may be found in George C. Groce and David H. Wallace, *The New-York Historical Society's Dictionary of Artists in America, 1564-1860*, p. 395.

Drawing 729, a sketch of two Indians, one with a rifle, Baton Rouge, is not shown here. In addition to the drawings mentioned there are a number of others regarding Indian remains which are not shown here: 444. "Mont Jolliet à St. Louis, Mississippi. Plan du Tumulus Jolliet." and 526-531. "Bony Bank, Wabash River," regarding archeological remains. 553. "Indian mount. Bluefort." 728. Two pipestone (red) calumets, one with feathered stem. These pipes are similar to those Catlin painted in the hands of members of the "Five Civilized Tribes." Oklahoma. 1834. 730. "Sandusky-Bay sur le Lac Erie." Several articles have been written about the work of Lesueur: La Cité Universitaire de Paris, *Dessins de Ch. A. Lesueur exécutés aux Etats-Unis de 1816 à 1837*. Paris. c. 1933. E. T. Hamy, "Les Voyages du Naturaliste Ch. Alex. Lesueur dans l'Amerique du Nord (1815-1837)," *Journal de la Société des Americanistes de Paris*, March, 1904. Par Mmm Adrien Loir, *Charles-Alexandre Lesueur, Artist et Savant Francais en Amérique de 1816 à 1837*. Le Havre, 1920. Waldo G. Leland, "The Lesueur Collection of American Sketches in the Museum of Natural History at Havre, Seine-Inférieure," *Mississippi Valley Historical Review*, June, 1923, pp. 53-78. Robert W. G. Vail, "The American Sketchbooks of a French Naturalist, 1816-1837, a Description of the Charles Alexandre Lesueur Collection, with a Brief Account of the Artist," *Proceedings of the American Antiquarian Society*, XLVIII, April 1938, 49-155.

182. Charles A. Lesueur. "JAMES. . . ." "Hamy reproduced as Plate V a map on which 'Petit Gulph' appears on the east bank of the Mississippi, south of Bayou Pierre, and north of Coles Creek." (correspondence with Bureau of American Ethnology). Note the turban-fashion, printed cloth headdress, silver head band? and leggings.

183—185. Charles A. Lesueur. "CHACTAS." "JEU DE PEAUNE INDIEN." "PEAU DE BISON."

186. Charles A. Lesueur. "CHAWCTAS. . . ." The man represented in the profile portrait appears to be wearing an animal skin cap with the ears and tail attached. Note the two small full-length portraits to the left. Each appears to have a pack on his back and to be walking. Many Indians migrating to the reservation west of the Mississippi River passed through Memphis. Some of the Indians sketched by Lesueur may have been transients.

187. Charles A. Lesueur. "CHAWCTAS. . ." He has a pack on his back; it is knotted in front, and his right hand loosely grasps the knot. Around his head appears to be a piece of printed cloth gathered into a band.

188. George Catlin. "STEEH-TCHA-KO-ME-CO. One of the Chiefs of the tribe with his rifle in his hand." Oklahoma. 1834. Catlin 288.

John C. Ewers, "George Catlin, Painter of Indians and the West," (Smithsonian Report, 1955, pp. 483-528—Publication 4251) lists Catlin's paintings owned by the United States National Museum and other major collections. He also discusses the life and work of George Catlin. Ewers writes:

"The collection of original paintings by George Catlin in the U. S. National Museum comprises 445 items, including the majority of the original oil paintings in Catlin's Indian Gallery exhibited by him in the United States and in Europe in the years 1833-1852. By actual count 422 of the 507 painting numbers listed in Catlin's exhibition catalog of 1840 are in this collection. (Catlin gave more than one number to portraits which included likenesses of two or more individuals. Hence painting numbers in his exhibition catalogs exceed the actual number of paintings.) In addition the collection includes 33 of the 100 paintings which Catlin executed and added to his exhibition between 1840 and 1848." . . . (p. 507).

Ewers states that most of the "large oil portraits are 28 x 23 inches." (p. 508). He lists and describes (pp. 525-527) eleven other major and several smaller collections of the work of Catlin. He remarks (pp. 483-484): "Today, a century and a quarter after vigorous, restless George Catlin braved the dangers and discomforts of the Indian country beyond the Mississippi to record on canvas the appearance of the land and its people, scholars and the public are gaining an understanding of the true significance of his paintings as pictorial documents of the old West."

Ewers describes the life of this remarkable recorder of Indian history:

"George Catlin was born in Wilkes-Barre, Pa., on July 26, 1796. As a boy his interest in American Indians was aroused by Indian legends and stories of Indian captivities which were current in his neighborhood. His own mother, as a girl, had been taken prisoner by Indians in the bloody Wyoming Massacre of 1778. . . .

"At the request of his lawyer father, George Catlin entered the law school of Reeves and Gould at Litchfield, Conn., in 1817. Next year he passed his bar examinations and began the practice of law in Lucerne, Pa. But his heart was not in the courtroom. Rather he was becoming more and more interested in art. Finally he sold his law books, abandoned his legal career, and moved to Philadelphia to devote full time to painting.

"As a painter Catlin was entirely self-taught. With characteristic enthusiasm and industry he worked at his art until he developed skill both as a miniature painter in watercolors and as a portrait painter in oils. In 1824 he was elected an academician of the Pennsylvania Academy of Fine Arts, a select company that numbered among its members such masters of the period as Charles Willson Peale, Rembrandt Peale, and Thomas Sully. In 1828, 12 of Catlin's works (including both drawings and paintings) were exhibited by the American Academy of Fine Arts. One of these was a full-length portrait of the late Gov. De Witt Clinton of New York State, which Catlin had painted for the Corporation of the City of New York.

"The frame of some of his sitters and the acceptance of his paintings in important exhibitions indicate that Catlin early achieved a degree of success as a portraitist. Yet he was restless, dissatisfied. As he himself later explained it, he was 'continually reaching for some branch or enterprise of the arts on which to devote a whole life-time of enthusiasm.' (Catlin, 1841, vol. 1, p. 2).

"While he was trying to find himself, Catlin saw some 10 or 15 Indian members of a delegation from the wilds of the 'Far West' who were passing through Philadelphia on their way to visit the Great White Father in Washington. Sight of their handsome features and picturesque costumes rekindled Catlin's youthful enthusiasm for Indians. It changed the course of his career and provided him with a goal for his life's work. In later years he worded his new resolve thus:

" 'Man, in the simplicity and loftiness of his nature, unrestrained and unfettered by the disguises of art, is surely the most beautiful model for the painter, and the country from which he hails is unquestionably the best study or school of the arts in the world; such I am sure, from the models I have seen, is the wilderness of North America. And the history and customs of such a people, preserved by pictorial illustrations are themes worthy the life-time of one man, and nothing short of the loss of my life, shall prevent me from visiting their country, and of becoming their historian.' (Catlin, 1841, vol. 1, p. 2).

"No missionary answering a call to service among a heathen people ever dedicated himself to a cause more steadfastly or energetically than did George Catlin to his self-determined task of 'rescuing from oblivion the looks and customs of the vanishing races of native men in America.' To this single purpose he devoted the best years of an amazingly active life.

"George Catlin gained his initial experience as a painter of Indians among the acculturated, reservation Iroquois of western New York. His earliest known Indian subject is an unfinished portrait of the Seneca orator, Red Jacket, signed and dated 'Buffalo, 1826.' . . . .

"In the spring of 1830, Catlin started on his great western adventure by traveling to St. Louis. . . . In July of that year Catlin accompanied General (William) Clark to Prairie du Chien and Fort Crawford to make treaties with the Iowa, Missouri, Sioux, Omaha, and Sauk and Fox. Early that fall he was at Cantonment Leavenworth on the Missouri painting Iowa Indians and members of tribes removed from the Eastern Woodlands—Delaware, Kaskaskia, Kickapoo, Peoria, Potawatomi, Shawnee, and Weah. Later that fall he accompanied General Clark to Kansa Indian villages on Kansas River where he executed a series of portraits of tribal leaders.

"In the spring of 1831 Catlin accompanied Indian Agent (Major) John Dougherty up the Missouri and Platte Rivers to visit his charges, the horticultural Pawnee, Omaha, Oto, and Missouri. . . .

"The year 1832 marked another turning point in Catlin's career. Prior to that time he had been content to paint only portraits. Nor is there evidence that he had taken extensive field notes describing his previous experiences among the redmen. . . . (Ewers describes Catlin's travels in 1832 and 1833. He includes a map showing the extensive travels from 1830-1836.)

"In 1834 Catlin gained an opportunity to interpret the Indians of the Southern Plains much as he had the Upper Missouri tribes two years before. The Secretary of War granted him permission to accompany an expedition of Dragoons from Fort Gibson on Arkansas River to the country of the wild and little-known Comanche and Kiowa Indians. Prior to or following the Dragon Expedition Catlin painted portraits of recently displaced Cherokee, Creek, and Choctaw Indians in the neighborhood of Fort Gibson (Oklahoma). They had been removed from lands east of the Mississippi to make room for expansion of white settlement in the Southeast. He also painted a Choctaw eagle dance and lively views of the fast action in a Choctaw lacrosse game. Osage Indians also posed for their portraits near Fort Gibson. (Ewers then describes the Expedition and Catlin's work in 1835 and 1836).

" . . . This series of field trips (1830-1836) provided the source materials for the great majority of the oil paintings in what later became known as Catlin's Indian Gallery. Not shown on this map (Ewers, Fig. 1) are Catlin's earlier trips to western New York or his later 1838) journey from New York to Charleston, S. C., to obtain portraits of Osceola and those other Seminole and Yuchi Indian prisoners held at Fort Moultrie."

Regarding Catlin's painting methods, Ewers (pp. 492-493) comments:

"George Catlin rarely mentioned his painting methods in his own writings. His pictures, however, reveal two distinct styles. One of these may be termed his studio-portrait style. Its outstanding example is his portrait of Osceola executed in 1838. Osceola was then a Seminole War hero for whose portrait there was a popular demand. Catlin visited him in prison and slowly and realistically rendered Osceola's physical appearance and the details of his costume. Osceola's grandfather was a Scotchman and the Caucasian strain is apparent in the features and complexion of Catlin's portrait. Few other half-length portraits by Catlin approach this one as finished works of art.

"Catlin's second style we may term his impressionistic or field-sketching style. He achieved it through a remarkably disciplined coordination of eye and hand, quick observation, and rapid execution. If his subject was a person, Catlin tried to catch a likeness in a few deft strokes of his brush. If it was an Indian activity, he merely suggested the position and actions of the figures with a like economy of time and paint. If it was a landscape, he indicated the general character of the country without dwelling on the details. This bold simplification of man and nature is typical of the great majority of paintings in the Catlin Collection in the U. S. National Museum. . . .

"In addition to his oils, Catlin apparently made rapid full-length pencil or pen-and-ink sketches of many of his costumed Indian subjects and sketchbook renderings of some of his scenes of Indian activities. . . . (p. 493).

". . . Catlin never was content to portray generalized or idealized Indian types. He was a realist who tried to produce recognizable likenesses of real people. He possessed an uncommon genius for seizing upon those features of a sitter's face that defined its individuality. Catlin's Indians are sympathetically presented. They have a proud bearing and an expression of dignity which should be familiar to anyone who has photographed Indians on western reservations. (p. 495). . . .

". . . Most of his subjects were chiefs and their wives and children. They were Indians of considerable wealth who owned the most elaborate suits, dresses, and ornaments to be found in their tribes. . . .

"Catlin's interest in the details of Indian costume always was secondary to his keen desire to record his sitter's facial features. In some portraits Catlin ignored the details of his sitter's costumes. In others he called particular attention to some items while slighting the delineation of other details. . . . his treatment of costume details ranges all the way from omission, through generalization and exaggeration, to very accurate rendering of minute units in their true colors."

Ewers discusses Catlin's portraits, scenes of Indian life, and landscapes. He compares Catlin's work with that of Carl Bodmer. He also gives a bibliography of the articles and books discussing the collections and work of Catlin. In this he lists the books and catalogues published during the life-time of Catlin, best known of which was George Catlin, *Letters and Notes on the Manners, Customs and Conditions of the North American Indians*, 2 vols., London, 1841. The numbers shown in these notes, as "Catlin 289," refer to the numbers given to the painting by George Catlin in *A Descriptive Catalogue of Catlin's Indian Collection*, London, 1840 and 1848.

189. George Catlin. "HOL-TE-MAL-TE-TEZ-TE-MEEK-EE brother of the Chief above (i.e. 'Ben Perryman'), and a jolly companionable man." Oklahoma. 1834. Catlin 289. Catlin, 1841, vol. 2, p. 122—"These two men are brothers, and are fair specimens of the tribe, who are mostly clad in calicoes, and other cloths of civilized manufacture; tasselled and fringed off by themselves in the most fantastic way, and sometimes with much true and picturesque taste. They use a vast many beads, and other trinkets, to hang upon their necks, and ornament their moccasins and beautiful belts.

"The Creeks (or Mus-ko-gees) of 20,000 in numbers, have, until quite recently, occupied an immense tract of country in the states of Mississippi (actually Georgia) and Alabama; but by a similar arrangement . . . with the Government, have exchanged their possessions there for a country, adjoining to the Cherokees, on the South side of the Arkansas, to which they have already all removed, and on which, like the Cherokees, they are laying out fine farms, and building good houses, in which they live; in many instances, surrounded by immense fields of corn and wheat. There is scarcely a finer country on earth than that now owned by the Creeks; and in North America, certainly no Indian tribe more advanced in the arts and agriculture than they are. It is no uncommon thing to see a Creek with twenty or thirty slaves at work on his plantation, having brought them from a slave-holding country, from which, in their long journey, and exposure to white man's ingenuity, I venture to say, that most of them got rid of one-half of them, whilst on their long and disastrous crusade.

"The Creeks, as well as the Cherokees and Choctaws, have good schools and churches established amongst them, conducted by excellent and pious men, from whose example they are drawing great and lasting benefits."

190. George Catlin. "HOSE-PUT-O-KAW-GEE; a brave." Oklahoma. 1834. Catlin 291.

191. George Catlin. "TEL-MAZ-HA-ZA; a warrior of great distinction." Oklahoma. 1834. Catlin 293.

192. George Catlin. "TCHOW-EE-PUT-O-KAW, a woman." Oklahoma. 1834. Catlin 292.

193. George Catlin. "WAT-AL-LE-GO, a brave." Oklahoma. 1834. Catlin 290.

194. George Catlin. "COL-LEE, Chief of a band of the Cherokees." Oklahoma. 1834. Catlin 285. In many of his pictures he writes this name "Jol-lee." He also has drawings of another Cherokee not pictured among the oils here, "Tuch-ee, called 'Dutch,' Chief of a Band of Cherokees, and a very distinguished man, as a Warrior." (See Note 224). Regarding the Cherokees Catlin (1841, p. 119) states:

"Living in the vicinity of, and about Fort Gibson, on the Arkansas, and 700 miles west of the Mississippi river, are a third part or more of the once very numerous and powerful tribe who inhabited and still inhabit, a considerable part of the state of Georgia, and under a Treaty made with the United States Government, have been removed to those regions, where they are settled on a fine tract of country; and having advanced somewhat in the arts and agriculture before they started, are now found to be mostly living well, cultivating their fields of corn and other crops, which they raise with great success.

". . . with a great majority of the nation remaining on their own ground in the state of Georgia, . . . some six or 7000 of the tribe have several years since removed to the Arkansas, under the guidance and controul of an aged and dignified chief by the name of *Jol-lee*.

"This man, like most of the chiefs, as well as a very great proportion of the Cherokee population, has a mixture of white and red blood in his veins, of which, in this instance, the first seems decidedly to predominate. Another chief, and second to this, amongst this portion of the Cherokees, by the name of Teh-ke-neh-kee (the black coat), I have also painted and placed in my Collection, as well as a very interesting specimen of the Cherokee women. (1841, Plate 216).

"I have travelled pretty generally through the several different locations of this interesting tribe, both in the Western and Eastern divisions, and have found them, as well as the Choctaws and Creeks, their neighbours, very far advanced in the arts; affording to the world the most satisfactory evidences that are to be found in America, of the fact, that the Indian was not made to shun and evade good example, and necessarily to live and die a brute."

Cherokees listed in Catlin's *Catalogue*, 1848, were: 283. "John Ross, a civilized and well-educated man, Head Chief of the Nation." 284. "Tuch-ee, called 'Dutch;' first War-chief of the Cherokees; a fine-looking fellow, with a turbaned head. I travelled and hunted with this man some months, when he guided the regiment of dragoons to the Camanchee and Pawnee villages: he is a great warrior and remarkable hunter. 287. "Ah-hee-te-wah-chee; a very pretty woman, in civilized dress, her hair falling over her shoulders."

195. George Catlin. "TEH-KE-NEH-KEE, a Chief, also of considerable standing." Oklahoma. 1834. Catlin 286. See also Note 194.

196. George Catlin. "ETCH-EE-FIX-E-CO; a Chief of considerable renown." Oklahoma. 1837. Catlin 309. (not pictured in Catlin 1841 edition or Donaldson, Thomas, "The George Catlin Indian Gallery in the U. S. National Museum." *Annual Report, Smithsonian Institution for 1885.* 1887.) Description by SI-USNM: "Cloth turban (white, red, green) with black feather plume. Red cloth neckerchief. Figured brown and red cloth shirt. Bright red trade blanket. Buckskin leggings and moccasins." In Catlin's *Catalogue*, 1848, listed "Eu-chee."

197. George Catlin. "CHEE-A-EX-E-CO; quite a modest and pretty girl, daughter of the above (Etch-ee-fix-e-co) Chief. Oklahoma. 1837. Catlin 310. Description by SI-USNM: "Glass trade beads around neck of several different colors. Silver brooches on chest. Silver bracelet. Brown cloth dress. Red trade blanket with green stripe."

198. George Catlin. "TEN-SQUAT-A-WAY, brother of Tecumseh." Part Creek. Shawnee. Kansas River, Oklahoma, 1831. Catlin 279. Though a few bands of Shawnee were scattered in the Southeast, the main body of the tribe lived north of the Ohio. However, their forays frequently took them south of the Ohio, and they are included because of their close location, and frequent trespassing on the Southeast. They had been removed to Oklahoma at the time Catlin drew the pictures. The biographies in McKenney and Hall, 1838-1844, tell of the relation of this tribe to the Southeast. Other Sha-wa-no (Shaw-nee) not shown here, but listed in Catlin's *Catalogue*, 1848 are: 278. Kate-Quaw, the Female Eagle; a fine-looking girl, daughter of the above chief. 282. Coo-ps-saw-quay-te; woman.

199. George Catlin. "LAY-LOO-AH-PEE-AI-SHEE-KAW; half civil, and more than half drunk." Shawnee. Kansas River, Oklahoma. 1831.

200. George Catlin. "PAW-TE-COO-CAW. Semi-civilized." Shawnee. Kansas River, Oklahoma. 1831. In Catlin's *Catalogue*, 1848, he spelled this, "Pah-te-Coo-Saw."

201. George Catlin. "LAY-LAW-SHE-KAW; a very good man, Chief of the tribe." Shawnee. Kansas River, Oklahoma. 1831.

202. George Catlin. "OS-CE-O-LA; a warrior of very great distinction." Seminole (Florida). Fort Moultrie, South Carolina. 1838. Catlin 301. The picture is described by the SI-USNM: "Turban of red cloth with green figures; white and black feather plumes. Amber trade beads in close fitting necklace. Tubular shell and large round red and green glass trade beads in outer necklace. Reddish brown neckerchief (cloth). Three silver gorgets on chest. Light colored, figured cloth vest. Figured dark brown background cloth shirt sleeves. Woven red and green yarn belt. Cloth bandolier dark green background, designs in light green with dark red centers."
Catlin's *Catalogue* (1848, p. 32) lists two other Seminole pictures not shown here: "306. How-ee-da-hee, a Seminolee woman." and "308. Os-ce-o-la, the Black Drink. Full-length, with his rifle in his hand, calico dress, and trinkets, exactly as he was dressed and stood to be painted five days before his death." See Plate 286. (Catlin, 1841, vol. 2, Pl. 298).
Catlin (1841, vol. 2, p. 218) writes: ". . . the Seminolees, . . . are a tribe of three or four thousand; occupying the peninsula of Florida—and speaking the language of the Creeks. . . . The word Seminolee is a Creek word, signifying runaways; a name which was given to a part of the Creek nation, who emigrated. . . ."
From Fort Moultrie, South Carolina, (1838) Catlin writes (1841, vol. 2, pp. 218-222):
"The prisoners who are held here, to the number of 250, men, women and children, have been captured during the recent part of this warfare, and amongst them the distinguished personages whom I named a few moments since (Mick-e-no-pah, Os-ce-o-la, and Cloud, King Phillip); of

these, the most conspicuous at this time is Os-ce-o-la, commonly called Powell, as he is generally supposed to be a halfbreed, the son of a white man (by that name), and a Creek woman.
"I have painted him precisely in the costume, in which he stood for his picture, even to a string and a trinket. He wore three ostrich feathers in his head, and a turban made of a vari-coloured cotton shawl—and his dress was chiefly of calicos, with a handsome bead sash or belt around his waist, and his rifle in his hand.
"This young man is, no doubt, an extraordinary character, as he has been for some years reputed, and doubtless looked upon by the Seminolees as the master spirit and leader of the tribe, although he is not a chief. From his boyhood, he had led an energetic and desperate sort of life, which had secured for him a conspicuous position in society; and when the desperate circumstances of war were agitating his country, he at once took a conspicuous and decided part; and in some way whether he deserved it or not, acquired an influence and a name that soon sounded to the remotest parts of the United States, and amongst the Indian tribes, to the Rocky Mountains.
"This gallant fellow, who was, undoubtedly, *captured* a few months since, with several of his chiefs and warriors, was at first brought in, to Fort Mellon in Florida, and afterwards sent to this place for safe-keeping, where he is grieving with a broken spirit, and ready to die, cursing white man, no doubt, to the end of his breath.
"The surgeon of the post, Dr. Weedon, who has charge of him, and has been with him ever since he was taken prisoner, has told me from day to day, that he will not live many weeks; and I have my doubts whether he will, from the rapid decline I have observed in his face and his flesh since I arrived here.
"During the time that I have been here, I have occupied a large room in the officers' quarters, by the politeness of Captain Morrison, who has command of the post, and charge of the prisoners; and on every evening, after painting all day at their portraits, I have had Os-ce-o-la, Mick-e-no-pa, Cloud, Co-a-had-jo, King Philip, and others in my room, until a late hour at night, where they have taken great pains to give me an account of the war, and the mode in which they were captured, of which they complain bitterly.
"I am fully convinced from all that I have seen, and learned from the lips of Osceola, and from the chiefs who are around him, that he is a most extraordinary man, and one entitled to a better fate.
"In stature he is about at mediocrity, with an elastic and graceful movement; in his face he is good looking, with rather an effeminate smile; but of so peculiar a character, that the world may be ransacked over without finding another just like it. In his manners, and all his movements in company, he is polite and gentlemanly, though all his conversation is entirely in his own tongue; and his general appearance and actions, those of a full-blooded and wild Indian. (pp. 219-220). . .
"Since I finished my portrait of Os-ce-o-la, and since writing the first part of this Letter, he has been extremely sick, and lies so yet, with an alarming attack of the quinsey or putrid sore throat, which will probably end his career in a few days. Two or three times the surgeon has sent for the officers of the Garrison and myself, to come and see him '*dying*'—we were with him the night before last till the middle of the night, every moment expecting his death; but he has improved during the last twenty-four hours, and there is some slight prospect of his recovery." (footnote which he added to his letter later): "From accounts which left Fort Moultrie a few days after I returned home, it seems, that this ill-fated warrior died, a prisoner, the next morning after I left him. And the following very interesting account of his last moments, was furnished me by Dr. Weedon, the surgeon who was by him, with the officers of the garrison, at Os-ce-o-la's request.
"'About half an hour before he died, he seemed to be sensible that he was dying; and although he could not speak, he signified by signs that he wished me to send for the chiefs and for the officers of the post, whom I called in. He made signs to his wives (of whom he had two, and also two fine little children by his side,) to go and bring his full dress,

which he wore in time of war; which having been brought in, he rose up in his bed, which was on the floor, and put on his shirt, his leggings and moccasins—girded on his war-belt—his bullet-pouch and powder-horn, and laid his knife by the side of him on the floor. He then called for his red paint, and his looking-glass, which was held before him, when he deliberately painted one half of his face, his neck and his throat—his wrists—the backs of his hands, and the handle of his knife, red with vermilion; a custom practiced when the irrevocable oath of war and destruction is taken. His knife he then placed in its sheath, under his belt; and he carefully arranged his turban on his head, and his three ostrich plumes that he was in the habit of wearing in it. Being thus prepared in full dress, he laid down a few minutes to recover strength sufficient, when he rose up as before, and with most benignant and pleasing smiles, extended his hand to me and to all the officers and chiefs that were around him; and shook hands with us all in dead silence; and also with his wives and his little children; he made a signal for them to lower him down upon his bed, which was done, and he then slowly drew from his war-belt, his scalping-knife, which he firmly grasped in his right hand, laying it across the other, on his breast, and in a moment smiled away his last breath, without a struggle or a groan.' "

203. George Catlin. "MICK-E-NO-PAH, first chief of the tribe." Seminole (Florida). Fort Moultrie, South Carolina. 1838. Catlin 300. Catlin (1841, vol. 2, Pl. 305, p. 221) describes his painting of this picture:

"Mick-e-no-pah, is the head chief of the tribe, and a very lusty and dignified man. He took great pleasure in being present every day in my room, whilst I was painting the others; but positively refused to be painted, until he found that a bottle of whiskey, and another of wine, which I kept on my mantelpiece, by permission of my kind friend Captain Morrison, were only to deal out their occasional kindnesses to those who sat for their portraits; when he at length agreed to be painted, 'If I could make a fair likeness of his *legs*,' which he had very tastefully dressed in a handsome pair of red leggings, and upon which I at once began, (as he sat cross-legged), by painting *them* on the lower part of the canvass, leaving room for his body and head above; all of which, through the irresistible influence of a few kindnesses from my bottle of wine, I soon had fastened to the canvass, where they will firmly stand I trust, for some hundreds of years."

204. George Catlin. "CO-EE-HE-JO; a chief, very conspicuous in the present war." Seminole (Florida). Fort Moultrie, South Carolina. 1838. Catlin 304. Catlin (1841, vol. 2, Pl. 301, p. 220): "Co-ee-ha-jo, is another chief who has been a long time distinguished in the tribe, having signalized himself very much by his feats in the present war."

205. George Catlin. "YE-HOW-LO-GEE; a Chief who distinguished himself in the war." Seminole (Florida). Fort Moultrie, South Carolina. 1838. Catlin 303. Catlin (1841, vol. 2, Pl. 299, p. 220): "Ye-how-lo-gee, (the cloud), generally known by the familiar name of 'Cloud.' This is one of the chiefs, and a very good-natured, jolly man, growing fat in his imprisonment, where he gets enough to eat, and an occasional drink of whiskey from the officers, with whom he is a great favourite." SI-USNM describes the picture: "Figured red cloth turban with green feather plume. Silver ear bobs; silver(?) brooch. Green trade bead necklace (glass beads). White shirt. Black cloth coat with red figures. Grey trade blanket."

206. George Catlin. "BEAUTIFUL SAVANNAH IN THE PINE-WOODS OF FLORIDA. One of thousands of small lakes which have been gradually filled in with vegetation. Catlin 349. (Catlin 1841, vol. 2, Pl. 147, Desc. p. 33. Listed in Donaldson 1887, p. 257).

207. George Catlin. "WHITE SAN BLUFFS, ON SANTA ROSA ISLAND; and Seminoles Drying Fish, near Pensacola, on the Gulf of Florida. Catlin 354.

208. George Catlin. "A SEMINOLE WOMAN." Catlin 307. SI-USNM describes the picture: "Red cloth cap with some green figures and red ribbon. Glass trade beads in necklace of many colors, but each bead a single color. Silver brooches on chest. Figured red and brown cloth shawl. Note: Painting unfinished, the cloth dress and the moccasins not colored." (Catlin, 1841, vol. 2, Pl. 304, pictures a woman, but it is probably his 306, since it does not appear to be the 307 referred to here).

209. George Catlin. "EE-MAT-LA, King Phillip; an old man, second chief." Seminole (Florida). Fort Moultrie, South Carolina. 1838. Catlin 302. Catlin (1841, vol. 2, Pl. 300, p. 220) writes: "Ee-mat-la is also a very aged chief, who has been a man of great notoriety and distinction in his time, but has now got too old for further warlike enterprise. (footnote) This veteran old warrior died a few weeks after I painted his portrait, whilst on his way, with the rest of the prisoners, to the Arkansas." SI-USNM describes the painting: "Cloth turban (red background with small green figures); Dark colored figured cloth neckerchief. Gray trade blanket. Figured reddish brown cloth shirt." (Donaldson, 1887, Pl. 61, p. 216).

210. George Catlin. "OSCEOLA NICKANOCHEE, a Seminole Boy." Seminole (Florida). England? 1840? Catlin 307½? This is not listed in Catlin's *Catalogue*, 1848, with the other Seminole pictures, pp. 31-32. It is however mentioned in Catlin, 1842, vol. 2, p. 221, Pl. 303, ". . . portrait of a Seminolee boy, about nine years of age." Catlin adds in a footnote on that page, "This remarkably fine boy, by the name of *Os-ce-o-la Nick-a-no-chee*, has recently been brought from America to London, by Dr. Welch, an Englishman, who has been for several years residing in Florida. The boy it seems, was captured by the United States troops, at the age of six years: but how my friend the Doctor got possession of him, and leave to bring him away I never have heard. He is acting a very praiseworthy part however, by the paternal fondness he evinces for the child, and fairly proves, by the very great pains he is taking with his education. The doctor has published recently, a very neat volume, containing the boy's history; and also a much fuller account of Os-ce-o-la, and incidents of the Florida war, to which I would refer the reader." With some of Catlin's sketches of this boy he refers to him as the nephew of the warrior, Osceloa, and a boy of 12 years. There is some doubt of his close relationship to Osceola, and of the authenticity of this costume as representative Seminole dress. SI-USNM describes the painting: "Feathers in hair. Three silver gorgets on chest. Multiple strand glass bead necklace. Red paint on body. Red cloth breechclout with dark colored figures. Buckskin leggings. Buckskin moccasins with red cloth ankle flaps." Carolyn Thomas Foreman, *Indians Abroad, 1493-1938*, University of Oklahoma Press, Norman, 1943, p. 161 states that this boy was taken into captivity in August 1836, and given to Dr. Andrew Welch, who took him to England to school in 1840, and there he visited Catlin's exhibition. In George Catlin, *Catlin's Notes of Eight Years. . .*, vol. 2, he referred to "Os-ce-o-la Nick-a-a-no-chee . . . Painted 1837." See also Andrew Welch, *A Narrative of the Early Days and Rememberance of Oceola Nikkanochee, Prince of Econchatti*. 1841. On p. 217 it mentions a "splendid painting similar to the frontispiece, has been made of the Young Prince, by Mr. Wilkin." (Foreman, p. 162.) The Bureau of American Ethnology states: ". . . the only items which resemble Seminole or other Southeastern artifacts are the silver gorgets and perhaps the belt and earrings. None of these are appropriate for a boy of his age."

211. George Catlin. "LAH-SHEE; a half-breed warrior, called 'Creek Billy.' " Seminole (Florida). Fort Moultrie, South Carolina. 1838. Catlin 305. Catlin (1841, vol. 2, Pl. 302, p. 221) states:

"La-shee, is a distinguished brave of the tribe, and a very handsome fellow." SI-USNM describes the painting: "Multicolored cloth turban with red feather plume. Silver ear ornaments. Three silver gorgets at neck. Blue glass trade bead necklace. Red figured cloth shirt. Dark cloth coat with red figures. Red woven yarn sash. Red cloth bandolier decorated with white beads. Grey trade blanket."

212. George Catlin. "KUT-TEE-O-TUB-BEE, a noted brave." Oklahoma. 1834. Catlin 295.

213. George Catlin. "MO-SHO-LA-TUB-BEE, first Chief of the tribe." Oklahoma. 1834. Catlin 294. Catlin (1841, p. 123, Pl. 221) writes: "Their famous and excellent chief. . . . a distinguished and very gentlemanly man, who has been well-educated, and who gave me much curious and valuable information, of the history and traditions of his tribe."

214. George Catlin. "A WOMAN, hair in braid; remarkable expression." Oklahoma. 1834. Catlin 297.

215. George Catlin. "HA-TCHOO-TUC-KNEE, half-bred and well-educated man." Oklahoma. 1834. Catlin 296.

216. George Catlin. "TUL-LOCK-CHISH-KO." Oklahoma. 1834. Catlin 298. See Plate 217.

217. George Catlin. "TUL-LOCK-CHISH-KO, full length, in the dress and attitude of a ball player." Oklahoma. 1834. Catlin 299. Catlin (1841, pp. 224-225, Pl. 223) writes: "The mode in which these sticks are constructed and used, will be seen in the portrait of Tullock-chish-ko, . . . the most distinguished ball-player of the Choctaw nation, represented in his ball-play dress, with his ball-sticks in his hands. In every ball-play of these people, it is a rule of the play, that no man shall wear moccasins on his feet, or any other dress than his breech-cloth around his waist, with a beautiful bead belt, and a 'tail,' made of white horsehair or quills, and a 'mane' on the neck, of horsehair dyed of various colours." (See Pls. 230, 273, 281).

218. George Catlin. "EAGLE DANCE." Oklahoma. 1834. Catlin 449. Catlin (1841, pp. 126-127, Pl. 227) describes this:
"After this exciting day (that of the ball game), the concourse was assembled in the vicinity of the agency house, where we had a great variety of dances and other amusements, the most of which I have described on former occasions. One, however, was new to me, and I must say a few words of it: this was the *Eagle Dance*, a very pretty scene, which is got up by their young men, in honour of that bird, for which they seem to have a religious regard. This picturesque dance was given by twelve or sixteen men, whose bodies were chiefly naked and painted white, with white clay, and each one holding in his hand the tail of the eagle, while his head was also decorated with an eagle's quill. Spears were stuck in the ground, around which the dance was performed by four men at a time, who had simultaneously, at the beat of the drum, jumped up from the ground where they had all sat in rows of four, one row immediately behind the other, and ready to take the place of the first four when they left the ground fatigued, which they did by hopping or jumping around behind the rest, and taking their seats, ready to come up again in their turn, after each of the other sets had been through the same forms.
"In this dance, the steps or rather jumps, were different from anything I had ever witnessed before, as the dancers were squat down, with their bodies almost to the ground, in a severe and most difficult posture, as will have been seen in the drawing."

219. George Catlin. "BALL PLAY OF THE CHOCTAW— BALL UP." Oklahoma. 1834. Catlin 428. "One party is painted white; each has two sticks with a web at their ends, in which they catch the ball and throw it. They all have tails of horse-hair or quills attached to their girdles or belts." (Catlin, 1841, Pl. 225, desc. p. 125-6. Donaldson, 1887, Pl. 72.)

220. George Catlin. "BALL PLAY OF THE CHOCTAW— BALL UP." Variant of above. Oklahoma. 1834. Catlin 428 variant. SI-USNM Cat. No. 386412. Catlin (1841, pp. 123-126) describes Choctaw amusements and the ball-game:
"These people seem, even in their troubles, to be happy; and have, like all the other remnants of tribes, preserved with great tenacity their different games, which it would seem they are everlastingly practicing for want of other occupations or amusements in life. Whilst I was staying at the Choctaw agency in the midst of their nation, it seemed to be a sort of season of amusements, a kind of holiday; when the whole tribe almost, were assembled around the establishment, and from day to day we were entertained with some games or feats that were exceedingly amusing: horse-racing, dancing, wrestling, foot-racing, and ball-playing, were amongst the most exciting; and of all the catalogue, the most beautiful, was decidedly that of ball-playing. This wonderful game, which is the favourite one amongst all the tribes, and with these Southern tribes played exactly the same, can never be appreciated by those who are not happy enough to see it.

"It is no uncommon occurrence for six or eight hundred or a thousand of these young men, to engage in a game of ball, with five or six times that number of spectators, of men, women and children, surrounding the ground, and looking on. And I pronounce such a scene, with its hundreds of Nature's most beautiful models, denuded, and painted of various colours, running and leaping into the air, in all the most extravagant and varied forms, in the desperate struggles for the ball, a school for the painter or sculptor, equal to any of those which ever inspired the hand of the artist in the Olympian games or the Roman forum.

"I have made it an uniform rule, whilst in the Indian country, to attend every ball-play I could hear of, if I could do it riding a distance of twenty or thirty miles; and my usual custom has been on such occasions, to straddle the back of my horse, and look on to the best advantage. In this way I have sat, and oftentimes reclined, and almost dropped from my horse's back, with irresistible laughter at the succession of droll tricks, and kicks and scuffles which ensue, in the almost superhuman struggles for the ball. These plays generally commence at nine o'clock, or near it, in the morning; and I have more than once balanced myself on my pony, from that time till near sundown, without more than one minute of intermission at a time, before the game has been decided.

"It is impossible for pen and ink alone, or brushes, or even with their combined efforts, to give more than a *caricature* of such a scene; but such as I have been able to do, I have put upon the canvass, ...

"While at the Choctaw agency it was announced, that there was to be a great play on a certain day, within a few miles, on which occasion I attended, and made the three sketches which are hereto annexed; and also the following entry in my note-book, which I literally copy out.

"Monday afternoon at three, o'clock, I rode out with Lieutenants S. and M., to a very pretty prairie, about six miles distant, to the ball-play ground of the Choctaws, where we found several thousand Indians encamped. There were two points of timber about half a mile apart, in which the two parties for the play, with their respective families and friends, were encamped; and lying between them, the prairie on which the game was to be played. My companions and myself, although we had been apprised, that to see the whole of a ball-play, we must remain on the ground all the night previous, had brought nothing to sleep upon, resolving to keep our eyes open, and see what transpired through the night. During the afternoon, we loitered about amongst the different tents and shantees of the two encampments, and afterwards, at sundown, witnessed the ceremony of measuring out the ground, and erecting the 'byes' or goals which were to guide the play. Each party had their goal made with two upright posts, about 25 feet high and six feet apart, set firm in the ground, with a pole across at the top. These goals were about forty or fifty rods apart; and at a point just half way between, was another small stake, driven down, where the ball was to be thrown up at the firing of a gun, to be struggled for by the players. All this preparation was made by some old men, who were, it seems, selected to be the judges of the play, who drew a line from one bye to the other; to which directly came from the woods, on both sides, a great concourse of women and old men, boys and girls, and dogs and horses, where bets were to be made on the play. The betting was all done across this line, and seemed to be chiefly left to the women, who seemed to have martialled out a little of everything that their houses and their fields possessed. Goods and chattels—knives—dresses— blankets—pots and kettles—dogs and horses, and guns; and all were placed in the possession of *stake-holders*, who sat by them, and watched them on the ground all night, preparatory to the play.

"The sticks with which this tribe play, are bent into an oblong hoop at the end, with a sort of slight web of small thongs tied across, to prevent the ball from passing through.

The players hold one of these in each hand, and by leaping into the air, they catch the ball between the two nettings and throw it, without being allowed to strike it, or catch it in their hands.

"The mode in which these sticks are constructed and used, will be seen in the portrait of Tullock-chish-ko (he who drinks the juice of the stone), . . . See Plate 217.

"This game had been arranged and 'made up,' three or four months before the parties met to play it, and in the following manner:—The two champions who led the two parties, and had the alternate choosing of the players through the whole tribe, sent runners, with the ball-sticks most fantastically ornamented with ribbons and red paint, to be touched by each one of the chosen players; who thereby agreed to be on the spot at the appointed time and ready for the play. The ground having been all prepared and preliminaries of the game all settled, and the betting all made, and goods all 'staked,' night came on without the appearance of any players on the ground. But soon after dark, a procession of lighted flambeaux was seen coming from each encampment, to the ground where the players assembled around their respective byes; and at the beat of the drums and chaunts of the women, each party of players commenced the 'ball-play dance' (See Plates 222, 229, 272, 283). Each party danced for a quarter of an hour around their respective byes, in their ball-play dress; rattling their ball-sticks together in the most violent manner, and all singing as loud as they could raise their voices; whilst the women of each party, who had their goods at stake, formed into two rows on the line between the two parties of players, and danced also, in an uniform step, and all their voices joined in chaunts to the Great Spirit; in which they were soliciting his favour in deciding the game to their advantages; and also encouraging the players to exert every power they possessed, in the struggle that was to ensue. In the mean time, four old *medicine-men*, who were to have the starting of the ball, and who were to be judges of the play, were seated at the point where the ball was to be started; and busily smoking to the Great Spirit for their success in judging rightly, and impartially, between the parties in so important an affair.

"This dance was one of the most picturesque scenes imaginable, and was repeated at intervals of every half hour during the night, and exactly in the same manner; so that the players were certainly awake all the night, and arranged in their appropriate dress, prepared for the play which was to commence at nine o'clock the next morning. In the morning, at the hour, the two parties and all their friends, were drawn out and over the ground; when at length the game commenced, by the judges throwing up the ball at the firing of a gun; when an instant struggle ensued between the players, who were some six or seven hundred in numbers, and were mutually endeavouring to catch the ball in their sticks, and throw it home and between their respective stakes; which, whenever successfully done, counts one for game. In this game every player was dressed alike, that is, *divested* of all dress, except the girdle and the tail, which I have before described; and in these desperate struggles for the ball, when it is *up* (See Plates 219, 220, 274, 282) (where hundreds are running together and leaping, actually over each other's heads, and darting between their adversaries' legs, tripping and throwing, and foiling each other in every possible manner, and every voice raised to the highest key, in shrill yelps and barks)! there are rapid successions of feats, and of incidents, that astonish and amuse far beyond the conception of any one who has not had the singular good luck to witness them. In these struggles, every mode is used that can be devised, to oppose the progress of the foremost, who is likely to get the ball; and these obstructions often meet desperate individual resistance, which terminates in a violent scuffle, and sometimes in fisticuffs; when their sticks are dropped, and the parties are unmolested, whilst they are settling it between themselves; unless it be by a general *stampedo*, to which they are subject who are down, if the ball happens to pass in their direction. Every weapon, by a rule of all ball-players, is laid by in their respective encampments, and no man allowed to go for one; so that the sudden broils that take place on the ground, are presumed to be as suddenly settled without any probability of much personal injury; and no one is allowed to interfere in any way with the contentious individuals.

"There are times, when the ball gets to the ground (See Plate 221), and such a confused mass rushing together around it, and knocking their sticks together, without the possibility of any one getting or seeing it, for the dust that they raise, that the spectator loses his strength, and everything else but his senses; when the condensed mass of ball-sticks, and shins, and bloody noses, is carried around the different parts of the ground, for a quarter of an hour at a time, without any one of the mass being able to see the ball; and which they are often thus scuffling for, several minutes after it has been thrown off, and played over another part of the ground.

"For each time that the ball was passed between the stakes of either party, one was counted for their game, and a halt of about one minute; when it was again started by the judges of the play, and a similar struggle ensued; and so on until the successful party arrived to 100, which was the limit of the game, and accomplished at an hour's sun, when they took the stakes; and then, by a previous agreement, produced a number of jugs of whiskey, which gave all a wholesome drink, and sent them all off merry and in good humor, but not drunk." (A more complete description of ball play is contained in an article by James Mooney in the *American Anthropologist*, 1890.

221. George Catlin. "BALL PLAY. BALL IS DOWN." Oklahoma. 1834. Catlin 429. This is similar to Catlin's 428 (Plate 219 and 220). There is a change of play. (Catlin, 1841, vol. 2, p. 126, Pl. 226 and Donaldson, 1887, p. 301, Pl. 73). Baldwin Möllhausen, *Diary of a Journey from the Mississippi to the Coasts of the Pacific. . . .*, London, 1858, pp. 46-49 describes Choctaw ball play and Indian enthusiasm for the game in terms similar to those of Catlin. In 1853 Möllhausen saw a game at the Choctaw reservation, Oklahoma, near the Agency at Sculleville. He writes (p. 46):

". . . No matter how far they may have advanced in civilization, the Indian gentleman educated in the Eastern States is as ready as the still wild hunter of the same tribe to throw aside all the troublesome restrains of clothing, and painted from head to foot in the fashion of the 'good old times,' to enter the lists with unrestrained eagerness for a grand national game of ball.

"This ball or ring playing is practiced more or less among all the North American Indians. . . . The ball playing of the Choctaws, Chickasaws, Creeks, and Cherokees, is, however, carried on with such grand formalities, and has such a great charm or 'medicine' ascribed to it, that it deserves more particular attention." He describes this, pp. 46-49. On page 48 he writes:

"Accustomed from their childhood to manage these sticks, these people display astonishing dexterity both in flinging the balls to an immense distance, and in catching them as they fly through the air. Only one ball is used in the game, and the possession of this, so as to be able to throw it through the gate of his party, is the object of every one's exertions, for the side which first does this for the hundredth time gains the victory and wins the prizes."

222. George Catlin. "BALL PLAY DANCE." Oklahoma. 1834. Catlin 427. "Ball-play dance. Choctaw men and women dance around their respective stakes, at intervals, during the night preceding the play. Four conjurors sit all night and smoke to the Great Spirit, at the point where the ball is to be started, and stakeholders guard the goods staked." For a clearer picture see Plate 229. (Catlin, 1841, vol. 2, p. 126, Pl. 224 and Donaldson, 1887, p. 300, Pl. 71).

223. George Catlin. "HOL-TE-MAL-TE-TEZ-TE-NEEK-E." See Pls. 188, 189, 246, 263, and 278. Two are single portraits and three groups. Note variations in the directions they face and the numbers included in the groups.

Another collection of water colors by George Catlin is owned by the Thomas Gilcrease Institute of American History and Art. Tulsa. Portraits of Southeastern Indians in that collection are: Choctaw: Ha-tchoo-tuck-nee (222); woman (unnamed); Mo-sho-la-tub-bee (221); Wa-pa-heo; Tullock-chish-ko; Tullock-chish-ko (full-length. 223). Cherokee: Tuch-ee (218); Teh-ke-neh-kee; Ah-hoo-loo-tak-kee (The Drum Thrower, Jol-lee 217.) Creek: Stee-cha-co-me-co (219); Tel-maz-ha-za; Wat-al-le-go (signed Geo. Catlin 1832); Hose-put-o-kaw-wee-ge; Tchow-ee-put-o-kaw; Hol-te-mal-te-tez-te-mehk-ee; (220). (Correspondence with C. C. Proctor, Curator, April, 1958).

224. George Catlin. "TUCH-EE." See Pls. 248, 261, 269, and 280. Catlin (1841, vol. 2, p. 121) writes:

"Besides the Cherokees in Georgia, and those that I have spoken of in the neighborhood of Fort Gibson, there is another band or family of the same tribe, of several hundreds, living on the banks of the Canadian river, an hundred or more miles South West of Fort Gibson, under the Government of a distinguished chief by the name of Tuch-ee (familiarly called by the white people, 'Dutch,' Plate 218—Catlin, 1841). This is one of the most extraordinary men that lives on the frontiers at the present day, both for his remarkable history, and for his fine and manly figure, and character of face.

"This man was in the employment of the Government as a guide and hunter for the regiment of dragoons, on their expedition to the Camanchees, where I had him for a constant companion for several months, and opportunities in abundance, for studying his true character, and of witnessing his wonderful exploits in the different varieties of the chase. The history of this man's life has been very curious and surprising; and I sincerely hope that some one, with more leisure and more talent than myself, will take it up, and do it justice. . . .

"Some twenty years or more since, becoming fatigued and incensed with civilized encroachments, that were continually making on the borders of the Cherokee country in Georgia, where he then resided, and probably, foreseeing the disastrous results they were to lead to, he beat up for volunteers to emigrate to the West, where he had designed to go, and colonize in a wild country beyond the reach and contamination of civilized innovations; and succeeded in getting several hundred men, women, and children, whom he led over the banks of the Mississippi, and settled upon the head waters of White River, where they lived until the appearance of white faces, which began to peep through the forests at them, when they made another move of 600 miles to the banks of the Canadian, where they now reside; and where, by the system of desperate warfare, which he has carried on against the Osages and the Camanchees, he has successfully cleared away from a large tract of fine country, all the enemies that could contend for it, and now holds it, with little band of myrmidons, as their own undisputed soil, where they are living comfortably by raising from the soil fine crops of corn and potatoes, and other necessaries of life; whilst they indulge whenever they please, in the pleasures of the chase amongst the herds of buffaloes, or in the natural propensity for ornamenting their dresses and their war-clubs with the scalp-locks of their enemies."

225. George Catlin. "OS-CE-O-LA. (the black drink) a Seminolee Boy 12. years old, nephew of the celebrated chief of that name; and like his uncle, captured by the U. States troops, at the close of the Seminolee War." See Pls. 210, 243, 255, 265, 267 and 277).

226. George Catlin. "YE-HOW-LO-GEE." See Pls. 205, 244, 265 and 277.

227. George Catlin. "LA-SHEE." See Pls. 211, 237, 265 and 277.

228. George Catlin. "CHOCTAW EAGLE DANCE." Oil on cardboard. Mounted on board 28 x 21¾ inches; length of ellipse, 22¾ inches. Painted about 1835-40. See Pls. 218 and 270.

229. George Catlin. "CHOCTAW BALL PLAY DANCE." This is the same dimensions as "Eagle Dance," Pl. 228. See Pls. 222, 272 and 283. In addition to the paintings shown in Pls. 228, 229 and 286, the American Museum of Natural History owns several other paintings of Southeastern Indians by George Catlin. These are: "Choctaw Indian Ball-Play 'Ball Down'" (322606); Two choctaws (same men and pose as Pls. 213, 215, 262, 271 and 276)—Mo-sho-la-tub-bee and Ha-choo-tuck-ne. (324237). Group Seminole pictures (as Pls. 264, 265, 267, 275 and 277) (324238 and 324239). Ewers, 1955,

describes "Catlin's Cartoon Collection." American Museum of Natural History. New York City: "418 oils on cardboard of the 603 items in Catlin's Cartoon Collection exhibited by him in New York in 1871. Includes many replicas executed in Europe of original Indian Gallery subjects. Portraits commonly full-length and three or more to a painting. In addition there are many pictures based on Catlin's travels in South America and North America west of the Rockies in the 1850's and a series of historical paintings interpreting La Salle's explorations in America intended for King Louis Philippe of France. (George Catlin, Catalogue Descriptive and Instructive of Catlin's Indian Cartoons. New York, 1871).

Another major collection of oil paintings by George Catlin, the O'Fallon Collection, at the Chicago Museum of Natural History, consists of 35 oil paintings, produced by him before 1833, and includes western Indians. They are described in George Quimby, Indians of the Western Frontier. Chicago Museum of Natural History, 1954.

230-240. George Catlin. See names in index.

241. George Catlin. "SEMILOLEE WOMAN, wife and child of the Chief, on the foregoing page." According to this she was the wife of "Ye-how-lo-gee. (the Cloud) a celebrated warrior of the Seminole War." (NL 133)? In several group pictures she (woman with baby in cradle) is sitting beside La-shee and may be his wife? The other woman with a baby is Mic-e-no-pah's wife. See Pls. 264 and 265.

242-248. George Catlin. See names in index.

249-260. George Catlin. See names in index. These are found in YUL Souvenir . . . Vol. II. The number with each plate indicates the page number. In addition to the individual drawings shown, they also have similar sketches of Choctaw (Mo-sho-la-tub-be—p. 200; Ha-choo-tuck-ne—p. 201; Tullock-chish-ko—p. 211). Creek (Stu-cha-co-me-co—p. 202; Hol-te-mal-te-tez-te-neek-e—p. 203). Cherokee (Tuch-ee—p. 209; Jol-lee—p. 210). This collection is similar to that of the Newberry Library (See Pls. 230-248). Plates 249-260 are from the Yale University Library, MS. 69, Western American Collection.

261-265. George Catlin. See Pls. 266, 267, 269, 271, 275, 276, 277, 278, 280 and names in index.

266—274. George Catlin. See Pls. 218, 219, 220, 221, 222, 228, 229, 275-283 and index.

275-280. George Catlin. See Pls. 261-271 and index.

281. George Catlin. "SIOUX AND CHOCTAW BALL PLAYERS, in Ball Play Costume. Tullock-chish-ko (he who drinks the juice of the stones) . . . Choctaw. . . . This tribe play with two rackets, one in each hand, and wear a tail made of white horse-hair,. . . . We-chush-ta-doo-ta. (the Red man) one of the most celebrated players in the Sioux tribe. This tribe play with one racket, carried in both hands, and wear a tail made of Eagles feathers, or of long grass. Ah-no-je-nahge. (he who stands on both sides) said to be the most distinguished player of his tribe (in the manuscript of the New-York Historical Society Pl. 83, Catlin refers to this man as an Ojibbeway ball player), and to have entered upon several of his last plays, with the fixed and unalterable determination not to outlive the event, if his side were beaten." NYPL Vol. II, 79.

282-283. George Catlin. "CHOCTAW BALL PLAY AND BALL-PLAY DANCE." See Pls. 219, 220, 221, 222, 229, 272, 273, 274 and 281.

284. "OSEOLA." Information beneath lithograph—"J. H. Bufford, del. Bufford's Lith. Sketched from life at Lake Monroe, Florida, while he was on parole at that post in May 1837 by Capt. J. R. Vinton of the United States Army. Published by Wm. W. Hooper, 126, Nassau St., N. Y." and "Entered according to act of Congress by Wm. W. Hooper in the year 1838 in the Clerk's Office of the Southern District of New York."

Two articles discuss the portraits of Osceola. They are: Joseph Edward McCarthy, "Portraits of Osceola and the Artists Who Painted Them," *Papers, The Jacksonville Historical Society,* Vol. II, 1949, pp. 23-44; and John M. Goggin, "Osceola: Portraits, Features, and Dress," *Florida Historical Quarterly,* Vol. xxxiii, Nos. 3 & 4, Jan.-Apr., 1955. This contains a good bibliography. Goggin included in the paper a description of "a number of personal objects, including ornaments, belonging to Osceola which aid in establishing the authenticity of detail of some of the paintings." Regarding Vinton, Goggin writes: (pp. 162-163).

"John Rogers Vinton (1801-1847) served as a captain in the United States Army during the Second Seminole War. During this period he met Osceola at least once and perhaps later. The known meeting was at the Armistice at Fort Mellon on Lake Monroe in May, 1837. He subsequently appears as the leader of an expedition across the Everglades into the Big Cypress in 1842 (Sprague, 1948, p. 380). Following his Florida campaign, Vinton played a conspicuous part in the Mexican War—dying in the battle at Vera Cruz, March 22, 1847 (Anon, 1907, 370-371).

". . . During his Florida experiences Vinton drew at least three, and perhaps more sketches of Osceola, as well as several landscapes. . . .

"It now seems clear that there was an original full-length sketch made in 1837. Although it is now lost, there does exist a very rare print which can only have been based on such a sketch (Shown in Plate 284). Actually we don't know whether this was done from the sketch Vinton mentions in 1840 or from another smaller copy which would have been sent to the engraver in New York. . . .

"Osceola is dressed in a typical Indian hunting shirt of the period which reaches to the knees. . . ." *Quoted by permission from the Florida Historical Quarterly.*

285. John Rogers Vinton. "OSEOLA." "Pencil copy made in 1845 by Captain J. R. Vinton from an original sketch made by him at Fort Mellon in May, 1837." Of this Goggin states: (p. 164)

"It was one of five pencil sketches prepared by Captain Vinton in 1845 at the request of a fellow officer of the Florida War, Dr Jacob R. Motte. They were designed as illustrations to accompany Motte's book on the Seminole War. (1836-1838). After more than a hundred years this work has finally been published and four surviving original sketches have been reproduced (Dr. J. Rhett Motte, *Journey into Wilderness,* edited by James F. Sunderman, University of Florida Press, 1953.)"

Regarding this picture (Pl. 285) Goggin writes:

". . . While in very much the same pose as the 1838 portrait the picture varies greatly in details. Legging and moccasins are not differentiated and the buttons are on the front of the leg. Garters are very carelessly depicted and quite unrecognizable as to form; the same is true with the belt.

"The hunting shirt is radically different. It is short sleeved (a feature not seen in any other contemporary shirt) and the top ruffle covers the shoulders like epaulets and does not extend across the chest. The four silver crescent gorgets are present but the earrings are lacking, while the turban and plumes are essentially similar. Additional items are a rifle in Osceola's right hand and a shoulder pouch.

"An even greater difference can be seen in the head. It is much better proportioned but more European and delicate in line.

"Because of these differences one might suspect that the 1845 drawing was made from memory without the aid of his original sketch. . . . However, Jacob Motte (1953, p. 141) states that 'I can testify to (this portrait) being the most correct likeness ever taken of him. The face is a remarkably striking likeness, as he appeared previous to his capture.' " *Quoted by permission from the Florida Historical Quarterly.*

This picture is the frontispiece in Mark F. Boyd, *Florida Aflame, Reprint from the Florida Historical Quarterly,* Vol. XXX, No. 1, July, 1951, and distributed by the Florida Board of Parks and Historic Memorials. In this booklet, Dr. Mark F. Boyd, Historian, Florida Board of Parks and Historic Memorials, discusses "The Seminole War: Its Background and Onset." This contains an excellent bibliography. This

picture is also reproduced in Mark F. Boyd, "Asi-Yaholo or Osceola," Reprint with revisions from *Florida Historical Quarterly* XXXIII: 3 and 4; January-April, 1955.) An interesting bibliography regarding Florida Indian history, is found in J. Clarence Simpson, *Florida Place-Names of Indian Derivation,* edited by Mark F. Boyd, Florida Geological Survey, Special Publication No. 1, 1956.

At the time Dr. Boyd purchased this and other Vinton sketches, their full significance was not known to him. Later, he learned that they were the sketches designed by Vinton for inclusion with Motte's Journal. The Florida Historical Society had received the original Motte manuscript without the sketches. The manuscript and sketches had undoubtedly become separated after the death of Motte, and neither had been published at the time they came into possession of the present owners. The "p. 193" on the drawing probably refers to the page on which it was to be inserted in the manuscript.

286. George Catlin. OSCEOLA. On October 12, 1837, Osceola and other Seminole leaders were captured at Camp Peyton, and imprisoned at St. Augustine. They were removed to Fort Moultrie, South Carolina, January 1, 1838. No records indicate that sketches or paintings were made at St. Augustine; however, several were produced at Charleston. On January 17, George Catlin (Goggin, 1955, pp. 168-169) arrived in Charleston, and by January 25 had completed two portraits— one waist length, listed as 301 in his catalogue; the other full length, listed as 308. It is Goggin's opinion (p. 169) that the waist length portrait is the more finished, though the full length portrait "is perhaps much better known, if not in the original, in terms of prints and prints derived from copies." See Pl. 202.

287. W. M. Laning. "OSCEOLA, CHIEF OF THE SEMINOLES." (signed). According to Groce and Wallace, 1957 *(New-York Historical Society's, Dictionary of Artists in America),* p. 384, Laning was working as an artist in 1837-38 in Charleston, at the time Osceola was in prison there.

288. John Vinton. "OCEOLA." Goggin (1955, p. 165) describes this: "An undated and unsigned pencil sketch attributed to J. R. Vinton and undoubtedly drawn by him, ... The small sketch is mounted above two neatly cutout cards bearing the following notes:

" 'A correct likeness of Oceola the Seminole Chief engaged in the Florida War 1835, and taken prisoner by me under orders of Genl. Jessup, in October 1837. Joseph M. Hernandez. Brigd. Gnl. Commd. E.F.M.'

"This drawing is a bust of Osceola depicted in the same shirt and with the same ornaments as in the 1838 print. The delineation of the features falls between the 1838 and 1845 portraits but perhaps a little closer to the earlier example. A sketch close to this was undoubtedly used by J. H. Bufford in engraving the 1838 print.

"The verification of this drawing as a likeness of Osceola by General Joseph A. Hernandez is of considerable interest. Under orders from General Jesup this commanding officer of the Florida Militia was the man who seized Osceola under a white flag at Camp Peyton. He should have had some familiarity with Osceola.

"This sketch or one closely similar seems to have been the source of the engraving of Osceola made by 'N. Orr and Richardson' of New York to illustrate Sprague's history of the Florida War (1848, opposite p. 101). In turn, a much cruder engraving derived from the same original or the first engraving, signed 'N. Orr Co.' is found in Giddings (1858)." From Goggin, 1955, pp. 165-166, *Quoted by permission from the Florida Historical Quarterly.*

289. John Rogers Vinton. "OSEOLA." Unsigned portrait attributed to Vinton. This painting was owned by General W. F. Tompkins' grandfather, Lt. C. Tompkins. In a letter addressed to Lt. C. Tompkins, U. S. Artillery, Fredericktown, Md., Vinton wrote of his observations and sketches. The letter is headed, "St. Augustine, July 18th, 1840, My dear friend," and it is signed, "Your attached friend, J. R. Vinton." An excerpt from the letter follows: *(quoted by permission from General W. F. Thompkins).*

"It is some weeks since I had the pleasure to receive your letter of the 28th April. Interested as I certainly was, in the subject of young Hubard and his design of an historic painting illustrative of Indian characters, I have endeavored to provide something 'pour servir,' as the French say, in the way of sketches to aid him in the matter of costumes. My Oseola is on thick pasteboard and too large to send by mail, and as yet I have not had time to make up any thing worthy of Mr. Hubard's attention with my pencil. But I shall not lose sight of the subject, and by the time I come to the North may possibly have some sketches that will be at his service. I shall certainly try to see him, & shall be proud to make his acquaintance. Suppose you & I concoct something, picturesque & striking, illustrative of some of the scenes we have witnessed here among the Indians! Hubard is just the man to paint a group & we (& you especially) have had opportunities of beholding some active scenes which are well worthy of being consigned to canvass. I am glad to find you so much interested in this beautiful art. There is none I doat on more. As to costume, my Oseola would serve Mr. H. but imperfectly as a guide or copy. You know how plain & vulgar the Seminoles dress in general & the artist must therefore borrow largely from his fancy if he wd. paint their vesture by any wiles of taste. On occasions of ceremony however there are certain peculiarities of costume which are seldom departed from. For instance The ostrich plumes which decorate the heads of the Chiefs. These are worn differently by different individuals. CoaHarjo wore his on the front part of his head and so did most of the other chiefs I saw, with certain modifications,—but Oseola was peculiar for wearing his always on the opposite side and hanging off to the rear, as I have drawn them. Then the gorget of 4 or 5 silver crescents hanging from the neck over the breast;—then the red sash round the waist,—sometimes a silver band round the forehead—never the plumes I believe, or the gorgets. Still I know not whether these are imperative distinctions, or how far the privates are interdicted from indulging their passion for finery. I only recite what has happened to fall under my own observation."

Regarding this oil portrait, Goggin (1955, p. 168) writes:
"Presumably Vinton must have supplied Mr. Hubard or some other artist sketches of some sort. The figure is in the Vinton style, depicting Osceola sitting on the bank of a stream bordered by cabbage palms, prairies, and hammocks. The costume is basically the same as in the other Vinton pictures but much less precise. Whatever the sketches were like, the result, if not anthropologically accurate, is certainly 'picturesque' as Captain Vinton desired.

Comparative Notes. In all of the works attributed to Vinton we can see a definite style. This is especially apparent in the treatment of the head. Then too, the clothing and accoutrements are basically the same although there has been a tendency to simplify and generalize them from the 1838 print, through the 1845 drawing, and the undated painting. This tendency may have been due to working from memory or in an attempt to make Seminole clothing more attractive to the American audience as Vinton seemed to feel necessary." (Goggin, 1955, p. 168).

290. "OCEOLA. (Powell)/The Celebrated Seminole Chief who died at Fort Moultrie 30th January 1838. (Landscape Fort Moultrie Sullivan's Island)/ From the Portrait Painted by R. J. Curtis Esq./Pub. by W. Keenan Engr. 51 Broad St. Charleston S. C." There is no indication as to whether Curtis produced a small or large portrait for the engraver. He states that it was painted, and presumably it was full length. The Picture File of the South Caroliniana Library, University of South Carolina shows that the library also owns a similar engraving. It is in *Osceola; or Fact and Fiction . . . By a Southerner* (James Brickett Ransom). N. Y. Harper, 1838. The caption with it reads: "J. Pierce del. N. Currier's Lith. N. Y." opp. p. 143. Page size 7⅜ x 4½ inches. It does not mention Curtis, and the background is omitted except for the rock by the left foot, and the inscription is shortened to the name only, correctly spelled.

291. Robert John Curtis. OSCEOLA. "The artist was a native of Charleston. He studied under Neagle of Philadelphia. The portrait was painted for Dr. Robert L. Baker who sent Mr. Curtis over to Ft. Moultrie to paint the portrait. The suit is of dark material with white collar—coat with red figures on dark background, red sash, cap with red design and white plume; three gorgets of silver." Description by Mr. E. Milby Burton, the Director of the Museum. For a detailed description see Goggin (1955, 171-172). This is an excellent portrait and said to be a good likeness.

292. George Catlin. "OSCEOLA. of Florida. Drawn on Stone by Geo. Catlin, from his original portrait. New York. 1838." This Lithograph is also owned by the Library of Congress, 15843, 7747. Rollins College, Winter Park, Florida, owns a similar picture.

293. Winslow Homer. "INDIAN HUNTER IN THE EVERGLADES." It is believed to have been painted in 1886; but it has also been called "Hunting, Nassau," where Homer was a year earlier. There has been no check of the tribe and locale. Homer (1836-1910) began his art career as a lithographer and illustrator. He produced many drawings for *Harper's Weekly*. His watercolors, especially, earned for him a place of distinction in 19th century American art.

294. "OSEOLA." Frontispiece. *Microfilm courtesy P. K. Yonge Library, of Florida History, University of Florida Libraries. Gainesville.* (also microfilm for Pl. 296).

295. OSCEOLA. Engraved by Bobbett-Edmonds, S. C. Faces p. 129. It may have been drawn by S. Waldo, as some of the other pictures are initialed SW. It is discussed in McCarthy, 1949 (cited in Note 284). *Photograph Courtesy of the New York State Library, Albany.*

296. "OSEOLA OR POWELL. . . Drawn, Engraved and Printed by W. Keenan. Pub. by Burgess & Honour, No. 18 Broad St. Charleston. So. Carolina." Frontispiece.

297. "BILLY BOWLEGS . . . From a photograph by Clark, of New Orleans." Seminole. *Courtesy the Smithsonian Institution,* Bureau of American Ethnology, S. I. Neg. 44,430.

298. "BEN BRUNO, Billy Bowlegs' Negro slave and interpreter." Seminole tribe. New Orleans, 1858. S.I. Neg. 44,-430-D. (Numbers 297-301 are Line Reproductions from *Harper's Weekly*, June 12, 1858).

299. "LONG JACK, brother of Billy Bowlegs' young wife." Seminole. New Orleans, 1858. S.I. Neg. 44,430-C.

300. "NO-KUSH-ADJO, brother of Billy Bowlegs' 'old wife.'" Seminole. New Orleans, 1858. S. I. Neg. 44,430-A.

301. "YOUNG WIFE OF BILLY BOWLEGS." Seminole. New Orleans, 1858. S. I. Neg 44,430-B.

302-305. Indians and Negroes. Seminole tribe. Engraved by N. Orr Co.sc. From Joshua R. Giddings, *The Exiles of Florida*, Columbus, 1858. This book has a frontispiece much like Pls. 288 and 294. The quality of engravings varied with books. That of Osceola in this book was not as good as in Williams, and the other engravings may also be relatively poor likenesses.

306. "BILLY BOWLEGS AND HIS SUITE OF INDIAN CHIEFS.—FROM A DAGUERREOTYPE BY MEADE, BROTHERS, N. Y." 1 to r. Sarparkee Yaholo Fasatchee Emanthla. John Jumper, Abram. Billy Bowlegs. Chocote Tustenuggee. Identified from a similar group in *Gleason's Pictorial Drawing Room Companion*, Vol. III, No. 17, Oct. 23, 1852, p. 257.

307. "VILLAGE INDIEN SUR L'APPALACHICOLA." Reproduced in *Florida Historical Quarterly*, Vol. 26, No. 3, 1948. Seminole or Lower Creek.

308. "MASSACRE OF WHITES. . . The above is intended to represent the horrid Massacre of the Whites in Florida, in December 1835, and January, February, March and April 1836, when near Four Hundred (including women and children) fell victims to the barbarity of the Negroes and Indians." (Description beneath picture.)

309. "CHIEFS OF THE CREEK NATION, & A GEOR-GIAN SQUATTER. Drawn with the Camera Lucida by Captn. B. Hall R. N. Engraved by W. H. Lizars."

310. "BILLY BOWLEGS." A photographic portrait is listed in the "Shindler Catalogue," *Smithsonian Miscellaneous Collections*, Publ. No. 216, 1867—"72. Oh-lach-ta Miko, Billy Bowlegs, A Seminole Chief, Indian T. West of Ark. Shindler, photog., Washington, 1858." The Bureau of American Ethnology states that:

"It seems probable that Shindler made this plate, now in the Bureau's possession, copying a daguerreotype in his Washington studio in 1858.

"Bowlegs, however, was not in Washington in 1858, but in New Orleans, en route to Indian Territory. His portrait was made there by Clark in May 1858. (Heye Museum print No. 18411). . . Clark may well have been the artist who made the daguerreotpye copied by Shindler."

"A line reproduction from a photograph by Clark of New Orleans, 1858, reproduced in *Harper's Weekly*, June 12, 1858, p. 376 shows Bowlegs wearing a costume similar to that worn in the pictures disclosed above. . . ."

315. Edward Troye. CHEROKEE WOMAN. oil on canvas. 23 x 30½ inches. "Troye (1808-1874) is best known for his sporting pictures, particularly paintings of horses. He traveled through the south after 1835 in search of subjects, and probably did this painting on one of his trips. It is undated, and of an unknown subject." TGIAHA. Groce and Wallace, 1957, p. 637 state that he spent much time in Kentucky; visited Charleston; and taught art at Spring Hill College, Mobile, Alabama. (A picture of a Cherokee woman by Troye, has been listed as a part of the Whitney Collection of Sporting Art, Yale University Art Gallery?)

316. A. Zeno Shindler. JOHN ROSS. We include this photograph to call to the attention of the reader the work of an outstanding early photographer. After 1850 many photographic shops began to take the place of artists who were formerly hired by the government to make sketches. Tintypes, daguerreotypes, and photographs covering the period following 1850 are located at many sources, as the Bureau of American Ethnology (including the DeLancey Gill photographs—1888-1934), The Oklahoma Historical Society and Creek Indian Memorial Association, Okmulgee, Oklahoma.

Wimar. FIVE INDIANS AND A CAPTIVE

311. Carl Wimar. "BILLY BOWLEGS." This picture is discussed in the *Bulletin of the City Art Museum of St. Louis*, Vol. XXIV, No. 1, January, 1939, pp. 8-9. Wimar traveled extensively among the Western Indians, and produced many remarkable printings of them. There is no record that this was made from life, and was probably made from one of the photographs produced in New Orleans in 1852 or 1858. Since he never visited the southeastern tribes, his ornaments and costumes are too generalized for identification, with the sole exception of the turban band, plumes, and gorget. (Corresp. with Smithsonian Institution).

Many of Wimar's paintings are listed in *Charles Wimar, 1828-1862, Painter of the Indian Frontier*, City Art Museum of St. Louis, 1946. The above mentioned arched top (cut square here) portrait of Bowlegs and another similar oil are listed as numbers 32 and 33 in the exhibition catalogue. Among the others listed are: No. 6, a picture of Indian discovering Boone's encampment in Kentucky (painted 1853); and numbers 7 and 13 (painted in Duesseldorf, 1853 and 1855) referred to as the capture of Boone's daughter by the Indians. Number 13 is shown here *Courtesy of August A. Busch, Jr., St. Louis*. It is oil on canvas, 45 x 60 inches, and is signed Carl Wimar, Düsseldorf 1855. It pictures five Indians on a raft with a captive white woman. *Photograph by Anheuser Busch, Inc.*, St. Louis.

312-313. SEMINOLE AND CADDO INDIANS.

314. P. Romer. A CHOCTAW BELLE. Probably represents one of the Indians living in the Mobile, Alabama, area in 1850.

Among those described by Theda Wammack, Curator of the latter, (correspondence July, 1958) are: "Inter-tribal meet of 1868, Old Log Council House. Brush Arbor Camp Meet, 1874. Last Creek Indian Election, 1899. Indian Court House, 1880. Orphans Home and Alexander Posey, Creek Poet, Superintendent." In addition they have a series of oil piantings by Mini Hammond produced in 1930 after various old photographs. Other sources of photographs are the Oklahoma Archives at the University of Oklahoma Library; the National Archives; the Bureau of Indian Affairs; the Museum of the American Indian; the American Museum of Natural History; the Cherokee Historical Association, Cherokee, N. C.; the Chicago Museum of Natural History (and other larger museums which collect ethnological specimens); The Murrell Home and the John Vaughn Library, Northeastern State College, Tahlequah, Oklahoma and many individuals in the Oklahoma tribal areas. A letter from the Muskogee Area Office, Bureau of Indian Affairs, states that there is interest in the possibility of restoring for museum purposes several tribal buildings in Oklahoma including the old capitols of the Cherokee Nation, Tahlequah; of the Chickasaw Nation, Tishomingo; of the Choctaw Nation, Tuskahoma. The old capitol of the Creek Nation at Ocmulgee is a Museum. The old capital of the Seminole Nation burned. Restoration of those buildings for the purpose of displaying and preserving the history of the tribes, doubtless would result in the gathering together of many valuable photographs and paintings, now in private hands. *Cherokee Cavaliers* by E. E. Dale and G. Litton and other books by the University of Oklahoma Press contain pictures of Southeastern Indians.

Some of the photographs in the collection of the Archives of The University of Oklahoma Library, are described by A. M. Gibson, Archivist (correspondence, September 1958):

"I have found tintypes and photographs for General Stand Watie, Cherokee, and family members including Sarah & Saladin Watie; Colonel James Madison Bell, Cherokee; John Rollin Ridge, Cherokee; Narcissa Owen, Cherokee; Moty Tiger, Creek; Alexander Posey, Creek; Basic L. LeFlore, Choctaw; Isaac Garvin, Choctaw; Thompson McKinney, Choctaw; Elias C. Boudinot, Cherokee; Joel B. Mayes, Cherokee; John Ross, Cherokee; John Brown, Seminole; William L. Byrd, Chickasaw; Tom Buffington and Lewis Downing, Cherokees.

"Besides these we have several hundred photographs of miscellaneous scenes depicting life among the Five Civilized Tribes including Council Houses, Council Members, Schools, Churches, Military Installations, Farms and Factories."

In the *Chronicles of Oklahoma* by the Oklahoma Historical Society, there are many reproductions of paintings and photographs. One of Reverend Jesse Bushyhead, which belongs to Mrs. James W. McSpadden, Tahlequah, Oklahoma, accompanies an article by Carolyn Thomas Foreman, Vol. 9, no. 1, p. 55. Other photographs of Indians of that area are included in *Indian Territory*, a Frontier Photographic Record by W. S. Prettyman, selected and edited by Robert E. Cunningham, University of Oklahoma Press. See also various books by Grant Foreman and Angie Debo (*Rise and Fall of Choctaw Republic*, 1934; *Five Civilized Tribes*, 1951).

Photographs of the Catawbas (Southern Siouan) are located in the University of South Carolina Library, Prints Division; the Bureau of American Ethnology; and the Catawbas are discussed in C. J. Milling, *Red Carolinians*. In Fort Mill, South Carolina, in 1900 a monument was erected to the Catawbas. It is a kneeling warrior on a granite base. (Correspondence with Mrs. R. L. Meriwether, University of South Carolina Library). An Indian memorial in the form of a weathervane stands on the Old Opera House turret of Camden, South Carolina. It is a representation of Chief King Haiglar, Catawba, who was a friend to the settlers, 1750-63. He was killed from ambush by Shawnees. The iron statue was cut in 1826 by a French artist, J. B. Mathieu, who lived in Camden. It is 5'1" high. Haiglar is shown with a drawn bow, quiver on shoulders, feather decoration in hair, and horn of a stag at his feet. (*Photograph Courtesy of the Camden and Kershaw County Chamber of Commerce*). For a detailed picture and description of this. See T. J. Kirkland and R. M. Kennedy, *Historic Camden, Part I*. The Camden and Kershaw Country Chamber of Commerce have a photographic print of this which was made by Wilbert R. Williams, Camden.

The Bureau of American Ethnology has issued many publications which contain both reproductions of paintings and drawings or photographs or a combination. Among them are: The 5th Ann. Rpt. 1883-84 (1887), Cherokee, Seminole; 7th Ann. Rpt. 1885-86 (1891), Cherokee; 18th Ann. Rpt. 1896-97 (1899), Indian Land Cessions; 19th Ann. Rpt. 1897-98 (1900), Cherokee; 42nd Ann. Rpt. 1924-25 (1928), Creek. 44th Ann. Rpt. 1926-27 (1928), Chickasaw. BAE Bull. 30, Handbook of Tribes; Bull. 43, Tribes of Lower Mississippi Valley and Gulf of Mexico; Bull. 48, Choctaw; Bull. 69, Villages East of Mississippi; Bull. 71, Native Cemeteries. Bull. 73, Creek. Bull 77, Algonquian, Siouan, and Caddoan Tribes West of Mississippi. Bull. 88, Southeastern Indians. Bull 99, Cherokee. Bull. 103, Choctaw. Bull. 132, Caddo. Bull. 137, Southeastern Indians. Bull 164, Eastern Siouan. For bibliographical references, see John Swanton, BAE Bull. 137; William N. Fenton, *American Indian and White Relations to 1830*, Chapel Hill, 1957; and I. Rouse and J. M. Goggin,*An Anthropological Bibliography of the Eastern Seaboard*, Eastern States Archeological Federation, Publ. 1, 1947.

317. Samuel B. Waugh. THE JOHN AND MARY ROSS CHILDREN. "Children of John Ross and his second wife. The children would be less than 1/16 Cherokee."

318. Samuel Bell Waugh (1814-1885). MARY STAPLER ROSS. Wife of John Ross. Probably painted in Philadelphia or Washington. *Collection of the Philbrook Art Center, Tulsa.*

319. John Neagle (1796-1865). JOHN ROSS. Chief of the Cherokee Nation. Probably painted in Philadelphia or Washington. *Collection of the Philbrook Art Center, Tulsa, Oklahoma.* (This photograph was trimmed by mistake. It is a three-quarter length portrait, and he holds a copy of a treaty in his hand).

320. Artist unknown. PUSHMATAHA. See Pl. 139 and 157. Photographs 320-328 are by Mandell Matheson, Oklahoma Publishing Company, Oklahoma City, Oklahoma.

321. Artist unknown. R. M. JONES. "Came to Indian Territory in the Choctaw removal and was a rich man."

322. Artist unknown. LEMUEL COLBERT.

323. Artist Unknown. DAVID FOLSOM. See article "David Folsom," *Chronicles of Oklahoma*, Winter 1952-53, Vol. XXX, No. 4, opp. p. 453 for this picture. This canvas has "Washington" stamped on the back, and probably was painted there. It appears to be very old.

324. Artist unknown. GREENWOOD LEFLORE. "Chief of Choctaws in 1828. A district chief before removal in 1832."

325. Artist unknown. THOMPSON McKENNEY. The Oklahoma Historical Society states, "We think this could be a Stanley, but it is not signed. Excellent work."

326-327. John Neagle. JOHN ROSS and MARY STAPLER ROSS. See Pls. 164, 318, 319, and 333.

328. Self portrait. NARCISSA CHISHOLM OWEN. "Mother of Senator Robert L. Owen. Mrs. Owen, Cherokee, born at Webbers Falls, Cherokee Nation, Indian Territory, October 3, 1831, died in Lynchburg, Virginia, July 16, 1911." She painted a copy of the McKenney and Hall, "Sequoyah" which is owned by the Oklahoma Historical Society.

329. John Mix Stanley. "CHEROKEE COUNCIL, TEXAS." This represents a meeting attended by Colonel Pierce M. Butler, Cherokee Indian Agent, to which he probably invited artist John Mix Stanley. It includes many interesting details of Indian camp life as the two Indians crossing the river by walking over felled trees. The painting was first reproduced in an article by Carolyn Thomas Foreman, "Pierce Mason Butler," *The Chronicles of Oklahoma*, Vol. XXX, No. 1, Spring, 1952, (pp. 6-28), opp. p. 14. In this article Mrs. Foreman discusses the life and work of Pierce Mason Butler. He was the second United States Indian Agent to the Cherokee, who had been removed from the east and were living in the neighborhood of Fort Gibson, Arkansas Territory. In 1841 President Tyler appointed Colonel Butler to the position which he held for some six years. At that time he had completed a term as Governor of South Carolina. He had served in the army and had lived at Fort Gibson in 1824-26. He was familiar with the area. He was a man of notable ability and one sympathetic to the problems of the Indian Territory and the western frontier. His reports to the Commissioner of Indian Affairs, are excellent source material on the Cherokees of that period.

As tribes from the east were forced into the areas claimed by western Indians, the federal government was faced with the problem of negotiating for more western land, and settling many bitter clashes on the boundaries. In addition there were animosities between groups of the same tribesmen, who had removed to the west at different times, and there were increasing hostilities between the Indians and white men crowding into the area. See Grant Foreman: *Indian Removal, the Emigration of the Five Civilized Tribes of Indians*, (1932); *Advancing the Frontier, 1830-1860*, (1933); *The Five Civilized Tribes*, (1934); and *a Brief History of Ft. Gibson*, (1936). As a result of clashes in the Red River area and complaints of the people of the Republic of Texas, Agent Butler was ordered to attend a Council of Plains Indians at Tawakoni Creek, Texas, March, 1843. Later in that year with a military escort, he attempted further negotiations in the area. (Foreman, 1936, pp. 27-28).

330. John Mix Stanley. LEWIS ANDERSON ROSS. "He was the youngest son of John Golden Ross and Elizabeth Ross. He was born in the Cherokee country east of the Mississippi on July 2, 1834, and died in Tahlequah in April, 1885."

331. John Mix Stanley. ELIZABETH ROSS. "She was born in the old Cherokee Nation east of the Mississippi River in

1789. She married John Golden Ross (a Scotch trader) in 1819, and they moved west along with the rest of the Cherokee Nation in 1839. She kept house for her brother John Ross, the principal chief of the Cherokee tribe, from 1839 until his second marriage in 1844, but continued to live in his house for several years later. She died in 1876." The Gilcrease Institute also owns John Mix Stanley's painting of John Golden Ross. He was not an Indian, but was "prominent in the Cherokee Nation." They also own a portrait by Ralph E. Earle, "Daniel Ross," Savannah, 1815. He was the father of John Ross, Cherokee.

332. John Mix Stanley. ELEANOR ROSS.

333. John Mix Stanley. "INTERNATIONAL INDIAN COUNCIL." (BAE Neg. 1063-w and N.M. Neg. 4095-e). Painting depicting the famous Council at Tahlequah, Indian Territory (Oklahoma), convened by the Cherokee leader, John Ross, June, 1843, to which seventeen tribes sent delegates. Agent Pierce Mason Butler and General Zachery Taylor attended some of the meetings which lasted four weeks. Butler described the Council as an attempt by the Indians to produce intertribal friendship and laws, and to renew old ties and customs. He reported that three or four thousand Indians attended daily, and that it was very orderly. According to W. Vernon Kinietz, *John Mix Stanley and His Indian Paintings*, Ann Arbor, 1942, p. 5, in addition to painting the council, Stanley painted his guides, Jess Chisholm, Cherokee, and Jim Shaw, Delaware, and after that many of the other chiefs. "In J. M. Stanley, *Portraits of North American Indians*, Smithsonian Institution, (Pub. No. 53), Washington, December, 1852, p. 15, he lists 'Keeth-la or Dog. (Painted 1844.) Commonly called Major George Lowrey. . . He is painted in the attitude of explaining the wampum. . .' On p. 18, in describing his painting of the International Indian Council at Tahlequah, 1843, Stanley refers to Lowrey's explanation of the wampum at that council, and quotes his speech." (correspondence with Bur. of Am. Ethn.) In addition to painting many of the chiefs at the council. John M. Stanley probably painted others the following year (1844) while he was still in the same area. "Stanley describes 152 paintings relating to 40 tribes including Seminole, Creek, Cherokee, Chickasaw, and Shawnee. Pages 18-25 discusses two

GEORGE LOWREY

This oil painting of George Lowrey is 22 x 26 inches. It is undated and unsigned. It is owned by and pictured, herein, *Courtesy of the Thomas Gilcrease Institute of American History and Art, Tulsa.*

parts of the proceedings at the International Indian Council— the explanation of the Wampum by George Lowrey, and the speech by John Ross. The descriptions of the other paintings are also interesting."

Other Stanley portraits of Southeastern Indians, not shown here, which are listed by Kinietz (pp. 31-32) are: four portraits of members of the Schrimscher family(1844) owned by the Guleger family, Tahlequah, and two portraits of members of the Meigs family(1844) owned by Mrs. Annie Meigs (Frank J.) Boudinot, Washington, D. C. A portrait of Elias Boudinot, produced during the period before 1860 is owned by Mary Caroline Boudinot, Muskogee, Oklahoma, and reproduced in Ralph H. Gabriel, *Elias Boudinot, Cherokee, and His America,* University of Oklahoma Press, 1941. See Carolyn Thomas Foreman, *Park Hill,* Muscogee, 1948, for reference to the work of Stanley at that site. Kinietz (p. 35) lists "the Corn Dance" as as having been "mentioned" in a scrapbook of Mrs. Bayles, J. O. Jacobson, "Early Oklahoma Artists," *Chronicle of Oklahoma,* Vol. XXXI, No. 2, 1953, footnote 10, suggests that the "Green Corn Dance" may have been sketched at the time Stanley visited Creek Indians, who lived at the fork of the Canadian River. (1843-1844). There is no reference to the possible location of this.

Had more of Stanley's paintings escaped the Smithsonian fire of 1865, they would occupy one of the most important places in our record of 19th century Indian life. His quality of workmanship is excellent. He worked in the West almost continually from 1842-1854; he, as Möllhausen was an artist for one of the three Pacific Railroad surveys; his route began in Missouri. He is said to have painted portraits and scenes representative of some 43 tribes, and produced about 200 paintings (Kinietz, p. 14-15). See Groce and Wallace, 1957, pp. 598 and 599. See also, D. I. Bushnell, Jr., "John Mix Stanley, Artist-Explorer, "Smithsonian Institution, *Annual Report.* 1924, pp. 507-27.

For a summary and comparison of the work of various artists who produced pictures of the American Indians, see Frank Weitenkampf, "How the Indians were Pictured in Earlier Days," (pp. 213-221) and John C. Ewers, "An Anthropologist Looks at Early Pictures of North American Indians," (pp. 223-234), both in *The New-York Historical Society Quarterly, October* 1949, Vol. XXXIII, No. 4.

334. Francois Bernard. "CHOCTAW VILLAGE NEAR THE CHEFUNCTE." According to the records in the catalogue of the Bushnell collection, Peabody Museum, Harvard University, David I. Bushnell, Jr., purchased this picture for $100.00 from Stein's Auction Exchange, New Orleans in 1921.

Bushnell refers to this painting as the Choctaw settlement at Bonfouca, St. Tammany Parish, Louisiana. At this settlement, Pére Roquette erected his first chapel during the year 1845. Bushnell describes this painting in "Native Villages and Village Sites East of the Mississippi," *Bureau of American Ethnology Bulletin 69,* pp. 64-65:

"A part of this settlement as it was the next year (presumably he means after Pére Roquette erected the chapel) is shown in Plate 11, this being a reproduction of a painting made by Bernard, bearing the date 1846. . . .

"This represents a group of women in the foreground, near a fire in the open. Others are gathered beneath the shelter on the left, while to the right of the door of the far cabin a woman is busily engaged with mortar and pestle, probably preparing *kombo ashish.* The use of the large carrying basket, the *kishé* of the Choctaw, is clearly indicated, and the group in the foreground may be engaged in preparing dyes and the materials for basket making, with strips of cane scattered on the ground. The open shelter was probably in use throughout the South and the one which stood at Bonfouca in 1846 was undoubtedly typical of all." The date he states is on the canvas, does not coincide with the date (1856-1860) mentioned by Groce (1957, p. 46) as the time Bernard was living in New Orleans?

The carrying basket on the back of the standing woman is held on by a tump line, or strap around her forehead. Note the same method used by one of the Indians in Plate 335.

335. Alfred Boisseau. "LOUISIANA INDIANS WALKING ALONG A BAYOU." This probably represents a man and his family. He is carrying a gun and his legs appear to be wrapped. The boy has in his hand a cane blowgun and two

darts. The woman behind the boy appears to be carrying a burden basket full of pelts. A strap around her forehead holds the basket. The woman in the back carries a papoose wrapped in a blanket. They may be returning home from a winter hunt.

This picture appears as number 23, in the City Art Museum, St. Louis, *Mississippi Panorama*, p. 67. Harriet Martineau, *Society in America*, 1837, gives many word pictures of the natives, including one which goes well with this, and which was used with the picture in *Mississippi Panorama*:

> "The squaws went by, walking one behind the other, with their hair growing low on the forehead, loose, or tied back of the head. . . . These squaws carried large Indian blankets on their backs, and shuffled along, barefooted, while their lords paced before them, well mounted; or, if walking, gay, with blue or red clothing and embroidered leggings, with tuffs of hair at the knees, while pounches and white fringes dangled about them. They looked like grave merry-andrews; or, more still, like solemn fanatical harvest men going out for largess. By eight o'clock they had all disappeared; but the streets were full of them again the next morning."

336. Leon Pomarede. INDIAN BURIAL. The picture is signed in lower right corner. This picture has many very interesting details in it. In the center foreground are two Indians, one seems to be holding a gun. At the extreme right appears to be other figures, and women (one standing with a papoose) and children are watching from the bluff. On the right near the scaffold is a kneeling Indian. On the far side of the frame are two other Indians. One Indian is on top of the frame, pulling up the body which seems to be wrapped in skin. It is being pushed upward by four braves. In front of them is a man with uplifted hands. In one hand he has a large calumet with smoke rising from the bowl and with a typical fan-shaped feather decoration on the stem. They appear to be wearing 4 feathers in their hair. There is an old burial scaffold on a knoll nearer the river. This picture is now in the process of being cleaned and restored. Pomarede painted many church murals and landscapes. A ceremony of this type would therefore have appealed to him for depiction. In addition he must have been somewhat interested in the Indians, because in 1848 while living in St. Louis he produced a panorama of Indian life and life on the Mississippi. The panorama toured many American cities, until it was destroyed by fire in 1850. (See Groce and Wallace, 1957, p. 510). For more information about native burials see: BAE Bull. 71, "Native Cemeteries and Forms of Burial East of the Mississippi," by David I. Bushnell, Jr. Another panorama of the Mississippi Valley, showing in particular, archaeological remains was that of Dr. Montroville, W. Dickeson and I. E. Egan, 1850. It is 7½ x 348 feet sheeting with tempera. (The University Museum, Philadelphia).

337-338. Heinrich B. Möllhausen. SHAWNEES AND CHOCTAWS. Originals from manuscripts in the collection of the Oklahoma Historical Society. *Photo, Meyers Photographic Shop.*

339. "CREEK BOY. August 10th, 1853." This was first published in an article by Muriel H. Wright and George H. Shirk, "The Journal of Lieutenant A. W. Whipple." *The Chronicles of Oklahoma*, Vol. XXVIII, No. 3, Autumn, 1950, opp. p. 269. It was on the page of his *Journal* with the entry for Aug. 21, 1853, but he states that the boy is mentioned by him on Aug. 10; however, it is under the page August 11, that he writes: (Ibid., p. 261) "Pablo son of Manuel Melendez of City of Durango, bought of Comanches by Mr. Warren & sold to Mr. Stevens, is a boy of from 10 to 12 yrs. old, has been a slave of Shawnees for 3½ years. He looks as much like an Indian as any boy seen but speaks Spanish very well. He was stolen from his friends by Comanches & sold to Shawnees. His mothers name Guadalupe Gonsales. He says he prefers going back to his friends. But he seems very happy here. Indians speak of him & to him kindly. Another 'Spanish boy' as they are called lives with Johnson a Shawnee. Jesse Chisholm (footnote 50. Jesse Chisholm, of Cherokee descent, was a noted trader among the western Indians. . . .) the man I hope to make guide has 3 of them. I suppose that from two to three hundred dollars each is the value set upon these boys. Almost all of these Indians—Shawnees Creeks

Chickasaws Choctaws Cherokees and Delawares, posses either African or Mexican slaves. It is a singular state of things where almost universally the master appears to be in mental capacity inferior to his slave." (The papers of General Amiel Weeks Whipple are property of the Oklahoma Historical Society) *Courtesy of the Oklahoma Historical Society and the Chronicles of Oklahoma.* This drawing is sideways on a page of Whipple's Journal. It might have been drawn by Möllhausen, or J. C. Tidball, artists of the expedition, or by Whipple?

Two articles which discuss the life and work of Möllhausen are Muriel H. Wright and George H. Shirk, "Artist Möllhausen in Oklahoma-1853." *The Chronicles of Oklahoma*, Vol. XXXI, Winter 1953-54, No. 4, pp. 392-441. Also, O. B. and Jeanne Jacobson, "Early Oklahoma Artists," *The Chronicles of Oklahoma*, Vol. XXXI, No. 2, pp. 122-131. The latter also discusses the work of Stanley and Catlin.

340-341. CHOCTAWS. From Whipple, *Report . . . Indians . . . Choctaws*, pp. 24-26: "Their dress is fanciful, showing a fondness for bright colors and silver ornaments. Pendants of beads or shells are frequently attached to the ears, nose, or neck. The hair is sometimes cropped in front, to reach to the eyebrows; and red or blue paint is generally used to beautify their faces. A favorite style of wearing it is in half circles beneath the eyes. The moustache is not worn, nor is there the appearance of a beard. The features are rounded, and the cheek-bones have not the prominence which characterizes western prairie Indians. The eyes are large, oval, and brilliant; and, though not blue, have the mild expression that belongs to that color."

In Wright and Shirk, op. cit., p. 254, is an entry in Whipple's *Journal* referring to his attending church in the Choctaw nation and sitting behind an attractive young "Choctaw belle."

Heinrich Balduin Möllhausen, *Diary of a Journey from the Mississippi to the Coasts of the Pacific with a United States Government Expedition*, 2 vols, London, 1858, describes, vol. 1, Vol. 1, Chapter IV, p. 34, their camp near the Choctaw Agency, Sculleville:

> "Although the Indian population is of course accustomed to intercourse with whites, the appearance of our expedition, with its military escort, attracted a great deal of attention, especially as we proceeded to pitch our camp near Sculleville, evidently with the intention of making a stay of some days. It happened, also, that a council of Choctaw chiefs was being held at the same time, so that it was no wonder if people flocked to the spot from far and near, and that the town assumed its gayest aspect. Men and women all appeared in their best clothes, which, though cut in the European fashion, exhibited glaring contrasts of bright colours and many fantastic and most untasteful decorations. The camp was the great point of attraction, and as I had set up a kind of studio in my tent, many of the Indians came crowding that way, evidently speculating on the chance of having their portraits taken in their splendid full dress. Arrangements for running matches, shooting matches, horse races, dances, and especially for grand games of ball playing, which are peculiar in their kind, came off with great celerity; wonderful things were to be done in these few days; and certainly a traveller may esteem himself fortunate who arrives in Sculleville at the time of a great public meeting of the Choctaws, for he may then learn in a short time, from his own observations of this interesting people, more than he could gather by mere inquiry less satisfactorily in a much longer period." He also described a Choctaw Council and a ball game.

342-343. SHAWNEES. From Whipple, *Report . . . Indians . . . Shawnees*, pp. 26-27. ". . . portraits of Shawnees who live upon the right bank of the Canadian, opposite the mouth of Little river. Although further from the white settlements, they seem not less advanced in civilization than the Choctaws. They dress less gaudily, and care little for other ornaments than silver ear-rings, finger-rings, and brooches of their own manufacture, some of which are executed with taste and skill. The hair is parted in front, or cut so as to fall loosely upon the neck. Moustaches are usually worn by the men. The women are neater and better looking than the Choctaws." (Whipple's *Report*, from which pictures in Pls. 340-343 were photographed was secured by inter-library loan from the *Tennessee State Library and Archives*, Nashville, Tennessee).

Bibliography and Index

In addition to the bibliographical references made throughout the "Notes on the Illustrations," the following quotation indicates many of the basic source materials regarding the history and ethnology of Southeastern tribes. This is quoted from John R. Swanton, *Indians of the Southeastern United States,* Bulletin 137, Bureau of American Ethnology (Smithsonian Institution), 1946, pp. 827-832. The bulletin also contains an excellent bibliography, pp. 832-856 and 155 pictures. *Courtesy of the Bureau of American Ethnology.*

"Our knowledge of the history and ethnology of these tribes varies greatly. Of some we know little more than the names; of others we have a few notes by one or two early explorers and missionaries; of still others we have at least one fairly good description; and of a very few, such as the Creeks, Choctaw, Chickasaw, Cherokee, and Natchez, we have several fairly detailed sources of information, but it must be said emphatically that our records are imperfect in some particulars in every case. I will review rapidly our principal sources of information regarding the more important of these peoples.

"Material on the tribes of the Creek Confederation taken as a whole is fairly extensive, but we have few details regarding the differences between the constituent members of it which must once have been marked. It included all of those given under the heads Muskogee, Hitchiti group, and Alabama group, and at various times parts of the Guale Indians and Yamasee, Cusabo, Natchez, Tawasa, Yuchi, and Shawnee, and all of the Osochi, which were probably of Timucuan origin. The adherence of the Natchez, Yuchi, and Shawnee was comparatively recent. They were once large, independent tribes— the Shawnee always remaining such— and we have considerable bodies of material regarding them. The Seminole, including the Mikasuki, on the other hand, represent a late separatist movement, and there is available a somewhat independent set of authorities dealing with them.

"Our principal sources of information for the rest of the Creek Confederacy are the works of William Bartram, Benjamin Hawkins, Le Clerc Milfort, Bernard Romans, Caleb Swan, George Stiggins, James Adair, Ethan Allen Hitchcock, Albert S. Gatschet, Frank G. Speck, and my own notes.

"For the Seminole and Mikasuki we rely upon James Adair, William Bartram, Benjamin Hawkins, Clay MacCauley, Alanson Skinner, A. S. Gatschet, Alexander Spoehr, and some recent work by Minnie Moore Wilson and Frances Densmore, to which I have added a few notes drawn from the western Seminole.

"Practically everything regarding the Apalachee must be taken from the Spanish records beginning with those of the Narvaez and De Soto expeditions, and but little more outside of their history and one short text in their language.

"A small body of material which applies to the Alabama in distinction from the rest of the Creeks may be derived from Bossu, Hawkins, Schoolcraft, Gatschet, and some of my own notes.

"Adair and Stiggins give us a little information regarding the peculiarities of the Koasati, and there are a few notes from Hawkins, Gatschet, and myself.

"The Tuskegee have been made the subject of a special report by Frank G. Speck.

"In a recent publication (Swanton, 1931) I have assembled all of the more readily available source material on the Choctaw except that bearing on their material culture. Among the original sources must be mentioned an anonymous French document preserved in the Newberry Library, Chicago, of the Choctaw section of which I published a translation some years back, and I have reproduced the original in the appendix to the Bureau of American Ethology Bulletin just cited (Swanton, 1931). To these must be added Adair, M. Bossu, George Catlin, J. F. H. Claiborne, H. B. Cushman, Le Clerc Milfort, Bernard Romans, A. S. Gatschet, Henry S. Halbert, John Edwards, D. I. Bushnell, Jr., and the reports of some of the early French explorers, notably De Lusser and Régis du Roullet. (Swanton, 1931, is BAE Bull. 103).

"Chickasaw material is not so extensive, but here we have one great advantage in that it was the tribe which James Adair knew best, and his material regarding the Chickasaw is basal to everything in the Southeast inside and outside of that tribe. To this may be added many names of the Choctaw authorities already mentioned, such as the anonymous French memoir, Claiborne, Cushman, and particularly Romans, a paper printed in Schoolcraft's Indian Tribes, and recent notes by Speck.

"We learn most about the Houma from the narratives of Iberville and Gravier; most about the Pascagoula, Mobile, and Tohome from the Pénicaut narrative in the Margry documents; most of the Acolapissa from Pénicaut and Charlevoix; and most of the Bayogoula and Mugulasha from the journals of Iberville's two ships. Our knowledge of the Napochi is almost confined to material drawn from the narratives of the De Luna expedition edited by Priestly and the Historia of Padilla. To our material on the Acolapissa must be added the De Batz sketches of their temple made available by Mr. Bushnell.

"Our very meager knowledge of the Cusabo is furnished mainly by the French Huguenots, the narratives of Hilton and Sandford, Alexander Hewat's Historical Account of the Rise and Progress of the Colonies of South Carolina and Georgia, and materials from manuscript sources, now made partially available by Milling (1940) in Red Carolinians. We must also turn to the same French narratives for the greater part of our information regarding the Timucua except on the items of language and social organization, which the Franciscan missionary Pareja furnishes us. To this we must add the information contained in a report by Bishop Calderón of Cuba, under whose spiritual charge were the Florida settlements, and some recently published Franciscan documents. Fontaneda's Memoir is our chief source for the Calusa Indians of southwest Florida and Jonathan Dickenson for those of the east coast, though they are a century and a half apart.

"Turning now to the Natchez, we find that the two most extensive treatments were by Le Page du Pratz and Dumont de Montigny, but there are several other fairly considerable bodies of information, including an anonymous French narrative published at Luxemburg in 1752, letters by the missionaries Gravier, Le Petit, and Charlevoix, and a description by Pénicaut. The most that we know of the customs and usages of the Taensa is in the documents detailing La Salle's descent of the Mississippi to the Gulf in 1682, Iberville's visit in 1700, and those of the missionaries La Source, De Montigny, and Le Petit.

"Early data regarding Tunican peoples is scanty. Most that we have on the Tunica proper comes from the missionaries La Source and Gravier and the explorer De la Harpe. To this Dr. Gatschet and I have added some data on the language and the myths and a small body of ethnological information, and a very complete grammar of the language by Dr. Mary R. Haas has now appeared. Regarding the Koroa, Yazoo, and Tiou we have nothing except some incidental notes in the journals of La Salle's companions and two or three items in the Mémoires of Dumont de Montigny, Le Page du Pratz, and Diron d'Artaguette.

"A few items regarding the customs and beliefs of the Chitimacha Indians were recorded by, or for, Martin Duralde early in the nineteenth century and sent to William Dunbar, by whom they were transmitted to the American Philosophical Society in Philadelphia. A considerable body of material has since been collected by Dr. A. S. Gatschet, some by myself, and much fuller material, as yet unpublished, by Dr. Morris Swadesh. For the Atakapa we are dependent on the Duralde letter and a few notes in the manuscripts of early French and American travelers and explorers. There are some notes on the western Atakapa in the Spanish archives, but they are decidedly scanty. For the language, see Gatschet and Swanton (1932).

"Spaniards and English made contacts with several bands of Yuchi at different periods and the accounts supplied by them are most interesting, but the amount of ethnologic material is very small. Noteworthy among these are Bartram's and Hawkins' descriptions of the Yuchi towns among the Lower Creeks. Gatschet also collected some materials regarding this peculiar tribe, but the outstanding work on Yuchi ethnology has been done in modern times by Speck. An excellent body of texts in the Yuchi language has been collected and published by Günter Wagner, and I have done considerable in Bureau of American Ethnology Bulletin 73 (Swanton, 1922) to unravel the somewhat involved early history of these people.

"The Catawba Indians were once so prominent in colonial history that it is surprising that no definite attempt was ever made in the earlier period to prepare a description of them, yet it happens that the first notes on any tribe in the Southeast which may pretend to the term extensive come from a related people. This is the material obtained by Peter Martyr d'Anghierra from the Indian Francisco of Chicora, probably a member of the Shakori tribe. The next important narrative in time is that of John Lawson, who traversed the country of the Siouan Indians of the two Carolinas and the Tuscarora in 1700-01, and third we may place the narrative of John Lederer, which antedates Lawson's material by about 30 years. Catesby copies considerably from Lawson but adds items from his own experience. Brickell copies to the extent of plagiarism. We are also obliged to rely considerably on Lawson and Lederer for our knowledge of the Tutelo and other Virginia Siouans. More recently, notes have been taken down from the survivors of these tribes by Hale, Sapir, Frachtenberg, and Speck. The greater part of the manuscript and early printed material regarding them was published by Mooney in The Siouan Tribes of the East, a work which is still an authority on the subject. Recent Bureau of American Ethnology Bulletins by Bushnell provide an identification of the sites of the Manahoac and Monacan towns and supply some notes regarding them. Mooney's work has been supplemented most effectively now by the Red Carolinians of Dr. Milling. Nearly all of the later original work among both the Catawba and Tutelo has been done by Speck.

"Dumont de Montigny gives us an interesting description of the manner in which the Biloxi and Pascagoula disposed of their dead, and in the closing decade of the last century J. O. Dorsey collected some details regarding the social organization of the former. Little remains of the Ofo except their remarkable history and a brief vocabulary (Dorsey and Swanton, 1912).

There is no extended treatment of the marginal tribe of Quapaw, and we must rely upon the writings of early travelers such as Marquette, the chroniclers of La Salle, Le Sueur, La Harpe, on Father Poisson the Jesuit, some notes by Dumont de Montigny, and later material from Thomas Nuttall. J. O. Dorsey published some notes on their social organization.

"For the Cherokee the standard work is Mooney's Myths of the Cherokee, which, including its notes, covers a very much wider field than the title indicates. Mooney also published a smaller report on The Sacred Formulas of the Cherokees, and collected a much greater body of formulas, some of which have been published under the editorship of Dr. Frans Olbrechts (Mooney and Olbrechts, 1932), who added much new material. In the Newberry Library, Chicago, is a considerable body of unpublished notes by John Howard Payne. Besides Mooney, the later history of the tribe has been treated at length by Dr. Grant Foreman and Dr. Chapman J. Milling. Considering the importance of the tribe, ethnological information regarding it is decidedly meager. The best of the published sources is William Bartram, to whose name we must add those of Timberlake, Adair, Haywood, and Hicks. Studies of Cherokee social organization have been made recently by Eggan, Gilbert, and Bloom, and an extensive paper by Gilbert was published by the Bureau of American Ethnology in 1943. (See Gilbert, 1943.) (BAE Bull. 133, pp. 169-413.)

"The writings of Lawson and De Graffenried give our fullest notes regarding the Tuscarora and their allies, and in modern times they have been especially studied by J. N. B. Hewitt, himself of Tuscarora descent.

"When we turn to the North Carolina Algonquians, our main reliance is the writings of the Raleigh colonists, particularly Thomas Hariot's First Plantation of Virginia, illustrated with John White's drawings, while for the Powhatan Indians we must rely on the works of John Smith, and William Strachey's Historie of Travaile into Virginia Britannia, to which Robert Beverley's History of Virginia adds important items, though it is in part compiled from the works of Smith and Hariot. Although mainly devoted to Maryland, Raphael Semmes' Captains and Marines of Early Maryland throws much light on Indian life south of the Potomac. Along with Smith's narrative must be placed the relations of Newport and Spelman, and work in this field is now being pursued energetically by Dr. Maurice A. Mook.

"There is as yet no single good work on the Shawnee. Henry Harvey's History of the Shawnee Indians, published in 1855, is useful; Mooney has many notes on them in his various writings; and The Wilderness Trail, by Charles A. Hanna, is important for the movements of the Shawnee bands. In Bureau of American Ethnology Bulletin 73 I have brought together considerable material bearing on the movements of those Shawnee who went south (Swanton, 1922). More recently Drs. Charles F. and Erminie W. Voegelin have added greatly to our knowledge of the Shawnee language and along with it their history and institutions. The appearance of Shawnese Traditions, by C. C. Trowbridge, edited by Vernon Kinietz and Erminie W. Voegelin, has been of special service to students of this ubiquitous people. In the present paper our interest in this tribe and the Quapaw is purely marginal.

"The most important sources of information regarding the Caddo are the narrative of Henri Joutel, La Salle's companion during the Texas misadventure, and the reports of the Spanish Franciscan missionaries Casañas de Jesus Maria, Francisco Hidalgo, and Isidro Felis de Espinosa. The Historia, and particularly the Memorias, of Juan A. de Morfi are also important, but he derives his material mainly from Hidalgo and Espinosa. Items regarding this tribe were collected by Prof. H. E. Bolton and incorporated into articles contributed to the Handbook of American Indians, especially part 2, and printed in his own works. Reference may also be made to the concluding chapters of M. R. Harrington's monograph entitled 'Certain Caddo Sites in Arkansas,' and to a sketch of these people by Mrs. Lee C. Harby in the Annual Report of the American Historical Association for the year 1894, pages 63-92. A collection of Caddo Myths was made by Dr. G. A. Dorsey some years ago and printed by the Carnegie Institution, and in 1941 Dr. Parsons added some 'Notes on the Caddo.' Most of the essential parts of this material I brought together in Bulletin 132 of the Bureau of American Ethnology (Swanton, 1942).

"The later history of the Five Civilized Tribes has been completely covered by Foreman and Debo. For my few notes on the physical characteristics of the Indians of this section, I have relied mainly upon the writings of Boas, Hrdlicka, Collins, and Krogman."

In addition to the prints, drawings, and paintings presented herein, there are others in the above publications and in individual and museum collections. Three watercolors of Choctaw Indians painted (1832-33) by Karl Bodmer are pictured in Westward the Way, City Art Museum of St. Louis. A Choctaw camp by Bodmer was in a Smithsonian exhibition. These are owned by the estate of Prince Maximilian of Wied, Germany. They were not included in his book, Travels in the Interior of North America, Koblenz, 1839. Others are: Alfred Sully, "Battle of Lake Okeechobee, 1837." J. H. B. Latrobe, "Landscape with three Indians" and "Landscape with Two Indians." (Maryland Historical Society). Four prints of Louisiana Indians (Tulane University Library). Harold Rudolph, "Indian Lodges on the Bluff." (1871-77); two carved figures, "Indian Chief and Squaw," 1869, and an oil painting by Dwight Benton, 1879, from the steamboat "Natchez." (Louisiana State Museum). Mississippi Panorama, City Art Museum of St. Louis, lists no. 105. g. "Fort Rosalie—Extermination of the French in 1729." Northern and western Indians imprisoned in the Southeast are not included, as Black Hawk (Sauk), Fortress Monroe, Virginia, by R. M. Sully (1833) (Virginia Historical Society and Wisconsin Historical Society).